ABOVE: Bulleid West Country light Pacific No. 34046 *Braunton* leaves Chelsfield Tunnel on the approach to Knockholt with the Great British Railway Journeys' 'The Golden Arrow' from Eastleigh to Canterbury West on April 9, 2014. JOHN TITLOW

COVER PICTURE: 1924-built GWR 5205 class 2-8-0T No. 5239 heads past the colourful row of beach huts on Goodrington Sands towards Kingswear with a Dartmouth Steam Railway service. DSRRC

THE SUNNY SOUTH OF ENGLAND

AUTHOR: Robin Jones
DESIGN: atg-media.com
PRODUCTION EDITOR: Sarah Palmer
COVER DESIGN: Michael Baumber
REPROGRAPHICS: Jonathan Schofield
PUBLISHER: Steve O'Hara, Tim Hartley
COMMERCIAL DIRECTOR: Nigel Hole
PUBLISHING DIRECTOR: Dan Savage

PUBLISHED BY: Mortons Media Group Ltd, Media Centre, Morton Way, Horncastle, Lincolnshire, LN9 6JR
Tel: 01507 529529

PRINTED BY: William Gibbons And Sons, Wolverhampton

CREDITS: All pictures marked * are published under a Creative Commons licence. Full details may be obtained at http://creativecommons.org/licenses

ISBN: 978-1-911276-04-3

© 2016 Mortons Media Group Ltd. All rights reserved. No part of this publication may be reproduced or transmitted in any form or by any means, electronic or mechanical, including photocopying, recording, or any information storage retrieval system without prior permission in writing from the publisher.

Contents

4		Introduction
6	CHAPTER 1	Dreaming of Sunny South steam
18	CHAPTER 2	Purbeck perfection!
37	CHAPTER 3	The Bluebell blueprint
42	CHAPTER 4	So much more than a seaside railway!
46	CHAPTER 5	Double Devon delight!
54	CHAPTER 6	Britain's first electric railway
58	CHAPTER 7	Watercress by rail
64	CHAPTER 8	Thirty years of Moors Valley marvels
68	CHAPTER 9	Sea change in the Sunny South!
74	CHAPTER 10	The return of the Hayling Billy
78	CHAPTER 11	Secondhand Rose of the Sunny South
84	CHAPTER 12	The hop-pickers' line
89	CHAPTER 13	Big heritage, small locomotives!
92	CHAPTER 14	'Slim Jim' from the Sunny South!
96	CHAPTER 15	Steaming to the Severn sea
101	CHAPTER 16	Hollycombe Steam in the Country
102	CHAPTER 17	Royal steam through the rhododendrons
104	CHAPTER 18	Exmouth goes to war!
106	CHAPTER 19	Reviving the Somerset & Dorset
113	CHAPTER 20	Chalk, steam and a Polar Bear!
114	CHAPTER 21	It's a small world!
116	CHAPTER 22	Top of the Southern!
122	CHAPTER 23	Steaming back to East Wheal Rose
124	CHAPTER 24	The most southerly steam of all!
126	CHAPTER 25	Retracing the 'ACE'

Introduction

ABOVE: Westwards bound: Bulleid Battle of Britain light Pacific No. 34067 *Tangmere* departs Waterloo with the 'Atlantic Coast Express', one of the Sunny South's most famous named trains, on April 7, 2013. The 'ACE' had its origins in the 'North Cornwall & Bude Express', which was launched by the LSWR in 1907, and was named early in Southern Railway days. The train had five main destinations west of Exeter, Plymouth, Ilfracombe and Torrington via Bideford in Devon and Bude and Padstow in Cornwall, reached via Halwill Junction west of Okehampton. The train comprised different portions, coaches labelled for their destinations being taken off at the appropriate junction. Suspended during the Second World War, the 'ACE' reached its zenith in the 1950s with the first mile-a-minute timing on the Southern Region. The last 'ACE' to Padstow, and indeed anywhere, ran on September 5, 1964. However, in 2008, First Great Western introduced a single daily HST summer service to Newquay under the banner of the 'Atlantic Coast Express', as an extension to the 9.06am Paddington to Plymouth train, with a return from Newquay at 3.04pm. The pictured 'ACE' was run by the Railway Touring Company and ran to Exeter St David's and back. JOHN TITLOW

The year 2017 will see two major landmarks on railways in the south of England.

Firstly, it will be 50 years since the end of steam on the Southern Region.

Secondly, real public services – as opposed to tourist or enthusiast trains – will again be running the full length of the London & South Western Railway's branch from Wareham to Swanage, at the conclusion of a marathon restoration effort lasting 45 years.

Steam specials on the Southern main lines are today a regular occurrence. However, it took years of persuasion that steam locomotives could be operated safely on the third-rail electric network.

This volume covers the mission impossibles that have been worked in both sectors. Who would have thought back in 1967 that in the 21st century, you would still be able to board a steam train for the coast at Waterloo or Victoria?

When the Swanage Railway revivalists began running their first public trains over a few hundred yards of relaid track in the resort, how much credence would outsiders have given to their aims of rebuilding the entire branch, closed by British Rail in 1972 despite local opposition?

While there are many magnificent heritage and steam railways in today's Sunny South – the immortal advertising slogan used by the Southern Railway to promote holiday travel to the South and West – the Swanage Railway will be the first of them to offer public trains throughout the entire length of the original route.

In achieving this goal, it has worked many miracles along the way, not least of all creating a transport hub for the Isle of Purbeck, where holidaymakers can leave their cars and travel by steam train to the beach several miles away.

Its dream has been accomplished without trampling over the finer details of heritage and history: with its immaculately presented stations and locomotive fleet largely historically appropriate to the line, the Swanage Railway may easily be considered to be a microcosm of the Southern Railway and Southern Region.

But if you are looking for steam railway heritage in all its shapes and sizes, the Sunny South and West offers a plethora of absolutely brilliant destinations today.

Its wonders include the Bluebell Railway, the first revival of a closed section of the British Railways' network that established the blueprint for others throughout Britain to follow, and the world-famous main line in miniature, the Romney, Hythe & Dymchurch Railway.

Southern heritage is also honed to perfection on the Isle of Wight steam railway, Kent & East Sussex Railway and Mid Hants Railway, each of which offers a different angle on the theme.

And then there's the revivalists who have relaid track on three sections of the much-

4 Making Fresh Tracks to the Sunny South and West

ABOVE: One of the best loved of all railway posters enticing holidaymakers to take the Southern Railway to the seaside. It was one of numerous posters created around the SR slogan South for Sunshine. The company also created a fictional character, Sunny South Sam as the helpful member of staff waiting to help you on arrival at an unknown location. Advertising material played strongly on the fact that the Southern would take you to the places with the best records for summer sunshine.

TOP RIGHT: The Who frontman Roger Daltrey opened new £700,000 station facilities at the Romney, Hythe & Dymchurch Railway's Dungeness terminus on Tuesday, August 2, 2016, as hundreds of enthusiasts and fans packed the platform. The 72-year-old star, who first visited the line in 1956, alighted from a special train and officially unveiled a plaque to mark the completion of the railway's recently upgraded End of the Line Restaurant at Dungeness station, which replaced the previous wooden structure. The Who's 1973 hit 5.15 described a train journey from London to Brighton and was part of the group's second rock opera, Quadrophenia. Roger is seen in the cab of Davey Paxman Pacific No. 2 *Northern Chief*. RHDR

ABOVE: Heading for the beach: two young happy sandcastlers raring to go after arriving with their buckets and spades by steam train at Swanage station. Many more will be following in their footsteps in 2017 when the Swanage branch is re-opened throughout for new timetabled public services from Wareham after a 45-year gap. ROBIN JONES

BELOW: Other Big Four railway companies in their advertising literature adopted the term 'Sunny South'. This map shows the South coast and West Country resorts to which you could travel by booking with the LMS.

lamented Somerset & Dorset Joint Railway main line, which closed half a century ago.

Brighton's Volks Electric Railway is of tremendous historical importance, and it was the first electric railway in Britain and the oldest in the world still running today.

Looking to the West, there are the South Devon Railway and the neighbouring Dartmouth Steam Railway offering a dramatic contrast between an idyllic GWR country branch line and knock-me-for-six stunning coastal and estuarine scenery.

The similarly scenic West Somerset Railway is Britain's longest standard gauge heritage line, while the Bodmin & Wenford Railway has a splendid locomotive collection representing types that have worked throughout the delectable Duchy of Cornwall.

And there's much, much more. Miniature railways were once staple fare at most UK resorts in the days of steam, yet in the Sunny South the concept has been honed to perfection with one outfit, the Moors Valley Railway, building its own locomotives on site.

That slogan Sunny South inspired many generations of holidaymakers in the days of steam, and is still doing very much the same today.

Will you be on that first train to Wareham, or on the next Steam Dreams' special out of London?

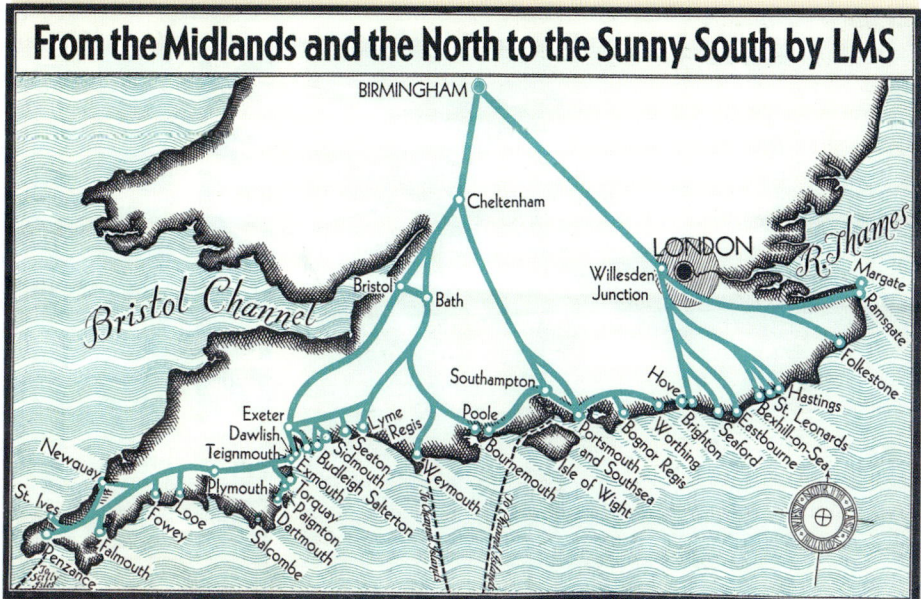

Chapter 1

DREAMING OF SUNNY SOUTH STEAM

Southern Region steam ended on July 9, 1967, when the modernisation programme of third-rail electrification and dieselisation was completed. However, steam trains are today a regular sight in the Sunny South. Here, Marcus Robertson, founder of Steam Dreams, whose 'Cathedrals Express' trips have become a byword for heritage excellence, explains how steam returned to the electrified region after 25 years, with several operators nowadays running specials, and how his own Mission Impossible to run walk-on steam tours from London succeeded against a mountain of odds.

LEFT: The end of Southern steam… or was it? Rebuilt Bulleid Pacific No. 35030 *Elder Dempster Lines* stands at Waterloo on July 9, 1967, with the last Southern Region steam passenger working.
STEAM DREAMS

The date July 9, 1967 is seared into the memories of all the many Southern steam fans who mourned the moment that rebuilt Bulleid Pacific No. 35050 *Elder Dempster Lines* came to a halt at the buffers at Waterloo on that sunny summer's evening.

Its run from Weymouth was the last 'proper' steam passenger haulage of the British Railways' era into London.

There had been rumours that a few of the Bulleid Pacifics and BR Standard locomotives that had survived to the last day would be retained for boat trains, but in the event No. 35030's unexpected foray to the capital was 'The End' as chalked on its smokebox.

Even that run happened only because of a diesel failure in Dorset as the locomotive had been destined for storing at Weymouth before scrapping.

Throughout British Rail's corporate restructure, steam was the enemy, and any opportunity to destroy the possibilities of running steam in the future was taken on the Southern just as it had been on the Western Region and as it was to be done on the rest of British Rail.

However, the sole incursion of steam on the main line in the south after July 9, 1967 were the light engine moves of two of artist David Shepherd's former BR locomotives from Cricklewood to Longmoor Military Railway in April 1968, but they were done without any fanfare or publicity.

The official end of steam haulage on BR was marked by the legendary 1T57 'Fifteen Guinea Special' excursion from Liverpool via Manchester to Carlisle and back from on August 11, 1968.

Steam was to successfully re-emerge in 1971, and the man credited with persuading the BR board to do a U-turn was Peter Prior, then chief executive of Bulmers, cider manufacturers in Hereford, which had sponsored the overhaul of National Collection GWR 4-6-0 No, 6000 *King George V*.

Peter wanted to see the engine haul the five-coach Bulmers Pullman exhibition train on a promotional tour of the country, and succeeded. A few extra coaches were added for fare-paying passengers and No. 6000 made a four-day tour of the Western Region, taking in Kensington Olympia and Birmingham in early October 1971.

After no serious problems were encountered, BR announced its very limited 'Return to Steam' commencing in June 1972.

This marked the start of today's main line steam operations.

Demarcation lines were laid down: lightly used routes, top speed 60mph, suitable steam locomotive based nearby, and triangles or other turning facilities at each end. By then BR had ripped out all steam infrastructure, few turntables existed and there were virtually no watering facilities.

While over the next few years steam settled into a small and controlled return, organised and run by British Rail, it was strictly limited to secondary routes such as the Settle & Carlisle, and Marylebone to Stratford-upon-Avon routes.

Yes, there had been several standout railtours on the Southern Region in the 1960s involving preserved steam locomotives. There were some interlopers such as GNR 0-6-0ST No. 1247; Caledonian Single No. 123; LNER K4 No. 3442 *The Great Marquess*; A3 No. 4472 *Flying Scotsman* and A4 No. 4498 *Sir Nigel Gresley*, but also native power in the shape of LBSCR 'Terrier' 0-6-0T No. 55 *Stepney* and E4 0-6-2T No. 473 *Birch Grove*; LSWR 4-4-2T No. 488, and T9 'Greyhound' 4-4-0 No. 120.

However, with third rail an added hazard in the minds of British Rail managers, steam on the electrified Southern Region was strictly forbidden particularly after enthusiasts trespassed on electrified track at Eastleigh Works during an open day on May 13, 1973. That incident led to the cancellation of a tour headed by Bulleid Merchant Navy Pacific No. 35028 *Clan Line* scheduled for October 13.

From that moment on there was absolutely no prospect of steam being allowed anywhere near the third rail in the South and it became a steam desert, even though some of the most-forward thinking heritage railways were springing up in the Sunny South.

There was virtually no main line steam action on the region throughout the 1970s and much of the 1980s, and main line certificated SR steam engines tended to be seen only north of London.

Nevertheless, *Clan Line* still became one of the first preserved locomotives to return on the network. On April 27, 1974, it hauled its first main line steam tour, from Basingstoke to Westbury and return, in what was then an exceedingly rare reappearance of steam in the Sunny South. BR Standard 9F 2-10-0 No. 92203 *Black Prince* subsequently ran on the same route.

ABOVE: Marcus Robertson, founder of 'Cathedrals Express' operator Stream Dreams. He is the son of author Elisabeth Beresford, who in 1968 created the Wombles, stars of a successful 1970s TV series... STEAM DREAMS
LEFT: BR Standard 5MT 4-6-0 No. 73096 leaves Clapham Junction with a Steam Dreams' 'Sunny South Special' on July 9, 2004. DON BENN

A breakthrough on the non-electrified part of the Southern Region came in 1986 when the then area manager at Salisbury, Gerry Daniels, was given permission to operate steam-hauled 'Blackmore Vale Express' trains on the 42 miles between Salisbury and Yeovil Junction.

Accordingly, on October 11 that year, Network SouthEast ran the 'Blackmoor Vale Express', hauled by Class 33 diesel No. 33007 from Waterloo to Salisbury, from where Bulleid Merchant Navy Pacific No. 35028 *Clan Line* took over for two runs to Yeovil Junction and back.

From Salisbury, diesel Nos. 33007 and 33048 headed the train back to Waterloo.

On July 23, 1988, Keighley & Worth Valley Railway-based unmodified Bulleid West Country Pacific No. 34092 *City of Wells* hauled the 'Blackmore Vale Express' between Salisbury, Yeovil Junction and Romsey. Respected recorder GAM Wood unofficially logged it at 93mph – the limit being 60mph – according to the Railway Performance Society database. Others on board the train hinted at 94mph, between Wilton and Dinton and also near Gillingham. There has never been any official confirmation of the speed on that day.

West Country Pacific No. 34027 *Taw Valley's* Folkestone Harbour branch shuttles in September 1991 brought steam back to the Eastern Section after many years.

Furthermore, steam ran beyond Yeovil on occasions, with *Taw Valley* reaching Exeter Central in June 1992 and even St Davids in September 1993.

LEFT: Did Bulleid West Country Pacific No. 34092 *City of Wells* haul the 'Blackmore Vale Express' at 94mph on July 23, 1988? The train is seen passing Barford St Martin. BRIAN SHARPE

RIGHT: Network South East's 'Blackmore Vale Express' on October 11, 1986 saw the first steam on the Southern Region in a decade. The two Salisbury round-trip legs on the day were hauled by Merchant Navy 4-6-2 No. 35028 *Clan Line*. The special is seen passing Stowell. BRIAN SHARPE

On its Green Train, not only did the Mid Hants turn out West Country No. 34016 *Bodmin* but moguls Nos. 31806 and 31625, followed by Merchant Navy No. 35005 *Canadian Pacific*.

Privatisation of the main line network really opened the floodgates for main line steam on the Southern, and steam is almost an everyday sight on the main line in the 21st century.

THE SUNNY SOUTH IN YORKSHIRE!

During the steam drought of the 1970s and 1980s, active Southern steam took the spirit of the Sunny South far away from home territory.

Clan Line was based at Bulmers in Hereford, and regularly ran to points even further north. S15 4-6-0 No. 841 made two trips in East Anglia in the late 1970s, before migrating to the North Yorkshire Moors Railway, a line that also played host to West Country light Pacific No. 34101 *Hartland* and Schools 4-4-0 No. 30926 *Repton*.

The Keighley & Worth Valley Railway had USA 'Yankee tank' 0-6-0T No. 72 and more importantly West Country Pacific No. 34092 *City of Wells*, which, as we saw, did make one memorable visit to the Southern Region from Yorkshire, but not until 1988.

The National Collection's two SR express 4-6-0s No. 777 *Sir Lamiel* and No. 850 *Lord Nelson* were very much northern engines in the 1980s after their restorations.

BELOW: On September 12 and 13, 1991, Network SouthEast ran a series of shuttles on the Folkestone Harbour branch with Bulleid West Country light Pacific No. 34027 *Taw Valley* and BR Standard 4MT 2-6-4T No. 80080 on the rear, as part of the Shepway Festival. The shuttle is seen heading out of the Folkestone sea terminal behind *Taw Valley*. BRIAN SHARPE

ABOVE: Rebuilt Bulleid Pacific No. 35030 *Elder Dempster Lines* as seen from the west end of the long Down platform at Bournemouth Central station on May 10, 1958. Built in April 1949, it was rebuilt in April 1958, and withdrawn in July 1967. BEN BROOKSBANK*

STEAM RUNS ON ELECTRIC LINES AGAIN

On a weekend at the beginning of June 1992, NSE organised shuttles between Ashford and Hastings using West Country light Pacific No. 34067 *Taw Valley* and BR Standard 4MT 2-6-0 No. 76059.

These went as far as to breach the third-rail embargo at the margins, leaving as they did from Ashford station and also travelling over the electrified short section between Ore and Hastings.

As a tester it was very successful, attracting sell-out trains and without report of trespass near the third rail (in those days away from the third rail minor trespass would probably have been overlooked anyway).

More intriguingly it was leaked to selected railway journalists that after the Sunday's shuttles were finished, there would be a return special to London Bridge hauled by "unusual traction". What could that possibly mean? Surely only one thing, as in those days something like Class 33 traction was not unusual, so it must have meant steam.

It was certainly enough of a carrot to get me to take a risk and drive down to Ashford for the 9.30pm start, and sure enough there was *Taw Valley* waiting to haul the coaches back to London with no diesel in sight!

What followed was quite surreal, as the cloak-and-dagger publicity meant that few enthusiasts had bothered to make the late Sunday evening pilgrimage to East Kent.

Boarding the train and paying a walk-up fare, the 100 or so passengers on board settled back to enjoy an absolutely magical time as we steamed off on a lovely summer's evening.

In the days before the internet and social media, almost no one had wind of it and as we steamed past houses and railway stations the sense of disbelief was quite palpable.

The trip ran as planned other than the fact that the 60mph speed restriction, then in place for steam, was definitely disregarded and a three-minute late start from Ashford had become an on-time arrival at London Bridge. Even more remarkable was while we were admiring *Taw Valley* at the buffers and marvelling at more than a quarter of a century's steam deprivation being swept away so unexpectedly – when No. 75069 and, I believe King Arthur class 4-6-0 No. 30777 *Sir Lamiel* almost silently slid up to the buffers doubleheading their support coaches.

From having no locomotives travelling across third-rail territory, suddenly here were three in the space of half an hour running up the South Eastern Railway main line, and while I retired home to a very happy night's sleep, even more remarkable things followed.

All three locomotives were sent with their three support coaches coupled together in a single train to Eastleigh, apparently travelling down the South Western main line shortly after dawn, passing bleary-eyed commuters who must have believed they were still asleep and enjoying a Steam Dream!

The jinx had been broken and the genie was well and truly out of the bottle. Steve McColl, Chris Green's right-hand man for steam, quickly realised the potential of steam on the Southern but continued to take the trespass worries seriously by announcing an 8pm departure with *Taw Valley* from Waterloo to Bournemouth on September 11, 1992, proving that steam really was back in the Sunny South!

With no serious trespass problems being encountered, steam was eventually permitted in daylight on electrified routes from 1994.

WATERLOO SUNSET – A NEW DAWN

It was to be yet again after sunset that we were to leave Waterloo, but the difference was that this time the whole world knew about it.

Once again, travelling with a friend, I was among the lucky hundreds who had managed to get tickets on a train that could have been sold out 50 times over.

For those that had watched the rebuilt Bulleids ply their trade on the old main line from Waterloo as steam gradually faded during the mid-1960s, this really was the holy grail. Echoing steam fan Ray Davies's hit for The Kinks, Waterloo Sunset, *Taw Valley* pulled out of Waterloo 25 years two months and two days since the last steam locomotive had been seen in the capital (other than the preserved A3 No. 4472 *Flying Scotsman* trip from King's Cross to Edinburgh in May 1968).

As the train gathered pace in the gloom, it soon became clear that this was not just an

RIGHT: Rebuilt Bulleid West Country light Pacific No. 34016 *Bodmin* heads past the Houses of Parliament with a 'Cathedrals Express' outing in 2002. STEAM DREAMS

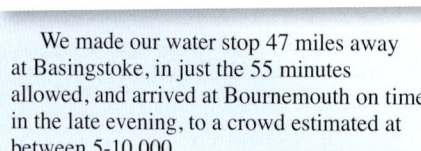

ABOVE: BR Standard 5MT 4-6-0 No. 73096 heads a 'Sunny South Special' from London to Weymouth in the summer of 2004. BRIAN SHARPE

RIGHT: SR King Arthur 4-6-0 No. 30777 *Sir Lamiel*, a National Collection locomotive, passing Battledown with the 'Cathedrals Express' from London Victoria to Swanage on July 9, 2010. DON BENN

epoch-making event, but also something that reached into the soul of the British psyche.

My wife had taken our two young children to Woking, and she could barely get on the platform but managed to be there as *Taw Valley* sped past the huge crowds in the gloaming at 77mph. Both crowds and speed were replicated all along the route.

We made our water stop 47 miles away at Basingstoke, in just the 55 minutes allowed, and arrived at Bournemouth on time in the late evening, to a crowd estimated at between 5-10,000.

RECLAIMING LOST TERRITORY
Over the coming months, the boundaries were pushed further back as each successive tour allowed more gradual daytime exposure of steam on the third-rail network. *Taw Valley* was undoubtedly the history maker and Merchant Navy 4-6-2 No. 35028 *Clan Line* soon joined the fun, as gradually what had seemed an impossible dream became the new norm.

The Mid Hants Railway unexpectedly took the plunge into main line operation in 1998 with its Daylight Railtours programme using its own locomotives and newly acquired stock, the Green Train. Paul Blowfield's LSW Railtours also sprang up specifically to take advantage of this new-found freedom for steam, as enthusiasts gradually sated their appetites.

Not only did the Mid Hants turn out West Country No. 34016 *Bodmin* but SR moguls Nos. 31806 and 31625 as well, followed by Merchant Navy No. 35005 *Canadian Pacific*.

Privatisation of the main line network really opened the floodgates for main line steam on the Southern.

Clan Line remained the spiritual leader of the Southern steam revival and spearheaded the use of air brakes on preserved main line steam in the UK in 1994, leading to its regular use on the Venice Simplon Orient-Express Pullmans, recreating the sight of the Southern Region's premier Pullman steam workings.

It eventually became clear that to survive long term, regular steam in the South would need to go the way of regular operations elsewhere in the country and provide a product attractive enough for non-enthusiasts… and just as importantly the wives of enthusiasts.

LEFT: No longer merely content to run walk-on day trips, Steam Dreams has successfully expanded into the land cruise market. Here, BR Pacific No. 70000 *Britannia* stands at London Victoria on May 18, 2012 waiting to head the seven-day 'Cathedrals Explorer' to Scotland among other destinations en route. JOHN TITLOW

ABOVE: Bulleid Battle of Britain Pacific No. 34067 *Tangmere* passing Lymington Junction with Steam Dreams' 'Sunny South Special' on July 9, 2009. DON BENN

ABOVE: Headed by LNER A4 Pacific No. 4464 Bittern, the Up 'Cathedrals Express' rushes through Teignmouth on May 21, 2013. BARRY LEWIS*

ABOVE: In 2016, the world's most famous steam locomotive, A3 Pacific No. 60103 *Flying Scotsman*, hauled several Steam Dreams' trips over the former Southern Region. Here, on May 25, 2016, it is preparing to depart London Victoria with a circular trip taking in Ashford, Staines, Woking, Dorking West, Redhill and East Croydon. TRAIN PHOTOS*

My 40th birthday celebration in the Harz mountains on February 4, 1996, which coincided with the first privatised train running on Britain's railways at 5.50am that Sunday on the newly created South West Trains franchise, were two events that ultimately led to the creation of Steam Dreams.

Whereas up until privatisation, steam on the main line had been carefully choreographed by British Rail, even where private promoters were involved, now the EU directive of open access had created a truly different situation.

The group in the Harz contained other enthusiasts and also journalists, and it was conversations in the bars and restaurants during that time that the real seeds of Steam Dreams were sown.

My wife, Marianne, who had treated me to this trip and brought the children with us, was convinced that done correctly there was an almost infinite market of people who were not enthusiasts but would enjoy a nostalgic day out behind steam.

Gill Trousdale, who was to become Steam Dreams' operations director, was someone with no intrinsic interest in steam, but quickly got the bug and bought into Marianne's vision.

Quite straightforwardly steam enthusiasts like myself really wouldn't care where we were going, what was on the menu for lunch or even how early we had to start, but Marianne and Gill of course did – and even more than all those things, they cared most that train loos needed to be at the forefront of any modernisation project for steam!

After nearly two years of planning, the first toe in the water for what was to become the 'Cathedrals Express' was a one-off tour on December 16, 1999 from London and Woking to Salisbury. For the first time in the heritage era, steam was going out of Waterloo in the middle of the day midweek, and remarkably given today's capacity constraints, it was going straight down the main line with BR Standard 5MT No. 73096 on the front of the Green Train that had been chartered from the Mid Hants Railway.

Looking back, Steam Dreams was lucky to even have got that far, and would not have done so without the help and enthusiasm of the Mid Hants board and its then locomotive superintendent, John Bunch. Their agreement to facilitate almost every aspect of the first few years meant that to a large extent our new firm was sheltered from the difficulties of running a main line steam trip.

While technically Railtrack, as it then was, could not block main line steam, shortly after Christmas, before we announced what our long-term plans would be, we were summoned to Waterloo to meet 'senior management'.

It was at this meeting that we met Stephen Cornish, head of special trains at Railtrack, for the first time, but also several members of the planning team responsible for the old Southern Region network, and they were not keen on regular steam from Waterloo, which had been our intention all along.

Stephen Cornish, in his inimitable style, persuaded us to compromise and instead visit Canterbury on a regular basis during the summer of 2000, as that part of the network was a lot emptier than the south-western main line on weekdays.

As the meeting was drawing to a close, we asked cheekily if that went well would we be allowed a few trials to Salisbury at the end of

Making Fresh Tracks to the Sunny South and West

ABOVE: New-build A1 Peppercorn Pacific No. 60163 *Tornado* leaving East Croydon with the 'Cathedrals Express' on November 29, 2012, having been repainted in the short-lived British Railways' express passenger blue livery. PETER TRIMMING*

RIGHT: Headed by LNER B1 4-6-0 No. 61306 *Mayflower*, the 'Cathedrals Express' passes Earley station between Waterloo and Reading on November 26, 2015. NH53*

the summer, and probably thinking that things would soon go wrong for us, Andy Bottom, the man in charge of the Railtrack planning team, finally said 'yes'.

As with all best-laid plans, Steam Dreams now had to tear up the concept of running the 'Wessex Belle' to Salisbury every week during the summer, and also think of a new name – 'Kentish Belle', 'Man of Kent', 'Golden Arrow' – any of these could be used, but then what would happen if, as hoped, we were then allowed to go to Salisbury, which clearly was nowhere near Kent?

Somebody piped up about how about the 'Cathedrals Express', as that would cover both destinations – and the name was born or rather revived as the GWR had, of course, used that name for its Oxford, Worcester and Hereford service!

The steam-era 'Cathedrals Express', which was, despite its name, at best a semi-fast service, had been introduced on September 16, 1957 and ran six days a week until June 12, 1965. It departed Hereford at 7.45am with the return service leaving Paddington at 4.45pm. Its coaching stock carried the GWR chocolate and cream livery, not the British Railways' standard maroon of this period.

The service also stopped at Oxford, while there was a restaurant car service east of Worcester. Through carriages from Kidderminster to London were also attached and detached at Worcester.

THE 21ST-CENTURY 'CATHEDRALS EXPRESS'

On Wednesday, June 28, 2000, with more than 40 media representatives from around the world on board, the first regular steam from London since the 20th century left Platform 2 at London Victoria heading for Canterbury behind John Bunch's rebuilt West Country Pacific No. 34016 *Bodmin*. Everyone on board was excited and the weather was there to match as we sped through the south-east London suburbs non-stop to Canterbury West.

Against all expectations, *Bodmin*, restored to the main line only two weeks previously, performed faultlessly throughout, and the train was constantly on or ahead of schedule.

Incredibly not one of the 13 trains to Canterbury that summer was ever late arriving into Canterbury or Victoria – where it was said you could set the big Platform 2 clock by the 8pm arrival of the 'Cathedrals Express'.

True to the input of the women involved in getting Steam Dreams going, not only were the trains destined to go to lovely cities, but there were also relatively short days, a new style of modern bistro catering, and most importantly of all, a full-time loo cleaner.

ABOVE: Steam Dreams' chef, Tony Keene. STEAM DREAMS

ABOVE: Luxury Pullman dining with Steam Dreams today. STEAM DREAMS

LEFT: BR Britannia Pacific No. 70000 *Britannia* hauls the 'Cathedrals Express' through Bickley with the April 6, 2011 'Cathedrals Express' from Oxford to Canterbury West and back. JOHN TITLOW

ABOVE: A1 Pacific No. 60163 *Tornado* safely back at Waterloo after not only completing its planned 'Cathedral Express' tour of the Kent coast in the sub-zero temperatures of December 21, 2009, but picked up stranded London commuters on the outward leg. ROBIN JONES

ABOVE: SR King Arthur 4-6-0 No. 30777 *Sir Lamiel* hauls the Railway Touring Company's 'Dorset Coast Express' from London Victoria to Weymouth on August 18, 2010. It is pictured just west of Southampton. DON BENN

There was though, just one glitch that reminds us of the world as it was then, as following a bombing by the still-operative IRA at Ealing station, there was a security alert at Victoria and the 'Cathedrals Express' scheduled for July 19 that year never got further than running as empty stock on the approaches to Victoria where it rested for four hours on the bridge over the Thames, before unfortunately it was cancelled.

Nevertheless, the whole programme was deemed a huge success even by 'senior management' at Waterloo and the extra trains to Salisbury were given a provisional go ahead subject to said 'senior management', travelling on the first one to check there were no serious issues.

The first one to run was on Wednesday, August 30, 2000 and was timed to depart around 11am as close to the time of the old 'Atlantic Coast Express' as possible, and duly did so from Platform 16 at 10.58pm. Again *Bodmin* was in charge as it was to be on all the services that summer, and with Peter Bassett from Railtrack's Special Trains Planning team timing throughout the day at every passing point, it was gratifying to know that not once were we more than a few seconds off our booked time. Indeed other 'senior management' decided by Basingstoke on the return that they were now off duty and were able to enjoy a celebratory glass or two on the fast run back from Eastleigh into Waterloo.

The success of this venture inspired the Steam Dreams' board to consider having its own Bulleid Pacific, and the firm was informed by John Bunch that Andrew Naish was selling his Merchant Navy No. 35005 *Canadian Pacific*.

By the end of 2000 the deal was done and the locomotive was moved to Ropley Works on the Mid Hants, where it was scheduled to haul a series of crew training runs from Eastleigh to Yeovil Junction during the early part of 2001.

Unfortunately No. 35005 had some issues with its tubes and lasted only the first few days. However, a new star was born and No. 34016 was able to deputise for that week of special trains.

Regular steam on a twice-daily basis was scheduled to stations along the route through Hampshire, Wiltshire and Dorset. Passengers were able to just turn up and have a day out by steam – this sort of thing would probably be unthinkable now, but in the early part of the century the network was nothing like as full as it is now.

Gradually, the 'Cathedrals Express' reached new destinations including most of the Cathedral cities across south-east England; Winchester, Chichester, Portsmouth and also the abbey city of Bath. At the end of the second summer in 2001, on September 13, No. 35005 was scheduled to take the first steam out of Liverpool Street since the 1960s to Ely.

As we all know now, that date was two days after the worst incident in modern times of terrorism, but after discussions with Railtrack and the British Transport Police, the trip was allowed to go ahead.

There had been fears that steam and smoke erupting from under the Broadgate centre in the heart of the city might spook people less than 48 hours after 9/11, but in the event the day passed off successfully and another landmark was achieved by steam.

There still remained a major dream for steam enthusiasts, which was to emulate the last express steam of the BR era and bring back the thrill of regular steam to Bournemouth and Weymouth on the historically traditional route for summertime excursions from London hauled by Bulleid Pacifics.

So it was that in 2004, Steam Dreams planned a series of trains to Weymouth during the summer season. Named the 'Sunny South Specials' they were in the end all hauled by No. 73096 as by then No. 35005 had expired in its infamous boiler tube failure at Paddock Wood, and at the time of writing, has not turned a wheel on the main line since.

As the itinerary required a rush-hour start from London the boarding point was not Waterloo but Platform 17 at Clapham Junction, but even this had echoes of the end of southern steam as the last regular steam-hauled branch service in London was the Clapham Junction to Kensington Olympian shuttles that ran up until July 7, 1967 from Platform 17. Fittingly the first Sunny South season started in May but included a trip on July 9.

No. 73096 undoubtedly made its name on these trips, including that train becoming briefly a local service between Brockenhurst and Poole after problems between Waterloo and Surbiton meant that South West Trains needed any train it could find to rescue its passengers who had been stuck for hours along the route through the New Forest because of signal failures.

Departing Brockenhurst, the train stopped at Sway, New Milton, Hinton Admiral, Christchurch and Bournemouth on its way to the Dorset coast. Not only did the passengers complete their journeys home, but were given a trip back to 1967 in the process.

In another instance, when a diesel multiple unit failed at Salisbury, an eastbound 'Cathedrals Express', hauled by LNER A4 Pacific No. 60009 *Union of South Africa*, ferried stranded passengers to Andover and Basingstoke as the train returned to London.

From the nadir of July 9, 1967 to the rebirth in 1992 to a point where in 2004, steam, on a train fittingly called the 'Sunny South Special', had become so normal that South West Trains was able to call upon it to serve its passengers with steam once more!

While the Mid Hants' Daylight Railtours proved very successful for seven years and raised the profile of the Watercress Line through the south and west of England, it became increasingly difficult to organise the tours, particularly getting the train in and out of Alton at reasonable times. So, the operation ceased at the end of 2004 with the coaches being sold, although still based on the railway and hired out for the Steam Dreams' expanding 'Cathedrals Express' programme for some years.

Steam Dreams differed from Daylight Railtours in being more orientated to the general public than the enthusiast, but has nonetheless always attracted a substantial enthusiast following.

The Guildford firm now proudly takes its place among several tour companies running steam specials over the Sunny South today, including the Venice Simplon Orient-Express 'British Pullman', The Railway Touring Company, Vintage Trains and Pathfinders Tours.

THREE-DAY TRIP TO MARK END OF SOUTHERN STEAM HALF-CENTENARY

Steam Dreams did not run a 'Cathedrals Express' on July 9, 2016 to celebrate the 49th anniversary of the end of Southern steam, as had been the firm's custom in recent years.

The train's absence was down to 'operational reasons'. With the official return to steam of A3 Pacific No. 60103 *Flying Scotsman* on February 25, following a £4.2 million overhaul by its owner the National Railway Museum, Steam Dreams instead ran a series of trips through the Sunny South behind the world's most famous steam locomotive.

However, Steam Dreams has big plans to mark the 50th anniversary in 2017.

Based on a three-day trip to the West Country, next year's anniversary special, 'The Devon Belle' offers a three-day break in either Torquay or Kingswear (Dartmouth) and Merchant Navy 4-6-2 No. 35018 *British India Line*, if its rebuild from Barry scrapyard condition by West Coast Railways at Carnforth is completed in time, is likely to head the proceedings.

On Thursday, July 6, the 'Belle' departs London – probably Waterloo – and runs down the South Western Main Line to Salisbury (water stop) then on over the hilly section to Yeovil Junction and from there to Exeter via Honiton bank.

At Exeter, the 4-6-2 is to be replaced by LMS Stanier 8F 2-8-0 No. 48151 for the second leg to Torquay and ultimately Kingswear.

On day two, Friday, July 7, passengers will be at leisure to explore as they wish or

BELOW: Passing Samphire Hoe on the Dover to Folkestone line with the Railway Touring Company's 'The Kentish Belle Armistice Day' special on November 11, 2012. JOHN TITLOW

LEFT: With the towers of Battersea Power Station in the background, Merchant Navy Pacific No. 35028 *Clan Line* passes Stewart's Lane Junction with the Venice Simplon Orient-Express 'British Pullman' circular tour from London Victoria on March 1, 2014. JOHN TITLOW

join optional excursions to the South Devon Railway, a walking tour of Dartmoor, boat trips from the Torbay coast, or to Greenway or Torre Abbey House.

On the Saturday the 'Belle' will most likely be in the hands of the 8F most of the day working from Kingswear to Newton Abbot then onwards over the South Devon banks to Plymouth, entering Cornwall over Brunel's Royal Albert Bridge spanning the Tamar bound for Penzance.

Passengers will have the option of visiting tourist attractions such as St Michael's Mount and the harbourside.

From Penzance, the train will be diesel hauled to St Blazey where the 8F takes charge for the run back to Kingswear.

On Sunday, July 9 – the significant date – the 'Belle' sets out from Kingswear, the 2-8-0

> From humble beginnings, Steam Dreams is now one of Europe's most prominent steam railtour operators.
> Not only has the Guildford-based operator returned regular main line steam to the Sunny South, but now ventures all over Britain, even offering holidays by steam to the Scottish Highlands and Islands and Ireland.
> The trains offer premier dining or Pullman-style dining tickets so you can dine in comfort along the way, while friendly on-board waiting staff can take your order from a range of hot and cold snacks.
> The extensive annual programme of tours can be viewed at www.steamdreams.co.uk
> For tickets and reservations, call 01483 209888 or email info@steamdreams.co.uk

working the train back though Dawlish, Newton Abbot and Exeter before picking up the Great Western main line via the Somerset levels to Castle Cary.

Reversing, the 'Belle' will head for Weymouth via Yeovil Pen Mill and Dorchester West for a short break on the Dorset coast.

As a final gesture towards that memorable day 50 years before, the 'Belle' departs Weymouth for London, provisionally with *British India Line* at the head of the train, the 8F acting as banker up through Upwey as far as Dorchester.

*Additional reporting: Robin Jones and Brian Sharpe.

WHEN THE SUN DOESN'T SHINE…
Of course the sun does not shine all the year round over the south and west of England, despite the Southern Railway's famous advertising slogan. It can get very overcast and chilly too.

That proved no problem for Steam Dreams on December 21, 2009, when the last 'Cathedrals Express' of the year, the 'White Cliffs' evening diner, headed by £3-million new-build A1 Peppercorn Pacific No. 60163 *Tornado*, was waiting to depart London Victoria for a tour of Kent – despite the fact that most of the local network had been hit by snow and sub-zero temperatures.

That evening, Victoria was jammed with commuters eager to return home but badly delayed by disrupted and cancelled services.

Many found themselves stranded because of the failure of modern traction. Steam, however, had no problem with 'the wrong kind of snow'.

With seats to spare, Steam Dreams then chief, Graeme Bunker, invited a group of stranded commuters to join the train, which was scheduled to stop at Swanley and Maidstone East en route to Canterbury.

Grateful in the extreme, they filled the empty seats, mostly in standard class, to experience a 'new' form of rush-hour travel in cosy steam-heated carriages.

That they enjoyed Steam Dreams' generosity was evident when alighting at their respective destinations many backed their thanks by proffering fivers and tenners.

On its return journey via Folkestone, the train swept through Ashford International station, which was denuded of Eurostar trains following the wrong-type-of-snow blocking the Channel Tunnel.

THE LAST 'REAL' STEAM ON THE SOUTHERN
While Merchant Navy 4-6-2 *Elder Dempster Lines* pulled the last steam train over the Southern Region in 1967, the service was not the final end of steam on that part of the network.

Although the official date for the end of Southern steam is given as July 9 that year, two S100 'USA' class 0-6-0T dock tanks soldiered on until September in use as Ashford shed pilots.

Designed by Col Howard G Hill in 1942 and built for the United States Army Transportation for use in the Second World War, a total of 382 were turned out by a series of manufacturers stateside.

They arrived in the UK in 1943 in anticipation of D-Day, after which most were shipped to the continent.

A few remained in store at Newbury racecourse having seen little use. Like other Big Four companies, the Southern Railway found itself short of locomotives after years of wartime austerity and sought to replace the E1, B4 and D1 tanks used in Southampton Docks.

The locomotives needed to have a short wheelbase to negotiate the tight curves found in the dockyard, but be able to haul heavy freight trains as well as full-length passenger trains in the harbour area.

SR Chief Mechanical Engineer Oliver Bulleid ran the rule over the S100s, and recommended that 14 were bought, plus another one for spares.

Other S100s went to the National Coal Board, the Longmoor Military Railway and Austin Motors.

Of the 15 acquired by the Southern Railway, 13 were built at the Vulcan Iron Works in Wilkes-Barre, Pennsylvania in 1942, with the other two coming from HK Porter of Pittsburgh.

Once in Southern hands, they were fitted with steam heating, vacuum ejectors, sliding cab windows, additional lamp irons and new cylinder drain cocks.

Further modifications became necessary once the locomotives started to enter traffic, including large roof-top ventilators, British-style regulators (as built they had US-style pull-out ones), three rectangular cab-front lookout windows, extended coal bunkers, separate steam and vacuum brake controls as well as wooden tip-up seats.

Telephones were later installed on the footplate to improve communication on the vast network of sidings at Southampton.

It took until November 1947 for the entire new class – which became known as 'Yankee tanks' – to be ready for work.

Before Nationalisation, the locomotives were painted in Southern black livery with Southern in sunshine yellow lettering. The lettering on the tank sides was changed to British Railways' during 1948 as a transitional measure. Finally, class members were painted in BR Departmental malachite livery, with BR crests on the tank sides and numbers on the cabsides.

Thirteen of the locomotives were renumbered in a single sequence from 61-73 by the Southern Railway but No. 4326 retained its earlier War Department number instead of being renumbered 74. The locomotive used for spares was not numbered.

After 1948 they were renumbered 30061-30074 by BR. Six examples were transferred to Departmental use in 1962-63 and renumbered DS233-DS238.

They were used in Southampton Docks for 15 years and were powerful, economical to operate and initially relatively easy to maintain. However, because they were basic machines turned out as cheaply as possible during the years of wartime austerity, age took its toll more quickly than might be expected.

Their steel fireboxes rusted and fatigued quickly, and had to be replaced as early as 1951. At the docks, British Rail Class 07 diesel-electric shunters, replaced them in 1962, when the first member of the class was withdrawn. The six departmental locomotives went to Redbridge Sleeper Depot, Meldon Quarry, Ashford wagon works (two locomotives) and Lancing Carriage Works (two locomotives).

Other survivors were used for informal departmental purposes such as steam heating at Southampton or shunting at Eastleigh shed before withdrawal. Nine examples remained in March 1967 and five of these survived until the end of steam on the Southern Region that year.

Examples hold the distinction of being the last locomotives in steam on the Southern Region.

Thankfully, the Ashford Works pair, Nos. 30065/DS237 and 30070/DS238, developed hot boxes while being towed to Cashmore's scrapyard in South Wales, and were dumped at Tonbridge. Moving them by road for scrapping was considered too costly, and luckily the nascent Kent & East Sussex Railway intervened to buy them.

Two others survived: No. 30064, which ended up on the Bluebell Railway, and No. 30072, which was long part of the Keighley & Worth Valley Railway fleet and is now undergoing an overhaul at the Ribble Steam Railway. ●

BELOW: USA 0-6-0T No. 30065 passes Rolvenden signalbox on the Kent & East Sussex Railway on March 7, 2016. *KESR*

Chapter 2

PURBECK PERFEC

It has taken a marathon 45 years to restore services throughout the Swanage Railway, and a steady stream of innovations over the decades has seen it stake its claim to the title of the ideal Sunny South branch line today. Indeed, in so many ways, this enterprising heritage line has re-emerged as a microcosm of the Southern Railway and its successor the Southern Region. Here is the full story of this line's incredible journey back from extinction.

A black cloud descended over the Sunny South on January 3, 1972, when British Rail closed the Swanage branch.

The closure took place nearly seven years after the departure of British Railways' chairman, Dr Richard Beeching, who had pruned most of the seaside branches west of Weymouth.

Yet 45 years later, in 2017, regular public trains – as opposed to heritage or tourist services – are once again set to link Swanage with the main line at Wareham.

It has taken nearly half a century to rebuild the line, during which it has re-emerged as the epitome of a Sunny South branch with locomotives, rolling stock and stations perfectly recapturing the ambience of the Southern Railway/Region in its heyday, and much more besides.

Today's Swanage Railway encapsulates everything that was once so magical about travelling by train from the busy metropolis to the seaside. A time when families laden with suitcases – who had been enticed by slick advertising posters – and their children with buckets and spades would jostle on the platforms of Waterloo for a seat on south- and west-bound trains on peak summer Saturday mornings, for a week of delight at their chosen resort.

Such scenes died with the decline of rail travel in the 1970s and 1980s, when the car became king, and families found that they were no longer tied to resorts served by rail.

It was in 1847 that the first plan for a branch line from Wareham, which became served by the new Southampton to Dorchester line, to Swanage was drawn up.

line) Furzebrook and Corfe Castle, however, eventually proved more successful. Under his scheme, both routes would tap into ball clay and stone traffic, exploiting the rich mineral resources of the Isle of Purbeck.

In November 1880, a Bill was lodged in Parliament for a branch line despite yet more protests from Wareham residents and an initial lack of interest from residents in Swanage.

That December, a public meeting in Swanage showed support for a branch from Wareham after Burt presented a route proposal surveyed by London & South Western Railway's consulting engineers Galbraith & Church.

In July 1881, Queen Victoria gave Royal Assent to the Swanage Railway Act of 1881. It included a 2ft gauge tramway from the site of Swanage station to the town's pier tramway, which carried Purbeck stone.

Purbeck stone was already being exported from Swanage by coastal shipping. Captain Moorsom, chief engineer of the Southampton & Dorchester Railway, encouraged local promoters to found the Swanage Pier and Tramway Company, which obtained an authorising Act of Parliament on August 8, 1859. The scheme involved four miles of tramway, running on to the pier at Swanage, from which coastal vessels would be loaded directly.

However, objections from Wareham residents who feared damage to the town's Saxon walls, and Purbeck landowners, meant that it never got off the ground.

In 1862, the Isle of Purbeck Railway Company proposed a branch line from Wareham to Swanage via Stoborough, Furzebrook and Corfe Castle.

This plan too failed through similar objections and a lack of financial support, although wealthy Swanage businessmen George Burt and John Mowlem, founder of the Mowlem construction company, had supported it.

A proposal in 1877 from George Burt for a branch line from Wareham to Swanage along one of two routes – one via Stoborough, Furzebrook and Corfe Castle and the second via Worgret (where it would leave the main

ABOVE: The Southern Railway reclaims its own: on May 2, 2009, Bulleid Battle of Britain light Pacific No. 34067 *Tangmere*, which hauled the first heritage-era steam train from London in the form of Past-Time Rail's 'The Royal Wessex' from Victoria, is greeted by sister No. 34070 *Manston* as it approaches Corfe Castle. ROBIN JONES

RIGHT: A British Railways' poster from the 1960s advertising the Dorset section of the Sunny South. ROBIN JONES

ABOVE: The tracks of the pier tramway are preserved today in paving. ROBIN JONES

ABOVE: Corfe Castle viaduct under construction in 1884. ANDREW PM WRIGHT
BELOW: Swanage station staff in the early 1900s. ANDREW PM WRIGHT COLLECTION

However, only a short section was built, from the pier to an area on the sea front called The Bankers where stone blocks were prepared for transit. Only horse traction was used.

After the enabling Act was obtained, the Swanage Railway Company was formed to build the line from Wareham, with share capital of £90,000 and permitted debenture borrowings of £30,000.

The town previously had been comparatively cut off because of its valley location. Swanage is the capital of the Isle of Purbeck, although it is for the large part surrounded by water on three sides, it cannot technically be considered an island in the fullest sense of the word because it is firmly linked to Dorset to the west. However, communications had often left much to be desired: today, its main link to the rest of Dorset is by the A351, which acts like a spine road leading to Swanage, and the car chain ferry from Studland to Sandbanks.

Building of the branch started in the summer of 1883 at the Worgret Junction and Swanage ends with the cost of construction being estimated to be £77,000.

In the autumn of 1884, the track from Worgret reached the north side of the village of Corfe Castle where a three-arched Purbeck stone viaduct was built.

In February 1885, the building of the Purbeck stone Swanage station was completed by Bull & Company of Southampton.

THE FIRST TRAINS

May 20, 1885, saw the first trains run from Swanage with the 10¼-mile branch worked by the LSWR. There was but one intermediate station, at Corfe Castle.

The first passenger train comprised a LSWR Beattie well tank towing four London and South Western Railway carriages. Amid public celebration in Swanage and Corfe Castle, a special train also ran from London on that historic first day of operation.

The first timetable consisted of five passenger trains each way and a daily goods train; the latter was amalgamated with the passenger service by the operation of mixed trains from August 1, 1885.

The LSWR had taken over the Swanage Railway's liabilities of £2914 in 1881 and a full amalgamation took place through an Act of Parliament on June 25, 1885.

The introduction of the railway made Swanage much more accessible to visitors, with direct services running from London. The impact of the new railway on Purbeck was tremendous and changed the area. A Victorian train journey from Wareham to Swanage took 25 minutes and cost 11 old pence. Compare that with the one-and-a-half hour horse-and-carriage journey costing two shillings and sixpence.

However, the greatest increase in visitors to the town came with the building of the second 'new' pier in 1895, primarily for use by pleasure steamers.

The Swanage branch intersected the pre-existing Furzebrook Railway, a narrow gauge industrial line also known as the Pike Brothers' Tramway, which carried locally extracted ball clay to a river wharf, and the Middlebere Plateway, which conveyed the mineral to Poole Harbour. The proprietors of those lines were slow to arrange interchange facilities with the new branch line.

The extension from Swanage station to the pier tramway, which was authorised by the enabling Act was never built.

A larger station to the west superseded the existing small Wareham station east of the level crossing, which was capable of acting as the junction interchange point. The new station was opened on April 4, 1887.

In 1905, an interchange siding for the Furzebook 2ft 8½in gauge line was finally opened, allowing minerals to be carried out by rail.

In Edwardian times, with improvements in social conditions, taking holidays at seaside resorts became the norm for many working-class families as well as the better off, and through trains from London to Swanage began.

During both world wars, the branch was visited by long Army trains as Purbeck became a training area for soldiers, including preparations for the D-Day invasion of France in 1944.

The LSWR became a principal part of the new Southern Railway at the Grouping that followed the Railways Act of 1922.

By the winter of 1931 there were 13 daily passenger trains on the Swanage branch. After 1945, local trains on the branch were operated as push-and-pull services.

Some branch trains conveyed through carriages from Weymouth. If the branch engine was propelling the branch coaches, the attached main line coaches would be behind the locomotive, which was sandwiched.

BEECHING AND BEYOND

With the end of rationing and increased prosperity after the Second World War, the line declined as people travelled to Purbeck by car rather than train. Increasingly fewer passengers and less goods were carried during the 1950s.

From September 1962, through coaches from Swanage to Wareham, where they were added to the rear of the Weymouth to London 'Royal Wessex' train, were stopped. From then on, passengers had to change at Wareham.

On March 27, 1963 Beeching published his landmark report, The Reshaping of British Railways, which led to a seismic change in the nation's railways.

He recommended that out of 18,000 miles of railway, 6000 miles, mostly rural and industrial lines, should be closed entirely, and that some of the remaining lines should be kept open only for freight. A total of 2363 stations were to close, including 435 already under threat, both on lines that were to close and on lines that were to say open.

However, the Swanage branch was not listed by Beeching in his 1963 report. It seemed that it would, like Hastings, Bexhill-on-Sea, Seaford, Lymington and other Sunny South resorts, escape the dreaded axe.

Nevertheless, the economies being made elsewhere began to make their mark. In October 1965, Corfe Castle and Swanage goods yards closed to freight, the nearest freight depot afterwards being Wareham. In 1966, Swanage lost their stationmasters, and Eldon's Siding, a transhipment point – between the Swanage branch and the 3ft 9in gauge (later 2ft) Fayle's Tramway, another mineral-carrying concern – officially closed after last being used in the early 1960s.

In April 1967, the Swanage branch's two track gangs – one covering Worgret Junction to Corfe Castle and the second covering Corfe Castle to Wareham – were abolished with the maintenance of the branch line track covered by a 'mobile' gang based at Wareham. From September 1967, there was no winter Sunday service on the branch.

Sunday, September 4, 1966 was the last day of branch timetabled steam trains between Wareham and Swanage. The following day saw the start of a dieselised Swanage branch-service operated by three-coach Class 205 'Hampshire' diesel-electric multiple units (DEMUs) built at Eastleigh in 1957.

On Sunday, June 18, 1967 the final steam train ran to Swanage, in the form of a Railway Correspondence & Travel Society end-of-steam special from London. On the Swanage end of that 12-carriage train was Bulleid Battle of Britain Pacific No. 34089 *602 Squadron*, the last steam locomotive to be overhauled at BR's Eastleigh Works, in September 1966, while on the Wareham end was Salisbury-based BR Standard 4MT No. 80146.

When Harold Wilson's Labour party campaigned in the 1964 general election, it publicly promised to reverse all the closures that Beeching had instigated and sack him. After Wilson came to power, his administration not only retained Beeching's services and carried on with his closures but eventually made more over and above those that he had recommended.

In October 1967, British Railways issued a notice that the Swanage line was to be closed by September 1968. However, owing to opposition heightened by the problems in providing a replacement bus service during the summer months, the closure was deferred.

May 1968 saw a Transport Users' Consultative Committee hearing (the TUCC was set up under the 1962 Transport Act) held at the Mowlem Theatre, Swanage, to hear local council and public objections to closure plans for the branch.

That August, the TUCC ruled that British Rail could not close the Swanage branch because of the inconvenience to travellers and an insufficient local bus service in the absence of the railway.

In 1969, a through train from London was operated on summer Saturdays. The last direct Swanage to Bournemouth and London train ran during the first week of October 1969.

British Rail claimed the Swanage branch line lost £79,000 during 1968, and came back again in January 1969 with a proposal to close the line in October that year. Angry locals formed the Isle of Purbeck Preservation Group to prevent the line from being closed.

A Department of the Environment inspector ruled that the line should remain open, but that decision was later overturned by the secretary of state for the environment.

In October 1969, British Rail announced that the branch would close from May 1970. Travellers and local councils again objected to the proposed extra bus services aimed at replacing the trains, and staved off the closure.

In February 1971, British Rail proposed to close the line that September. The 1971 Southern Region timetable for the Swanage branch warns that the train service could be "withdrawn at any time".

In April 1971, Swanage station's remaining staff of three people – booking clerk, Maurice Walton, and porters Bill 'Taffy' Hazell and George Sims – were awarded third prize in the Southern Region's best-kept station competition.

That held no sway for those in power, for in November, 1971, British Rail came back with yet another closure proposal, and this time it was to be successful.

It announced that the branch was to close on the morning of Monday, January 3, 1972 – the line's 87th year of operation – with the last trains running on January 1, as there was no winter Sunday service.

On that cold Saturday night, crowds gathered at the near-derelict Swanage station to watch the departure of a special train driven by Johnny Walker who had driven the last steam train from Swanage to Wareham in 1966. Dirty Hampshire 3H DEMUs No. 1110

LEFT: A doubleheader passes Eldons siding in the 1930s. ANDREW PM WRIGHT COLLECTION
BELOW: Corfe Castle station in 1910. ANDREW PM WRIGHT COLLECTION

ABOVE: An early postcard lampooning the Swanage branch. ROBIN JONES **RIGHT:** Swanage station in the 1920s. LES HAYWARD via ANDREW PM WRIGHT

ABOVE: Was Corfe Castle the biggest sandcastle in the Sunny South? Generations of young holidaymakers may have asked this question on the last stage of the journey to the seaside. Ivatt 2MT 2-6-2T No. 41275 leaves the village station bound for Swanage in the summer of 1964. ANDREW PM WRIGHT COLLECTION

ABOVE: Before the rot set in: Swanage station in 1961, as an M7 0-4-4T runs round its Southern green-liveried branch train. JOHN CARTER via ANDREW PM WRIGHT

ABOVE: Drummond M7 0-4-4T No. 30108 leaves Swanage in 1963. ANDREW PM WRIGHT COLLECTION

and No. 1124 made the final trip to Swanage with the train packed and special Edmondson tickets having been produced.

A knock-on casualty of the closure was that of the surviving narrow gauge ball clay tramway system at Norden weeks later, with the track lifted soon afterwards. The last ball clay load was carried from the Norden mines to the lorry drop (now the site of the Swanage Railway's Norden station) in late 1971 or early 1972.

A FRESH BEGINNING

In June 1972, as a result of local anger at the loss of the branch, the Swanage Railway Society was formed to rebuild the line, with the objective of restoring an all-the-year-round community railway service linking to the main line at Wareham, which would be 'subsidised' by the operation of steam-hauled heritage trains during the holidays.

Meanwhile, as was normal practice at the time, following the closure, seven miles of track was lifted from Swanage to Motala, a point half a mile east of Furzebrook, by contractors hired by BR. The work took seven weeks, with the metal rails melted down for scrap and the wooden sleepers sold to farmers for fencing.

The new society organised protests, and eventually an agreement with BR followed to leave all the ballast in place along with an extra half a mile of track between Furzebrook and Motala.

The western section of the branch from Furzebrook to the main line junction at Worgret remained in use for ball clay traffic, and later also served the oilfield at Wytch Farm north of Corfe Castle.

BR originally intended to sell the Swanage station site to a property developer, but after the intervention of Evelyn King, the MP for south Dorset, at the society's request, offered it to Swanage Town Council, which bought it in 1974 – but then demolished the main platform and other buildings, and stripped the canopy of lead and glass.

As was typical of the times, when there were few examples of heritage railways making a major if not essential contribution to a local tourist economy, the society's plans received a less than lukewarm response from Dorset County Council or the town council.

In March 1974, the council acquired the railway land between the end of the line at

Furzebrook from the A351 Catseye bridge and Northbrook Road bridge in Swanage and planned to build a bypass for Corfe Castle on the trackbed, wanting to demolish a key bridge on the outskirts of Swanage, while the town council started to demolish Swanage station. It was planned to replace it with a shopping centre, pub and car park.

In response, the society formed two daughter organisations: the Swanage and Wareham Railway Group, composed of local residents prepared to lobby the local authorities; and the Southern Steam Group, to collect historic railway rolling stock and establish a museum of steam and railway technology.

After many interventions by local residents, in 1975, the town council finally granted the society limited facilities on the Swanage station site with a one-year lease, following a referendum among townspeople, after society supporters gathered a petition of town ratepayers.

The Southern Steam Group acquired charitable status, and subsequently both the society and the residents' group joined a new Southern Steam Trust.

It was on Saturday, February 14, 1976 that members of the fledgling society moved into the boarded-up Victorian Swanage station building.

Volunteer Jonathan Burke, then 14, who later became a station porter there, recalled: "My memories of that first day of restoration work at Swanage station are of achievement and a realisation that there was a very long way to go.

"Many people said it would never happen so it was good to gain access to Swanage station. The railway was very dear to my heart and it still is.

"My mother and father had been involved in previous attempts by the Isle of Purbeck Preservation Group to keep the railway open in the late 1960s. My dad died in 1976 but I stayed involved with the railway, as did my mother.

"We took the boards off the windows of Swanage station and gained access to the station. With a lot of enthusiasm we felt that we were going to do it, which we have."

Fellow teenage pioneer Peter Frost, who later became a steam driver at Swanage, remembered:

"When the opportunity came to rebuild the railway with the formation of the Swanage Railway Society, I leapt at the chance. Society chairman, Andrew Goltz, provided a real opportunity to achieve the dream when the group was given a lease of the station site.

"We were able to re-create part of our history and rebuild the railway. Swanage was in a recession in 1976 and the winter months in the town were dead because the visitors stopped coming.

"Eventually, we ground down the opposition through the power of our rationale behind rebuilding the railway and the progress being made on the ground."

The small group of volunteers laid some track inside the goods shed in readiness for the arrival of the first locomotive.

June that year saw the arrival of the first locomotive, *Beryl*, a small Hibberd Planet petrol shunter from Poole Quay.

It was followed in September 1976, by British Railways 4MT 2-6-4T No. 80078, which arrived from Dai Woodham's legendary Barry scrapyard in South Wales. It was the same type of locomotive that hauled trains on the branch in the 1960s.

In 1977 the town council permitted tracklaying outside the shed, while December 1978, saw an oil-loading depot opened at Furzebrook on the existing stub of the branch, for the BP Wytch Farm oil field.

In 1978, the Southern Steam Trust, which manages the railway restoration project, was formed as a charity out of the old Southern Steam Group.

TRAINS RETURN TO SWANAGE

August 1979 saw the first heritage-era passenger train service from Northbrook Road bridge to just beyond Swan Brook stream bridge behind the engine shed.

It comprised 1957-built Fowler 0-4-0 diesel mechanical industrial shunter No. 4210132 *May*, which had arrived in 1977 and Bulleid coach No. 4365.

Those first trains ran over just a few hundred yards of track and raised money to help rebuild the line and boost awareness of the revivalists' long-term ambition – to rebuild the branch to Wareham yard by yard.

The first steam-hauled passenger trains at Swanage since June 1967 ran at Easter 1981, hauled by oil-burning Barclay industrial 0-4-0T No. 2354 of 1954 *Richard Trevithick* (now at the Swindon & Cricklade Railway) and comprising two coaches. It was operated as a push-pull service from the main platform under the canopy to beyond the stream bridge behind the engine shed. When *Richard Trevithick* arrived at Swanage on August 6, 1979 it was the line's first operating steam locomotive. Indeed, many of today's top UK heritage lines began operations using humble industrial tank engine types that were historically inappropriate to their railway: the fledgling Swanage Railway relied on several for the first few years, until main line types became available.

With Dorset County Council allowing the volunteers to extend their track beyond Swanage station, the line reached the one-mile point at Herston during 1982, where a new halt was built out of wood, with a run-round loop installed.

The first passenger trains to Herston Halt ran on Good Friday 1984.

ABOVE: Bunker first, a BR Standard 4MT 2-6-4T approaches Worgret Junction from River Frome in May 1966. ANDREW PM WRIGHT COLLECTION

LEFT: The last steam train out of Swanage was this Railway Correspondence & Travel Society special in June 1967. ANDREW PM WRIGHT

ABOVE: In a scene typical of the post-Beeching years, Class 33 Crompton diesel D6531 stands at the head of a train in weed-choked Swanage station. ANDREW PM WRIGHT COLLECTION

ABOVE: BR Standard 4MT 2-6-4T No. 80146 heads the last steam train out of Corfe Castle in June 1967. ANDREW PM WRIGHT COLLECTION

In 1986 one of the four Corfe Castle bypass routes, which would have used the trackbed, was taken out of Dorset County Council's plans after a lengthy campaign by villagers and the Swanage Railway. Only the year before, the county council had announced that it would build its bypass on the trackbed so this about-turn was a colossal victory.

The track was slowly relaid towards the three-mile point at Harman's Cross. In July 1987, services were extended half a mile past Herston Halt to New Barn – giving a total run from Swanage of 1½ miles. Trains were pushed from Herston to New Barn where there was no run-round loop. On September 11, the 100,000th fare-paying passenger was carried since the service to Herston Halt began in 1984. The passenger was carried from Swanage to New Barn.

In 1987 the relaid tracks reached Harman's Cross where a new station was built, the first in Dorset for more than 50 years. Accepting its first public trains in March 1989, Harman's Cross station was opened by Gordon Pettit, the general manager of the Southern Region, which had closed and lifted the line to Swanage 17 years before.

The next challenge for the dedicated Swanage Railway volunteers was to extend their line two miles to Corfe Castle – and just under a mile beyond that to Norden.

There were two major obstacles to be overcome – the replacement of three bridges and government permission to return the railway to Corfe Castle and Norden.

Large girders were obtained from British Rail so underbridges could be reinstated ahead of the track re-laying operation. Dorset County Council had withdrawn the plan for a bypass on railway land at Corfe Castle in 1986.

ABOVE: The end is nigh: 'Hampshire' unit No. 1105 arrives at Swanage station in 1970, when British Rail had long since given up on weeding the track.

ABOVE: The last British Rail train at Swanage on January 1, 1972. TONY LEGG via ANDREW PM WRIGHT

LEFT: British Rail's last Wareham to Swanage train on January 1, 1972. ANDREW PM WRIGHT COLLECTION

ABOVE: Tracklifting at Corfe Castle in July 1972. ANDREW PM WRIGHT COLLECTION

A public enquiry planning hearing held before a government inspector ruled against objectors and decided that the volunteers could rebuild the line. The Purbeck stone station buildings at Corfe Castle were restored and the tracks relaid while at Norden, half a mile to the west, another completely new station was to be built.

December 1988 had seen Swanage Railway members travel on the first train to Harman's Cross, with passenger services starting the following March and in the summer of 1990, the relaid tracks reached Corfe Castle station.

OPERATION MILLSTONE

The extension plans sparked huge optimism among railway supporters – at last the new Swanage Railway would be going "from somewhere to somewhere".

However, Norden was at first the station that nobody wanted. Corfe Castle would have been the ideal temporary terminus for the fledgling line, connecting the seaside resort to a popular tourist attraction.

However, the local authority insisted that the line ran on to Norden instead of Corfe Castle, because of the acute lack of car parking facilities in the quaint picture postcard village. The railway found itself in the unenviable position of not being able to run trains from Harman's Cross to Corfe Castle until the next half-mile was built, and therefore found itself deprived of the ability to raise desperately needed revenue.

Wild rumours emanating from one of two dissatisfied volunteers "in the know" at Easter 1991 suggested that the railway was on the brink of financial ruin, with the new track still awaiting ballasting and much infrastructure unfinished.

Volunteers were then leaked an auditors' letter which stated that the accounts were two years behind and in an utter mess. It was discovered that Swanage Railway Company Ltd. had run up debts of more than £250,000, far worse than even the most disenchanted members had conjectured.

Then it was found that the company had not even applied for the Light Railway Order necessary to run trains to Corfe Castle.

The advice from insolvency practitioners was crystal clear – close the railway down.

However, volunteers were made of much sterner stuff. They had defied the outright

ABOVE: Derelict Swanage station in May 1975. ANDREW PM WRIGHT

ABOVE: Moving into Swanage station in February 1976. ANDREW PM WRIGHT COLLECTION

ABOVE: British Railways 4MT 2-6-4T No. 80078 is unloaded at Swanage in September 1976. ANDREW PM WRIGHT COLLECTION

ABOVE: Swanage Railway Society volunteers at work in 1976. ANDREW PM WRIGHT COLLECTION

RIGHT: The first locomotive for the revival arrived at Swanage in June 1976. ANDREW PM WRIGHT COLLECTION

Making Fresh Tracks to the Sunny South and West

closure of the branch, and would now fight the soaring debts against the odds. But desperate times called for desperate measures, as piles of bills several inches high mounted in the Swanage station office.

The composition of the railway company board and trust council was radically altered following a 'revolution' while the then general manager resigned, and 12 out of 13 paid staff were made redundant.

As the railway was well into the red, nobody would loan it a locomotive, and it was left with only the 1708 Trust's Midland Railway 1F 0-6-0T No. 1708 to haul trains.

Bill Trite, chairman of the then Southern Steam Trust, was named as chairman of an emergency committee formed to keep the railway in business.

Its policy was total transparency – not hiding anything from creditors, but explaining to each the current situation and asking for their goodwill in giving breathing space.

Summer came, and it was dull, wet and miserable – exactly what the railway needed.

On most days for several weeks, early sunshine gave way to mid-morning clouds and lunchtime drizzle – forcing beachgoers on to the train in droves, if only to keep dry.

Fares rolled in, and members paid £50,000 out of their own pockets to pay pressing creditors.

The Inland Revenue was due £32,000, and to pay it, the trust sold off No. 80078 to a group of members, arranging to lease it back in due course.

ABOVE: The first heritage-era train service at Swanage in August 1979. MICK STONE via ANDREW PM WRIGHT

By the end of that summer, many creditors had been paid, but it took until 1993 for the company to be brought back into financial security.

A £250,000 overdraft to pay for the extension was still outstanding, so the trust pushed hard on promotion of its premier membership scheme giving free travel for life for £230, and sold 1600. That proved another major milestone in the long road back to solvency.

December 1995 saw Bill and his team launch Operation Millstone in another bid to slash the overdraft. Over and above an appeal for donations to members, a leaflet asking for money was placed on every seat on the trains in a handwritten envelope.

Members of the emergency committee taught themselves how to apply for the Light Railway Order while a fresh appeal for funds for the half-mile to Norden was launched.

The relaid tracks reached Norden in April 1992. Finally, Norden station opened in August 1995, with LSWR M7 0-4-4T No. 30053 hauling the first train.

SOUTHERN CLASSIC BACK FROM EXILE

The M7s were a classic LSWR design, which was once part and parcel of the Sunny South scenario.

Designed by Dugald Drummond for use on the intensive London network, a total of 105 were built between 1897 and 1911.

ABOVE: Corfe Castle station in 1985: still a scene of dereliction, but within a decade all that was to change. ANDREW PM WRIGHT

LEFT: Tracklaying at Corfe Castle in September 1990. ANDREW PM WRIGHT

RIGHT: Barclay saddle tank *Richard Trevithick* hauls a short Swanage Railway train in 1980. ANDREW PM WRIGHT COLLECTION

BELOW: Midland Railway 1F 0-6-0T No. 41708 heads the first train to Harman's Cross in December 1988. ANDREW PM WRIGHT

26 Making Fresh Tracks to the Sunny South and West

ABOVE: In a scene oozing pure heritage, M7 No. 30053 heads the first heritage-era train to Corfe Castle and Norden on Saturday, August 12, 1995. ANDREW PM WRIGHT

Many of the class were fitted with push-pull operation gear that enabled efficient use on branch line duties without the need to change to the other end of its train at the end of a journey.

Very successful as suburban passenger engines, they were superseded by newer, standard designs; many of them were switched for branch line use, especially in southern England.

British Rail withdrew the last of the class in 1964 with two examples making it into preservation: No. 245 in the National Railway Museum, and No. 53 (BR 30053).

No. 30053, which was built at Nine Elms in 1905, and ran on the Swanage branch in the 1930s and 1940s as well as between December 1963 was withdrawn from 71B Bournemouth shed on May 17, 1964, and bought privately for preservation.

After a period of outdoor storage at Eastleigh, it was cosmetically restored and sold to the Steamtown museum in Bellows Falls, Vermont, USA, in 1967.

It was shipped abroad in April that year.

In 1983, the Southern Repatriation Group, mindful of its immense local historical importance, was formed to repatriate No. 30053 from the USA for use on the Swanage Railway.

On April 9, 1987 M7 No. 30053 returned to Swanage station, from which it last hauled trains for British Railways in 1964.

Owned by the Drummond Locomotives Society, the Edwardian-built locomotive has been running regularly on the railway since 1992, having taken five years to be overhauled to working order.

NORDEN'S RESOUNDING SUCCESS

Far from being an unwanted station imposed on the railway, Norden proved an outstanding success.

In 1979, railway volunteer, David Morgan, a local town planner, came up with the idea of creating a park-and-ride serving as a transport hub, whereby holidaymakers could park up and not only take the train to Corfe Castle and the beach, avoiding the narrow and winding A351 between Corfe Castle and Swanage but also to take buses to other beauty spots such as Lulworth Cove and Durdle Door.

Again, steam proved the big draw for the general public. Norden's park-and-ride station exceeded all expectations, and led to more trains being laid on; the railway claiming to be the most intensively used heritage line in Britain during the summer months.

While the railway was to all appearances a tourist attraction, it had begun doing exactly what the branch had been built for – offering 'real' public transport.

Norden took off, and within a few years the local council had spent £500,000 on expanding the car park from 130 to 250 spaces to cope with demand.

CHASING THE WAREHAM GOAL AGAIN

With Millstone a resounding success, and other recovery measures slowly but surely having pulled the railway back from the brink of a jaw-dropping £500,000 Purbeck financial precipice, the reorganised and revitalised company began looking westwards beyond Norden.

In March 1992, on the eastern stub of the branch that was still part of the national network, the last ball clay train left the Furzebrook siding of English China Clays. As we saw earlier, the first clay train had left the siding in 1905.

In 1997, a new signal box was opened at Harman's Cross so two trains could run on the line at once, instead of just one. Determined volunteers spent the late 1990s clearing the overgrown trackbed and re-laying the track for

ABOVE: LSWR M7 0-4-4T No. 30053 returns from exile in the USA as it is unloaded at Felixstowe docks in April 1987. ANDREW PM WRIGHT

Making Fresh Tracks to the Sunny South and West

ABOVE: BR Standard 2-6-4T No. 80104 passes visiting 515 4-6-0 No. E828 at Harman's Cross in July 1998. ANDREW PM WRIGHT

ABOVE: The Swanage Railway meets the Railtrack section of the branch at Motala in January 2002. ANDREW PM WRIGHT

ABOVE: Tracklaying to the A351 Catseye bridge beyond Norden in 2001. ANDREW PM WRIGHT

another mile – from Norden to Motala and the start of the national network.

In July 1999 track was relaid over the BP Wytch Farm oil field and Norden car park access road. In September the following year, the track was extended past Eldon's Siding and up through Woodpecker cutting. In May 2001 track was relaid to the A351 Catseye bridge.

On January 3, 2002 – 30 years after the line was lifted – the Swanage Railway's tracks met the line from Worgret Junction at Motala. A gap of just one inch divided the stopblock set up in the summer of 1972 from the Swanage Railway.

THE FIRST INCOMING TRAIN

Goliaths of the steam and modern traction eras stood shoulder to shoulder as the Swanage Railway and the preservation movement celebrated one of its biggest landmarks – the running of the first through train to the seaside town in more than 30 years.

On Sunday, September 8, 2002, gleaming red Virgin Trains' high-tech Class 220 Voyager train No. 220018 made the historic journey from the main line via Worgret Junction and a temporary weekend-only connection at Motala.

The Voyager's public arrival at Norden station saw the 125mph express train set off a pyrotechnic display before it ran through a special commemorative banner across the tracks.

Two thousand members, supporters and partisan local residents packed Swanage station when the train carrying a party of VIP guests from Norden drew into the seaside town for a naming ceremony.

Eighty-year-old Purbeck Line pioneer, Moyra Cross of Swanage, who had campaigned against BR's closure of the branch, and veteran Dorset steam locomotive driver Stan Symes of Bournemouth – named Virgin Trains' newest train, the £4-million *Dorset Voyager*, which began work carrying passengers between Dorset, the Midlands, the North and Scotland from the end of that September.

Moyra said: "I was very excited but also very emotional. It was the realisation of all our dreams. We all struggled and a lot of people said it would never happen but a few determined people were absolutely certain that it was going to happen so we pressed on and this is the result today."

On his arrival at Swanage on the historic train, the mayor of Wareham, Coun Charles Patterson, was welcomed by the mayor of Swanage, Coun Tony Miller, as the Swanage Town Band played Cliff Richard's 1968 hit, Congratulations, on the platform.

Virgin Trains chief executive, Chris Green, said: "Speaking on behalf of the rail industry – because we have Railtrack, Balfour Beatty, the Strategic Rail Authority and South West Trains here today – we are delighted to be rolling back Beeching with the Swanage Railway. To be standing here 30 years after the last train from Wareham is terrific."

After the official naming, he presented a mounted replica of the *Dorset Voyager* nameplate to Swanage Railway chairman, Bill Trite, and another to Michael Holden, boss of Railtrack's southern region.

In return, Bill presented Chris Green with a large replica of the nameplate that used to be carried by the unrebuilt West Country class Bulleid Pacific No. 34105 *Swanage*, which used to work to the resort during the 1950s.

Dorset Voyager had arrived on the branch the previous evening and was berthed at the heritage line's Eldon's sidings west of Norden. While HM Railway Inspectorate had given it permission to run over the half-mile between Motala and Furzebrook, it had to run at just 5mph and could not carry passengers west of Norden.

However, after the naming ceremony, the four-coach unit took the place of the 12.55pm service train from Swanage to Norden and ran regular public timetabled services for the rest of the day.

It alternated paths with Bulleid Pacifics No. 34072 *257 Squadron* and No. 35027 *Port Line*, which took turns on the remaining services. *Dorset Voyager* left the branch on the Sunday evening.

THROUGH TRAINS TO SWANAGE ARE BACK!

In 2003, the Swanage signal box was brought into use. Two years later, an original mid-1950s British Railways' signal box at Corfe Castle came back into use, allowing trains to pass for the first time since 1972 and steam trains to pass there for the first time since September 1966.

Also in July 2005 the final BP gas train left Furzebrook sidings and BP closed its Wytch Farm liquid petroleum gas terminal, just leaving the tracks. There was a danger that Network Rail could have demolished and 'plain lined' the junction after closing the Worgret Junction to Motala branch, but thankfully it didn't happen.

In 2006, the railway signed a connection agreement with Network Rail. A double-trap point signalling safety system was set up at Motala with a ground frame operated by Network Rail and Swanage Railway keys.

The permanent link between the two halves of the line at Motala was used for the first time to bring in visiting traction for the May 11-13, 2007 beer festival and diesel gala.

The day before the start of the May event, four heritage diesels ran from Eastleigh to Swanage via the main line connection, hauling South West Trains' preserved blue-liveried 4VEP EMU unit No. 3417. The 4VEP was used during the event for push-pull trains, the first on the branch since the BR era.

It was the first time that three of the four classes of ex-main line diesels – two Class 73 electro-diesels and a Class 47 diesel – had run to Swanage since the 1960s.

The two 73s, No. 73136, owned by the Class 73 Locomotive Preservation Group and No. 73208, owned and operated by GB Railfreight, and Serco Rail Class 47 No. 47635 were joined by Class 52 diesel hydraulic D1015 *Western Champion*, owned by the Diesel Traction Group.

On July 2 that year, BR 4MT 2-6-0 No. 76079 travelled by rail from the East Lancashire Railway to the Swanage Railway

ABOVE: Driver, Stan Symes, and revivalist, Moyra Cross, with the Virgin Voyager on September 8, 2002. ANDREW PM WRIGHT **LEFT:** Crowds greet Virgin Voyager No. 220018 as it arrives at Swanage on September 8, 2002. ANDREW PM WRIGHT

to star in a major gala to mark the 40th anniversary of end of Southern steam during July 7-9.

It was the first time that a class member had run to Swanage since May 1967 when an enthusiasts' end-of-steam railtour called the 'Dorset Coast Express' visited the resort.

Then Swanage Railway general manager, Nick Brown, said: "No. 76079's arrival at Corfe Castle and Swanage by rail was the first time since Sunday, June 18, 1967 when the Arab-Israeli six-day war and the Beatles' new Sgt Pepper's Lonely Hearts Club Band album were both making headlines – that a steam locomotive has run down the line from Wareham."

Wednesday, April 1, 2009, saw the first passenger-carrying train from the national network to the Purbeck resort in 37 years.

UK Railtours' sell-out 12-coach 'Purbeck Pioneer' carrying 420 passengers ran from Waterloo to Swanage behind DB Schenker Class 66 No. 66152, driven by Dave Gravell from Poole, with No. 66142 on the back to haul the return trip.

The train departed from Victoria station at 8.45am, travelling via Guildford, Petersfield, Fareham, Southampton, Brockenhurst, Bournemouth and Poole to Wareham and arriving at Swanage just after 2pm. It stayed until 4pm before heading back to Waterloo.

So great was the demand for tickets that a repeat railtour was run the following day, behind the same locomotives, this time carrying 340 passengers.

Again, crowds thronged the lineside and Swanage railway members eagerly snapped up spare tickets to travel on the train from Wareham to Swanage and return.

The specials were the first passenger trains to run between Wareham, Corfe Castle and Swanage since January 1, 1972.

They were also the first trains to run from London to Swanage since teatime that same day when the final railtour to visit the Swanage branch line ran over it.

RIGHT: The first movement of diesels from the main line to the heritage railway for use in a gala passes Motala in May 2007. ANDREW PM WRIGHT
BELOW: The last Furzebrook gas train departed in July 2005. ANDREW PM WRIGHT

BELOW: UK Railtours' April 1, 2009 'Purbeck Pioneer' from Waterloo to Swanage behind DB Schenker Class 66 No. 66152 was the first passenger train from London since 1972. ANDREW PM WRIGHT

ABOVE: On July 2, 2007, BR 4MT 2-6-0 No. 76079 become the first steam locomotive to use the Motala connection. ANDREW PM WRIGHT

Making Fresh Tracks to the Sunny South and West

ABOVE: History is made on May 2, 2009, as Bulleid Battle of Britain light Pacific No. 34067 *Tangmere* approaches the A351 bridge on Network Rail's section of the Swanage branch with the first heritage-era steam-hauled passenger train from London. ROBIN JONES

Saturday May 2, 2009 saw the first steam train run from London through to Swanage since Sunday, June 18, 1967.

Steam – in the form of Bulleid Pacific, Battle of Britain No. 34067 *Tangmere* – arrived in the resort at the head of Past-Time Rail's 'The Royal Wessex' from London Victoria.

The 10-coach train hauled by *Tangmere* left Victoria station on time at 8.05am, travelling to Swanage via Woking, Winchfield for a watering stop, Basingstoke, Winchester, Eastleigh, Southampton, Brockenhurst, Bournemouth, Branksome, Poole and Hamworthy before arriving 15 minutes early at Wareham.

Yet again, spectators lined the route at crossings and stations, including Bournemouth, Poole and Wareham, and at every overbridge and other vantage point along the heritage line.

The railway was already packed: clear blue skies and soaring temperatures had brought crowds pouring into the resort for the May bank holiday weekend regardless of the 'The Royal Wessex' – which had to be squeezed in between a normal Swanage Railway timetable over which more than 1500 passengers were carried.

The train slowed to a halt at the point where Swanage Railway metals meet those of Network Rail and stopped for a few tantalising minutes, in order to wait for a path to Swanage.

Approaching Corfe Castle, the special passed unrebuilt sister No. 34070 *Manston*, waiting in the loop with the next regular service to Norden.

Finally, the 'The Royal Wessex' pulled into Swanage, where, with the platform off limits because of the waiting VIP party and TV cameramen, there was standing room only alongside the top of the embankment and on the pavement behind the bufferstops, where rebuilt West Country light Pacific No. 34028 *Eddystone* was undergoing testing after recent repairs to wheel bearings at the West Somerset Railway. It was waiting to welcome the visitor with two blasts of the horn.

At the end of the track, a crowd of more than 1000 welcomed *Tangmere* with cheers and applause as it ground to a halt at 1.17pm – just two minutes late after a journey of more than five hours.

Swanage Railway Trust chairman, Mike Whitwam, said: "It was very emotional – I had a lump in my throat. I think a lot of people did – and it would never have been achieved without the volunteers over the years – it was a moment of elation.

"There was a huge throng of people around the steam engine – I've never seen so many people with cameras – there was a fantastic atmosphere. This was the most momentous occasion for the railway since January 1, 1972 when British Rail closed it.

"The first steam trains between London and Swanage is something that several generations of determined Swanage Railway volunteers have been working towards, against all the odds, for almost 40 years."

Another piece of history was made the next day when *Tangmere* ran light engine from Swanage to Eastleigh in Hampshire to be turned on the triangle.

The previous time that a steam locomotive ran light from Swanage to Wareham, Poole and Bournemouth was on Sunday, September 4, 1966, the last day of regular timetabled steam-hauled passenger trains between Wareham, Corfe Castle and Swanage.

The move was made so that *Tangmere* was facing London when returned to Swanage later that day, in readiness for its historic departure on Monday, May 4, at the head of Past-Time's 'Wessex Venturer', the first steam-hauled passenger train from Purbeck to Waterloo since 1967.

In 2010, the Swanage bay platform, crossover track and signalling were brought into use, with the first passenger trains using the bay platform since the end of branch steam trains in September, 1966.

The Swanage Railway secured local council funding in 2010 (from a developers' transport infrastructure improvement tax charged by Purbeck District Council and collected by Dorset County Council) for the essential £3.2 million resignalling of Worgret Junction for Swanage branch trains.

The following year, a new Corfe Castle signal box opened after a three-year construction project by volunteers. It was built on the site of the original 1885 signal box and the same height and depth but a third wider.

In December 2012, Worgret Junction was upgraded by Network Rail with new trackwork.

February 2013 saw the Swanage Railway awarded a £1.47-million Government grant from the Coastal Communities Fund to upgrade Network Rail's section of the Swanage branch between Motala and Bridge No. 2.

The grant also included finance for the overhaul and upgrade for main line running of two heritage diesel multiple units, and the running of a trial two-year trial passenger train service from Swanage to Wareham.

The summer of 2014 saw the long-awaited Network Rail resignalling work at Worgret Junction for Swanage Railway trains completed. The Poole to Wool resignalling scheme was commissioned, including the signalling system from Worgret Junction on to the heritage line.

Sadly, a side effect of the completion of the main line resignalling programme was that Wareham signalbox, which opened in 1928, was closed but not demolished.

In September 2014, Network Rail's three-mile western section of the branch was transferred to Dorset County Council and leased to the Swanage Railway for 99 years.

WAREHAM IN SIGHT AT LAST

In October, 2014, the former Swanage Railway boundary with Network Rail at Motala was removed and the track plain-lined.

That autumn, the new Norden Gates full-barrier level crossing – essential if the heritage line was to be allowed to run regular trains to Wareham – was under construction.

In April 2016, the Bridge No. 2 to Motala three-mile track restoration and upgrade

ABOVE: Back to back Bulleids: during No. 34067 *Tangmere's* groundbreaking visit on May 2, 2009, it hauled some Swanage railway service trains back-to-back with resident sister No. 34070 *Manston*. The pair are seen leaving Corfe Castle. ROBIN JONES

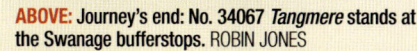

ABOVE: Journey's end: No. 34067 *Tangmere* stands at the Swanage bufferstops. ROBIN JONES

ABOVE: The replacement of the Worgret Junction point in 2012. ANDREW PM WRIGHT

was completed and the line speed on the extension raised to 25mph. The Norden Gates level crossing and nearby road-rail interchange were also complete.

Yet another landmark when the railway ran the first timetabled passenger train ran over four miles of newly restored line towards Wareham for the first time in 44 years during the line's April 8-10 spring steam gala.

The first train between Norden park-and-ride station and the River Frome departed Swanage at 9.45am on Friday, April 8, with Southern Railway U class 2-6-0 No. 31806 on the front. The choice of motive power was appropriate, as No. 31806 used to visit Swanage in the 1950s.

At Norden, gala guest locomotive GWR 1916-built 2-8-0T No. 4247 from the Bodmin & Wenford Railway in Cornwall was attached to the rear of the train for the journey to the river.

The day marked several firsts: the first timetabled passenger trains to the River Frome since January 1, 1972 and the last day of BR trains, and the first steam-hauled service trains to the river since September 4, 1966.

It also saw the first timetabled passenger train to be hauled to the river by a Bulleid Pacific since the weekend of September 3 and 4, 1966, when rebuilt No. 34004 *Yeovil* hauled the last steam morning train from Swanage to London. This time round, it was unrebuilt Battle of Britain No. 34070 *Manston* at the front.

The day also featured the first timetabled passenger train to be hauled to the river by an M7 tank since May, 1964.

Starting from Swanage, four such passenger trains each day ran beyond Norden station, over the newly installed Norden Gates level crossing and on past Motala, Furzebrook, Creech Bottom and East Holme before stopping at the river – within sight of the town of Wareham. It was also the first time that passenger trains had used the new crossing at Norden Gates.

Passengers were not able to board or alight the steam trains running over the four-mile extension beyond Norden station and the Frome river.

Swanage Railway Project Wareham director, Mark Woolley, said: "It was wonderful and very exciting to see the first timetabled passenger train run between Norden to within sight of Wareham at the River Frome for the first time since January 1972."

The railway had originally hoped to complete Project Wareham for the summer of 2016, but the date for the first timetabled public trains from Swanage to Wareham has now been deferred until the summer of 2017.

The new £500,000 Norden Gates level crossing will enable regular passenger trains to run from Swanage to the main line at Wareham was fully used for an incoming railtour for the first time on Saturday, June 11, 2016.

The newly commissioned level crossing – provided through the 'legacy' support of the Wytch Farm oilfield previous and current operators, BP and Perenoc respectively – had taken volunteers four years and more than 3000 hours of design, building and testing work to bring to fruition. The crossing called allows

RIGHT: The award-winning Victorian-style signalbox built at Corfe Castle by Swanage Railway volunteers – and set to control trains to the main line at Wareham – was officially opened by transport minister Theresa Villiers MP on May 17, 2012. Ninety invited guests travelled to the station on a diesel railbus from Norden. Before cutting a ceremonial green ribbon at the foot of the wooden steps to the signalbox, she congratulated the volunteers on a "fabulous job", adding that she was "so impressed with what you have managed to achieve here." After being given a guided tour of the signalbox on the Down platform pull two levers, she said she was "very impressed" by the commitment shown by the Purbeck Community Rail Partnership in working to reinstate passenger trains between Swanage and Wareham. Adding: "We are very supportive of heritage railways because we know they make a tremendous contribution to tourism and the economy of places like Swanage." The signalbox has been built in the Victorian style of the 1885 original demolished in 1956. The 32-lever 1920s-built and Westinghouse-designed A2 class lever frame has come from lever frames in two long-demolished signalboxes at Broadstone station between Poole and Wimborne, and Brockenhurst station in the New Forest. ANDREW PM WRIGHT

Making Fresh Tracks to the Sunny South and West

ABOVE: Maunsell U 2-6-0 No. 31806 rubs shoulders with visiting King Arthur 4-6-0 No. 777 *Sir Lamiel* at Swanage station in 2015. ANDREW PM WRIGHT

LEFT: The 'Purbeck Adventurer', a special day excursion from Waterloo to Swanage on June 29, 2013 saw SouthWest Trains Class 159 DMUs Nos. 159006/9 become the first train from London to use the bay platform at Swanage since the resort's station opened in May, 1885. The heritage line fully restored the bay platform specially to accommodate the six-coach charter (pictured). It was also the first passenger train from Wareham to use the bay platform since September 4, 1966, when regular BR steam trains on the branch line came to an end. ANDREW PM WRIGHT

trains to cross a busy access to the Wytch Farm on-shore oilfield as well as the car park next to Norden station.

The crossing was used for the first time to signal a Pathfinder Tours 12-carriage 'Purbeck and Bournemouth Explorer' excursion train from Derby headed by Class 50s No. 50007 *Hercules* and No. 50050 *Fearless* and operated by GB Railfreight.

Equipped with full barriers, warning lights and audible alerts, the signalbox level crossing has been built from wood, with a slate roof, in the style of the one at Lyme Regis station.

Approved by the Government's Department for Transport, the level crossing's computer-controlled safety systems, crossing barriers and road user warning systems were designed and installed by Schweizer Electronic of Switzerland.

Around 1500 sleepers have been replaced and an eroding embankment repaired during the restoration of the line from Norden to Wareham.

THE REBORN SWANAGE BRANCH OPEN THROUGHOUT

At the time of writing, the heritage line's detailed 2017 timetable had not yet been finalised but the Swanage-Wareham trial service is scheduled to commence on June 13.

It will operate for 60 days on Tuesdays, Wednesdays, Thursdays, Saturdays and Sundays. There will be four return trips a day between approximately 10am and 5pm.

The initial trial service will end on September 3.

A 90-day service is planned for 2018 but the operating dates and service pattern of this will be agreed only following a review of the 2017 service. Earlier and later trains catering for local traffic to places such as Poole, Bournemouth and Weymouth may be introduced in 2017 once the demand is estimated.

A three-car Class 117 DMU and a single Class 121 'Bubblecar' are being overhauled at Eastleigh with their wheelsets also being overhauled. Delays in upgrading the wheelsets on the railway's first-generation DMUs to main line standards saw the start date postponed until 2017. All rolling stock running into Wareham will need to be main line certified before it will be allowed to enter service.

The aim is to return the DMUs to Swanage in early 2017 for testing and route familiarisation.

If the trial seasons are successful, the Purbeck line may well emulate the North Yorkshire Moors Railway's Whitby operation with more regular timetabled trains into Wareham.

The big question, however, that everyone is asking is – will we see regular steam trains back at Wareham?

From 1885 until the Swanage branch closed in 1972, its trains ran into bay platforms at Wareham station.

However, from 2017, the branch trains will be using the main line platforms – while the surviving bay platform has been allowed to return to nature.

Deliberately left choked with blackberry briars and weeds, it is now a haven for rare smooth snakes and sand lizards, celebrated inhabitants of the Dorset heathlands.

Network Rail has been developing a strip of land to the north-west of the station, and needed to find an alternative site for the snakes and lizards, both of which are protected species. So they have now taken up residence in the bay platform next to Platform 2.

Mark Woolley, the Swanage Railway's Project Wareham director, said that the possibility of reusing the bay platform at the outset had been rejected on cost grounds. However, it is being protected for possible future use by trains, but if that happens, the snakes and lizards will have to be found new homes first of all.

The branch to Swanage diverges at Worgret Junction from the Down main line, so at first, most of the Wareham trains will run into and from the Down platform at the town's station to avoid crossing the main line. Another reason for the use of DMUs is that there is currently no run-round loop at Wareham.

Yet the biggest obstacle to Swanage steam trains running into Wareham is that none of the heritage line's steam locomotive fleet is main line certified.

Maunsell N 2-6-0 No. 31874, currently under overhaul at the railway's Herston Works, is now being rebuilt to MT276 main line standards.

In 2016, the railway was awarded a £75,000 grant from the Department for Transport's Heritage and Community Rail Tourism Innovation Competition to fit the required AWS, TPWS, OTM-R and GSM-R apparatus and upgrade a rake of five carriages to main line standards.

The N is likely to be followed to Wareham by Bulleid unrebuilt Battle of Britain Pacific No. 34072 257 *Squadron*, which was due back in traffic in late 2016 after an absence of many years following a heavy overhaul, sister No. 34070 *Manston*, BR Standard 4MT 2-6-4T No. 80104 and U class 2-6-0 No. 31625.

Because of the lack of run-round facilities at Wareham, all steam-hauled services will need

ABOVE: A Class 33 diesel heads a works train engaged on embankment upgrading near Furzebrook in April 2015. ANDREW PM WRIGHT

ABOVE: GWR 2-8-0T No. 4247, visiting from the Bodmin & Wenford Railway, runs over embankment 4 east of Furzebrook on Friday, April 8, 2016. ANDREW PM WRIGHT

ABOVE: The Motala boundary between the two parts of the Swanage branch is taken out in October 2014. ANDREW PM WRIGHT

ABOVE: The first full use of the Norden Gates level crossing as a Pathfinders Tour charter from Derby heads to Swanage on Saturday, June 11, 2016. ANDREW PM WRIGHT

ABOVE: Unrebuilt Battle of Britain No. 34070 *Manston* at Creech Bottom crossing on April 8, 2016. ANDREW PM WRIGHT

ABOVE: The first Swanage Railway train to the River Frome bridge, within sight of Wareham, was headed by GWR 2-8-0T No. 4247 on April 8, 2016. ANDREW PM WRIGHT

to be top and tailed. Both the Up and Down running lines are bidirectional, with crossovers at both ends of Wareham station offering Swanage trains greater operational flexibility to work around the 30-minute South West Trains main line services between Weymouth and Waterloo.

Three disused sidings just north east of the station on the Down side offer scope for future Swanage Railway developments.

Network Rail is to recommission the second and third sidings for Swanage trains. By reinstating the sidings and adding a loop, steam locomotives will be able to leave the train in the station and run-round out of the way of the main line.

In the longer term, both steam and diesel traction could be stabled there.

A NEW STATION FOR THE BLUE POOL AND CARRIAGE SHED FOR FURZEBROOK

The Swanage Railway has long-term plans to build yet another new intermediate station, this time at Furzebrook, to serve the much-loved Blue Pool local beauty spot.

Blue Pool is a flooded clay pit where ball clay was once extracted. It is now a lake within the Furzebrook Estate, a 25-acre park of heath, woodland and yellow gorse.

In 1985 the estate was declared a Site of Special Scientific Interest.

Next to the running line at Furzebrook are the Perenco (formerly BP) oil terminal sidings, which served the Wytch Farm oilfield.

Dorset County Council is negotiating a lease of the sidings with the intention of sub-letting them to the railway.

It is planned that these sidings become the site of a carriage shed, allowing the railway to store its rolling stock under cover for the first time.

Pride of place in that shed may well go to two Pullman carriages, Nos. 246 *Lydia* and 247 *Isle of Thanet*, which formed part of the funeral train of Sir Winston Churchill on January 30, 1965.

The two coaches were later bought from British Railways by the US National Railroad Museum at Green Bay in Wisconsin, along with another pair of carriages, which had formed part of General Eisenhower's British wartime command train.

When the world's most famous steam locomotive, Gresley A3 Pacific No. 4472 *Flying Scotsman*, embarked on a tour of North America in 1969, it was arranged that the two Pullmans could form part of its train provided they were delivered to the museum.

One of the coaches was delivered as planned – but the tour later went bankrupt, leaving the engine and the rest of the train stranded in

BELOW: Visiting GWR 2-8-0T No. 4247 heads the first steam train over the new Norden Gates level crossing in April 2016. ANDREW PM WRIGHT

ABOVE: Jon Denision in charge inside the new Norden Gates level crossing signalbox as the historic train movement takes place. ANDREW PM WRIGHT

Making Fresh Tracks to the Sunny South and West 33

ABOVE: A 1960s green-liveried DMU stands at Swanage station on the evening of August 29, 2015. Similar vehicles will form the basis of the first 21st century 'real' as opposed to tourist heritage trains from Swanage to Wareham. ROBIN JONES
RIGHT: The historic frontage of Wareham station. ROBIN JONES

ABOVE: One of the most dramatic landscapes anywhere on the British railway network and heritage railway portfolio must be that of the ruins of medieval Corfe Castle overlooking the Swanage railway station serving the village of the same name. ANDREW PM WRIGHT

ABOVE: Maunsell U class 2-6-0 No. 31625 on display at the Great Dorset Steam Fair in September 2015 to publicise its restoration appeal. ROBIN JONES

California. The operation was so penniless that it left the engine's owner Alan Pegler destitute: he had to work his passage home to Britain as a ship's entertainer. Money had to then be raised by the US museum to move the other Pullman across the States to Green Bay.

The Pullman pair were bought after months of secret negotiations for an undisclosed sum by a private enthusiast who supports the Swanage Railway, which wants to use them as part of a new first-class 'Wessex Belle' dining train on its line in the Isle of Purbeck. The coaches were found to be a living time capsule – with the dining cards from the ill-fated *Flying Scotsman* tour 30 years ago still on the tables inside!

Arriving at Newport Docks in the autumn of 2000, they were restored at West Coast Railways' Carnforth base where they have remained until the Purbeck line can provide secure undercover storage.

They are not the only items from the Churchill funeral train that were repatriated for the Swanage Railway.

The Southern Railway luggage van that carried the great wartime leader's coffin, No. S2464S, was repatriated from California in 2007, after spending four decades in use at a mock English station on a golf course.

Built in 1931, the carriage was specially repainted in Pullman colours and decorated for Churchill's funeral. Its status as part of the train saved it from being scrapped, and it was sold abroad in 1966, but it was allowed to come back to England in 2007 after the Los Angeles City of Industry declared it surplus to requirements following an approach by the volunteers of the Swanage Railway Trust.

A fourth vehicle repatriated for Swanage from across the Atlantic, and which itself comprises a significant slice of Sunny South history, is 'Devon Belle' Observation Car no. 14.

The 'Devon Belle' was a luxury express passenger train that ran between and Ilfracombe and Plymouth between 1947-54.

The Southern Railway was anxious to encourage the resumption of normal leisure activities after the Second World War, and began running the all-Pullman train on June 20, 1947. A marked feature was the Observation Car, attached at the rear for the benefit of passengers to and from Ilfracombe.

The train ran non-stop between London and Sidmouth Junction, a distance of 160 miles. The throughout journey time was about 5½ hours.

Despite initial popularity, the train was not as much of a success as hoped, and the Plymouth portion was dropped in September 1949 and the train withdrawn entirely at the end of the 1954 summer season.

In 1961 the Observation Cars were transferred to the Scottish Region for use on the lines between Inverness and the Kyle of Lochalsh, and from Glasgow to Oban.

ABOVE: Pullman carriage Nos. 246 *Lydia* on display in the National Railway Museum on January 30, 2015 to mark the 50th anniversary of the funeral of sir Winston Churchill. ROBIN JONES

ABOVE: Southern Railway parcels van No. S2464S which carried Sir Winston Churchill's coffin, and was later reimported from the USA to the Swanage Railway. ROBIN JONES

ABOVE: Another of the magnificent Bulleid Pacifics based at Swanage is West Country No. 34028 *Eddystone*. ROBIN JONES

ABOVE: Repatriated 'Devon Belle' Pullman Observation Car No. 14 behind Maunsell U 2-6-0 No. 31806 in 2015. ANDREW PM WRIGHT

Observation Car No. 13 ended up on the Dartmouth Steam Railway, while No. 14 was included on the abovementioned disastrous *Flying Scotsman* tour of 1969.

No. 14 ended up being used as an office annexe in San Francisco for many years, but following talks, was returned to the UK and the Swanage Railway in early 2007, having travelled by ship via the Panama Canal.

It was immediately transported by road to Ramparts railway workshops at Derby where restoration work was carried out, including the refitting of the classic interior and bar. It was officially relaunched into service on the Swanage Railway on July 16, 2008.

North of Furzebrook, the line runs through another SSSI, and to keep maintenance and disruption of local wildlife to a minimum, the railway has utilised continuous welded rail and concrete sleepers.

At Furzebrook station is one of many exciting new possibilities that will emerge in the years to come over this fully restored classic Sunny South seaside branch line, now restored and reinstated as it existed between 1885 and 1972, but already with many added benefits and facilities.

The railway's long-term strategic plan also includes lengthening the platform at Swanage to enable locomotives to run round six-coach trains.

Indeed, the prospect of yet more regular charters from London, giving the public the chance for an affordable day trip to the seaside leaving and returning at civilised hours, will bring massive benefits to Swanage, its traders and shopkeepers, with the potential to make it an all-year round resort.

NARROW GAUGE REVIVAL IN PURBECK TOO!

Nowhere along the coast of the Sunny South is as famous for its geology and mineral resources as Dorset.

The 95-mile coastline between Exmouth and Studland is designated as the Jurassic Coast because of the richness of the fossils that can be found in its rocks.

When British narrow gauge is mentioned, thoughts automatically turn to North Wales and the splendid former slate-carrying lines such as the Ffestiniog and Talyllyn railways.

RIGHT: Swanage was not only a classic Sunny South destination, but its branch hauled considerable mineral traffic too, thanks to the rich deposits of ball clay in the Isle of Purbeck. On May 2, 1966, BR standard 2-6-4Ts Nos. 80013 and 80094 pass at Furzebrook, the latter on a clay working. ANDREW PM WRIGHT COLLECTION

However, it is often overlooked that the Isle of Purbeck once had an extensive network of narrow gauge railways too, exploiting the mineral wealth including extensive deposits of ball clay, which is are commonly used in the production of ceramics. Its primary role, apart from its white colour, is to either impart plasticity or to aid rheological stability during the shaping processes.

The use of ball clay mined in Purbeck dates back to at least the Roman era. In 1771 Josiah Wedgwood signed a contract for 1400 tons a year of ball clay with Thomas Hyde of Purbeck, enabling him to fire thinner-walled ceramics.

Not only has the Swanage railway been restored throughout, but also one of the associated former clay tramways has also been reborn as a tourist attraction in its own right.

Norden station is much more than a park-and-ride and a local transport hub. It is also the home of the Purbeck Mineral and Mining Museum, part of Swanage Railway Trust.

There, volunteers have built a clay mine from scratch on the site of the old Pike Brothers Victorian ball clay works demolished during the 1970s.

It has a 2ft gauge system complete with running line, points, sidings and wagon turntables that run around the restored mine complex, allowing visitors to walk through the underground passages – which themselves have tracks laid inside.

One of the few places in Britain that ball clay can be found is on the Isle of Purbeck, far better known for its building stone, as evident in the magnificent restored Swanage Railway station buildings.

The aim was to recreate a working environment typical of the drift ball clay mining industry, including a short operational demonstration line around the Norden site, on which an industrial diesel locomotive usually runs. Planning permission for the museum was granted by Purbeck District Council on January 29, 2004, since when, progress has been sure and steady.

Norden No.7 mine transhipment building was donated by Imerys and moved to the park-and-ride site by the volunteers to form a museum building.

ABOVE: A collection of enamel signs in the Corfe Castle station museum. ROBIN JONES

ABOVE: One of only two steam locomotives built in Birmingham, Purbeck mineral railways veteran *Secundus* can be viewed in the Corfe Castle station museum. ROBIN JONES

ABOVE: Quarry Hunslet 0-4-0ST *Cloister* at home in a mineral setting, albeit Dorset and not Snowdonia! ANDREW PM WRIGHT COLLECTION

ABOVE: Visitors to the Purbeck Mineral and Mining Museum can walk down a ramp into this ball clay mine tunnel. ROBIN JONES

ABOVE: The beauty spot of Blue Pool could be served by a new station. ROBIN JONES

Over the years, many former workers have visited the museum and given their advice and photographs as well as donating personal equipment.

In September 2013, steam ran over a restored section of the Pike Brothers, Fayle & Company's 2ft gauge industrial railway system for the first time since 1953.

The locomotive in operation was freelance 0-4-0T *Emmet*, which was built by Jim Haylock at the Moors Valley Railway at Ringwood and in 2004 ran the first steam-hauled passenger services on the reborn Lynton & Barnstaple Railway.

It was that year when volunteers began work on restoring part of the Norden ball clay mine.

Although *Emmet* is a heritage-era new-build, it was a homecoming to the Fayle Tramway by the back door – as Jim built it on the chassis of an 1930 Orenstein & Koppel industrial diesel locomotive – one that had hauled trains at the same ball clay mine from the late '40s to 1970.

On static display at the museum during the weekend was Quarry Hunslet No. 542 *Cloister*, built by Hunslet in 1891 for the Dinorwic slate quarry in Snowdonia. Now belonging to the Hampshire Narrow Gauge Railway Trust after the locomotive retired in 1962, the 0-4-0 saddle tank was named after the Grand National winner of 1893 as the quarry owner was a horse-racing enthusiast.

Emmet, by contrast, was named after a cat who lived on the Moors Valley Railway.

It worked at the Kiel Docks before being shipped to England after the Second World War for a new working life hauling ball clay trains at the Norden clay mines.

The museum group has taken the unique Purbeck mining tramways veteran Bellis & Seekings 2ft 8in gauge 0-6-0WT of 1874 *Secundus* on long-term loan from Birmingham Museums.

At present, the former Furzebrook Railway locomotive is on view in the excellent small exhibits museum in the restored goods shed at Corfe Castle station, but it is planned to house it at Norden and display it in a purpose-designed facility.

Through the Swanage Railway Trust, the Purbeck Mineral and Mining Museum owns two flooded clay pits at Norden and it is planned to develop them to show the remains of the alternative ball clay extraction.

A structural survey and load assessment of the Swanage Railway's Bridge 15, also known as Skew Bridge, which carried the tramway across the LSWR branch at this interchange point, and was built only as a temporary structure in 1885, has been undertaken.

The group plans to relay track over the bridge and create a unique setting by where Swanage Railway passengers will see narrow gauge trains running above their heads.

The lattice steelwork, corbels and beam landings need some remedial work before they can carry trains again. However, the main foundations, abutments and wing wall are in good condition.

In 2013, the museum carried off a major Heritage Railway Association national award.

The Mortons Media (Heritage Railway) Interpretation Award was awarded for the operation and return to steam to a section of the former extensive narrow gauge mineral tramway network on the Isle of Purbeck, and for the creation of a unique museum devoted to the history and technology of ball clay mining complete with underground mine tunnel and associated rail tracks and rolling stock.

Very much long-term aims include the possibility of relaying further parts of Fayle's Tramway, maybe to take visitors through the environmentally sensitive and ecologically rich Purbeck heaths, allowing them to appreciate them from a slow-moving spark-free diesel-hauled train rather than walking through these delicate ecosystems. ●

ABOVE: Explaining the use of mine tub wagons inside the museum. ANDREW PM WRIGHT

ABOVE: The Norden clay mine museum building. ANDREW PM WRIGHT

BELOW: Ruston & Hornsby 48DL 0-4-0 diesel No. 392117 returned to Norden after 45 years on Sunday, May 8, 2016. Built in Lincoln in 1956, it is a compression ignition engined locomotive, with a four-cylinder Ruston engine, driving both axles by a chain drive via a three-speed gearbox. On completion, the locomotive was sent with several others to work on the building of the new tunnels at Hadley Wood on the East Coast Main Line, when a stretch of that route was being quadrupled. At the end of that contract, No. 392117 was moved to the ball clay works at Norden, where it worked until it was preserved in the early 1970s, along with Orenstein & Kopple No. 20777 (now at the Statford Barn Railway), at the then Hampshire Narrow Gauge Society's base at Durley near Bishop's Waltham. No. 392117 was purchased by Swanage Railway fireman Dave Knott in 1992 and was moved to the Old Kiln Light Railway, near Farnham. Richard Bentley purchased it from Dave Knott in 1999 and has placed it on loan to the Swanage Railway Trust, of which the Purbeck Mineral and Mining Museum is part. ANDREW PM WRIGHT

Chapter 3

THE BLUEBELL BLUEPRINT

The Swanage Railway's magnificent achievement in reopening the resort's branch owes a massive debt of gratitude to the inspirational Sunny South's Bluebell Railway, which in August 1960, became the first to reopen a closed section of the British Railways' standard gauge network.

ABOVE: South Eastern & Chatham Railway H class 0-4-4T No. 263 makes a storming exit from Sheffield Park. The standard type for the SECR's suburban services, H class locos were seen in later years on rural branch lines in Sussex. No. 263 ended up on the line between Three Bridges, East Grinstead and Tunbridge Wells and worked there until the last push-pull services on that line were withdrawn in January 1964. BRIAN SHARPE **BELOW:** The beginning of standard gauge preservation: LBSCR A1X 'Terrier' 0-6-0T No. 55 *Stepney* leaves the crowded platforms at Sheffield Park with the first Bluebell Railway public passenger train on August 7, 1960. Hayling Island branch veteran *Stepney*, later to be one of the characters in the Rev W Awdry's Thomas the Tank Engine series, was the fledgling line's first locomotive. BLUEBELL RAILWAY ARCHIVES

Making Fresh Tracks to the Sunny South and West

LEFT: Press report of the Bluebell Railway's first trains in 1960.

In 1951, transport history was made when the Talyllyn Railway became the first line in the world to be taken over by volunteer preservationists. Their feat was followed by a similar successful scheme to re-open the moribund Ffestiniog Railway, and then then the Welshpool & Llanfair Light Railway, the latter having been part of the British Railways' empire.

The Talyllyn milestone inspired The Titfield Thunderbolt, a 1953 Ealing comedy about a group of villagers trying to keep their branch line operating after British Railways decided to close it, and starred Stanley Holloway, George Relph and John Gregson. It was the first Ealing comedy shot in Technicolor.

Pure fiction, it planted the idea deep in the consciousness of the British public that it was possible to save a railway line from being closed, and you did not have to accept everything that the Ministry of Transport officers dictated.

However, saving a seven-mile narrow gauge line was one matter. Reviving a standard gauge line with far bigger locomotives and stock was another.

It was in the Sunny South that the first such section of the national network was saved.

It became the Bluebell Railway, and went on to become a world leader in railway preservation and a major visitor destination.

The line has its origins in the 1877 Act of Parliament that authorised construction of the Lewes & East Grinstead Railway, which was acquired by operator the London, Brighton and South Coast Railway under a subsequent Act a year later.

Both included the clause: "Four passenger trains each way daily to run on this line, with through connections at East Grinstead to London and to stop at Sheffield Bridge, Newick and West Hoathly." The clause imposed a legal requirement to provide a service and the only way to remove this obligation was to pass another Act.

In 1954, a British Railways' branch line committee proposed closing the line from East Grinstead to Culver Junction near Lewes. Despite a challenge by local residents, the closure was set for June 15, 1955, although it took place earlier, on May 29, owing to a rail strike.

Residents and rail users fought hard over the next three years to get the decision reversed.

Shortly after closure, Chailey spinster Madge Bessemer, the grand-daughter of Henry Bessemer, inventor of the Bessemer converter for converting pig iron into steel, discovered the clause in the 1877 and 1878 Acts relating to the 'Statutory Line' and demanded that British Railways reinstate services.

Aided by local MP Tufton Beamish, she forced BR to rethink. Faced with this statutory legal obligation, on August 7, 1956 BR re-opened the line, but with trains stopping only at stations mentioned in the Acts. As a result of this, it was nicknamed the 'sulky service'.

BR took the case to the House of Commons in 1957, resulting in a public enquiry. BR was censured, but later the Transport Commission was able to persuade Parliament to repeal the special section of the Act, and so the line was finally closed on March 17, 1958.

Madge was a lover of wildlife, and so it has been theorised that while picking spring flowers on the embankment near her estate that she may have herself come up with the nickname of the 'Bluebell Line'. The name was certainly appended to early reports of saving the line by Brighton's Evening Argus.

On that final day, Madge Bessemer encountered Carshalton Technical College student, Chris Campbell, who shared his many recollections of travelling on the line while spending school holidays with relatives. Inspired by her efforts to save the line, Chris, then 18, wondered if it might be possible that he could take up the cudgel.

Meanwhile, Martin Eastland, 19, a telecommunications engineering student of Haywards Heath, David Dallimore, a student at the London School of Economics, from Woodingdean, and Brighton-based Alan Sturt, 19, who was studying at the Regent Street Polytechnic, had mooted the idea of setting up a Lewes and East Grinstead Railway Preservation Society, drawing on the examples of those Welsh narrow gauge lines.

They sent a letter to interested parties highlighting Madge Bessemer's campaign and the unexpected public support that it had generated.

They initially hoped to save the entire route, re-opening it stages at a time, acquiring a GWR railcar for regular use and using steam during the summer months.

On March 15, 1959 a public meeting chaired by the future president of the society, Bernard Holden MBE, met at the Church Lads Brigade hall in Haywards Heath and duly formed the Lewes & East Grinstead Railway Preservation Society. Railwayman Bernard was involved with Burgess Hill Model Railway Club and was seen as a senior presence by the four students, when the powers that be at Waterloo would view them as 'minors'. At a later meeting, the society changed its name to the Bluebell Railway Preservation Society.

The society's initial, and very over-ambitious aim, was to re-open the whole line from East Grinstead to Culver Junction as a commercial service. However, the society failed to buy the whole line, and had to edit its dreams. The society then came up with the idea of using the line between Sheffield Park and Horsted Keynes as a

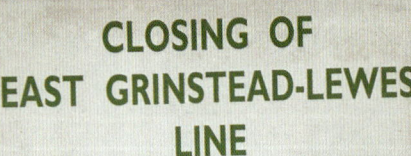

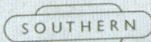

RIGHT: Anti-closure campaigner Madge Bessemer's name is remembered in the name of the Bessemer Arms pub and restaurant at the Bluebell Railway's Sheffield Park headquarters.

tourist attraction, with vintage locomotives and stock operated by unpaid volunteer staff. Sheffield Park was chosen for the HQ as it was on a main A-road and had a water source for locomotives.

As BR still ran an electrified line from Haywards Heath to Horsted Keynes via Ardingly, the society leased a stretch of track from just south of Horsted Keynes. The third-rail electric services came up from Seaford via Haywards Heath and Ardingly to Horsted Keynes. Though initially planned, extension of the third-rail electrification north from Horsted Keynes was halted as a result of the outbreak of the Second World War, and the scheme was never brought back into play.

On August 7, 1960, the first Bluebell Railway services ran to Bluebell Halt, 100yds south of Horsted Keynes, from Sheffield Park.

In 1962, the society extended services to Horsted Keynes, and invited Dr Beeching to open a halt at Holywell (Waterworks). It closed within 12 months, primarily as a result of parking problems.

The following year BR withdrew passenger services from Horsted Keynes to Haywards Heath and with complete closure of the line north of Horsted Keynes, the Bluebell Railway found itself severed from the BR system. In March that year, East Grinstead resident and BR chairman, Dr Richard Beeching, delivered his report The Reshaping of British Railways, a framework for closing thousands of miles of similarly unprofitable rural routes.

In retrospect, what is certain is that had the Bluebell Railway not started its operations in 1960, its blueprint of what was possible would not have been there for others to follow. If the UK railway preservation movement had taken several more years to reach that stage, how many now-priceless examples of classic locomotives and rolling stock would have been lost forever?

Indeed, it was to be another eight years before the next former BR line would be re-opened as a heritage route and the Keighley & Worth Valley Railway would run its public trains.

ABOVE: Sunny South survivor extraordinaire LSWR Adams radial 4-4-2T No. 488 is pictured in Bluebell action in the 1980s. Built in 1885 for inner suburban work, the class of 71 were made redundant by electrification and by 1927 all but three had been withdrawn and scrapped. Two were retained for the sharply curving Lyme Regis branch while No. 488 was sold to the Army for use during the First World War and in 1919 was bought by the East Kent Railway. In 1946 it was bought by the Southern Railway and overhauled to provide relief for the other two Lyme Regis engines; the three operated the branch until 1960. No. 488 was chosen for preservation by the Bluebell since, out of the three, it was closest to original condition at the time of withdrawal, having an original Adams' boiler – which now needs extensive repairs, hence the fact that the locomotive has not steamed since 1990 after three decades of heritage use. BRIAN SHARPE

ABOVE: *Stepney* is seen heading a special VIP train at Kingscote to mark the 40th anniversary of the Bluebell Railway in 2000. ROBIN JONES

RIGHT: South Eastern & Chatham Railway O1 0-6-0 No. 65 and C 0-6-0 No 592 doubleheading during celebrations in 1999 to mark the centenary of the South Eastern Railway and the London, Chatham & Dover Railway. ROBIN JONES

NORTHWARDS TO EAST GRINSTEAD

Looking to expand what had by then long been established as a sizeable visitor magnet, in 1974 the society bought the site of the demolished West Hoathly station, to make a start on what would eventually lead to a return to East Grinstead.

Kingscote station was bought in January 1985, and in the face of opposition from local councillors, a public enquiry resulted in both the Secretaries of State for the environment and transport giving planning permission and a Light Railway Order for an extension to East Grinstead that year.

Work on the seven-mile extension from Horsted Keynes to East Grinstead began in March 1988 with a golden spike ceremony. As with the Swanage reinstatement, it would not be a quick job.

The extension from Horsted Keynes as far as Kingscote was completed in 1994, including the relaying of track through the 731yd Sharpthorne Tunnel, but planning permission was not forthcoming for the rebuilding of West Hoathly station.

BR donated East Grinstead's spectacular Imberhorne Viaduct to the railway in 1992. However, the trackbed had been sold off into numerous portions, all of which had to be bought back one by one, a process that was not completed until 2003, from when physical civil engineering activity on the extension beyond Kingscote began.

The biggest blockage of all, however, was the 30ft-deep 1600ft-long Imberhorne cutting which, after the original line was lifted, was used as a landfill site. The rubbish had to come out if trains were to pass through again. Test borings established that the 96,000cu m of waste was not toxic, but it would cost £5 million to remove it.

The track north of the tip was relaid to allow it to be taken out by rail, not to local sites but to landfill sites one to the north of Aylesbury and the other north of Didcot.

BBC News presenter and Bluebell member, Nick Owen, publicly began the removal of the waste on November 25, 2008, and items of heavy machinery were donated from the Channel Tunnel Rail Link, which had just been completed through Kent. The first trial movements of excavated spoil by rail were made in 2009, and since then, GB Railfreight handled the bulk of the work.

Finally, the date for the public opening of the extension into East Grinstead was set for March 23, 2013, and the first two months of this year saw frantic tracklaying as the wintry weather permitted. On Friday, March

ABOVE: The South was not very sunny on March 23, 2013, when the first public train from East Grinstead was worked by a trio headed by No. 55 *Stepney*, followed by blue-liveried SECR P 060T No. 323 *Bluebell* and E4 0-6-2T No. 473 *Birch Grove*. ANDREW STRONGITHARM

8, shortly after a GB Railfreight Class 66 diesel made a clandestine late-night run over the extension the final section of track was formally joined using a white fishplate, with long-standing Bluebell extension catering lady, Barbara Watkins, tightening the four bolts amid a sea of orange jackets.

March 23 found the Sunny South locked in the grip of a last but severe gasp of winter, with snow to many parts including East Grinstead, but it would take more than that to deter the Bluebell battlers. Like their Swanage counterparts, they had fought far worse and won.

On the day, the first public train from East Grinstead was worked by a trio headed by No. 55 *Stepney*, followed by blue-liveried SECR P 060T No. 323 *Bluebell* and E4 0-6-2T No. 473 *Birch Grove*.

The first train north from Sheffield Park was headed by U class 2-6-0 No. 1638 and comprised the breakfast Pullman carrying 144 guests who were served champagne.

In the face of the Arctic blasts, a 45-minute service ran to time, with no engine failing.

Many of the passengers from the South alighted at East Grinstead and returned hours later with shopping bags – a sight that boded well for local traders.

Thursday, March 28 saw an eagerly awaited 12-coach UK Railtours' charter from Victoria, headed by Class 66 No. 66739, which had taken its turn on the GB Railfreight spoil trains, with two BR blue-liveried Class 73s on the rear.

After running though to Sheffield Park, the train was hauled back by the 73s to Horsted Keynes, where No. 66739 was named by GB Railfreight managing director, John Smith, Bluebell Railway.

Spades down, officials said that their railway would give itself a breathing space before embarking on any further extension projects, the restoration of the Ardingly branch from Horsted Keynes, and a possible link into Haywards Heath as well as an interchange with the London to Brighton main line, being a possibility.

But will the railway ever go south again, with trains running over Culver Junction into Lewes, finally realising the dreams of the society's founders? There are no plans at the moment, but in Sussex as at Swanage, railway preservation has proved itself to be the art of the possible.

■ The full history of the founding of the Bluebell Railway and its 42-year push to East Grinstead is to be found in a sister title, Battle for Bluebell, by Bluebell News and Old Glory magazines editor, Colin Tyson. It can be bought for £5.99 as a digital download from www.classicmagazines.co.uk/product/5443/bookazine-battle-for-bluebell

THE BLUEBELL TODAY

From that founders meeting, the Bluebell has grown to what it is today. The society boasts a membership of more than 10,400 is the governing body and sets the strategy, goals and objectives for the operating company – Bluebell Railway plc – of which it is the majority shareholder with a 75% stake.

The railway's headquarters are at Sheffield Park just a short walk away from the National Trust's Sheffield Park Gardens. As well as its main offices, restaurant and bar, the station accommodates a shop outlet, an accredited museum and the locomotive shed and works.

Housing one of the largest collections of steam locomotives outside of the National Railway Museum, visitors are able to see close up the static display of engines awaiting overhaul or just having a day's rest. A picnic area that adjoins the River Ouse is an ideal spot for taking time out.

Plans are underway at Sheffield Park to fundamentally upgrade the visitor experience of locomotive displays to create a more interactive experience and also make it accessible to all. The educational facets of steam motive power will include a rolling road display of a full-size locomotive as well as a cut-away replica of its famous engine *Stepney*. Round one funding from the Heritage Lottery Fund has made the working up of detailed plans possible. The Accessible Steam Heritage project, as it is known, should take less than a year to complete once the green flag is waved.

To enhance the nostalgic visitor experience each of the four stations are themed in terms of staff uniform, colour schemes and signage: Sheffield Park in the late 1800s of the LBSCR; Horsted Keynes in the Southern Railway, Kingscote in the 1950s of British Railways and East Grinstead in the 1960s.

Horsted Keynes with its five platforms is one of the largest on a preserved line and its size makes it an attractive location for not only many of the Bluebell's events but also for film makers – the versatility of the site and age of station buildings making a good backdrop for period dramas from the Victorian era all the way up to the 1960s.

The station became Downton (of Abbey fame) on numerous occasions as well being used for several of the railway scenes in the Poirot detective series. The railway has just released a book, The Line to the Stars, which covers more than half a century of filming at the Bluebell line from The Innocents in 1961 through to the Muppets Most Wanted in 2013. Revenues from filming, fashion and advertising shoots plus other corporate

ABOVE: SR U class 2-6-0 No. 1638 arrives at East Grinstead hauling 'The Grinstead Belle', forming the first passenger train to arrive at the new station. ANDREW STRONGITHARM

RIGHT: One of several posters produced by local schoolchildren and displayed in the Sainsbury's store opposite East Grinstead station celebrating the Bluebell Railway's arrival in the town in 2013.

40 Making Fresh Tracks to the Sunny South and West

ABOVE: What rubbish views from the train! LBSCR 0-6-2T No. 473 carries a 'Golden Arrow' headboard as it passes through Imberhorne cutting on March 27, 2013, with black matting either side concealing the landfill waste from the tip that did not need to be excavated in order to allow the railway back. ANDREW STRONGITHARM

ABOVE RIGHT: Maunsell U class 2-6-0 No. 1638 prepares to pull away from Sheffield Park on July 27, 2014. ROBIN JONES

RIGHT: SECR P CLASS 0-6-0T No. 323 heads a service train. BRIAN SHARPE

activity are an essential part of the cash flow required to sustain the railway and its ever-ageing buildings, infrastructure, locomotives, carriages and wagons – for which the costs of maintenance and restoration are ever increasing.

The East Grinstead extension, which allows visitors from London to travel to the Bluebell Railway by train, indeed brought a tourist boom to the town that Beeching once called home.

In the first years after steam trains returned to East Grinstead, figures showed that the railway attracted 188,144 visitors compared with 146,224 in 2012. Ticket revenue soared from £1,577,474 in 2012 to £2,294,145 in 2013.

East Grinstead tourism manager, Simon Kerr, said: "Everybody seems to be more than pleasantly surprised by the visitor numbers joining the Bluebell Railway at East Grinstead. All this seems to have been accomplished without any extra pressure on the town's existing car-parking capacity. Most of this extra passenger loading comes from the use of the Network Rail connection from London."

By 2015, the Bluebell Railway was forced to review its carriage fleet because of the overwhelming success of the northern extension.

Before the extension was opened, 60% of Bluebell trains were formed of four carriages, and only 30% of five or six. It was expected that demand for seats would tail off after the euphoria surrounding the opening to East Grinstead two years ago. But the railway needs five- or six-car trains through much of the peak season.

After the extension of the line to East Grinstead a period of consolidation was required but that has not stopped the successful completion in summer 2016 of the first building phase of Operation Undercover on land adjoining the carriage and wagon works at Horsted Keynes.

When finished this will provide cover from the elements for up to 20 carriages awaiting restoration or repair. The Bluebell Railway is a market leader in the recovery and restoration of Victorian and Edwardian carriage stock, renovating coach bodies that were used for decades as bungalows or chicken coops to as-built condition.

Vital to the successful operation of the Bluebell Railway is a core of around 60 employed staff supported by, and working with, an extensive array of volunteers – there being more than 700 of them on the list. Drivers, firemen, guards, booking office clerks, station staff, signalmen, buffet stewards, shop assistants, museum attendants and guides. The list goes on – track layers, lineside maintenance, fencing, painting as well as the volunteers working in the carriage and wagon and locomotive works, plus signalling. That is not to miss out on the enormous effort put in one weekend a month by youngsters in the 9F club who are forever cleaning, polishing, repairing and painting. Aged between 11 and 16 members of the 9F club often use this as source of training and experience for entry into voluntary work – but mainly the idea is to have fun. The youngsters of today are indeed the lifeblood for the success, preservation and continuation of the heritage railways of tomorrow.

Kingscote station is planned to become a more key attraction to some of the railway's younger visitors and a place to let off steam. At the same a time a project is currently being planned to have Kingscote as an operational goods yard and coal merchants so that visitors can see and understand how a railway goods yard worked before the days of universal road transport.

What does the Bluebell offer today? Operating a steam-hauled passenger train service every day from April to October – the chance for a nostalgic as well as educational experience for children, parents, grandparents and great grandparents – the day ticket puts travel on the railway throughout the day at your disposal. Gala events on certain weekends add variety to the offering, along with dining opportunities from a ploughman's lunch or cream tea on the main service train to relaxing in the luxury of one of four lounge cars on the 'Wealden Rambler' afternoon tea service that operates on selected dates.

Friday evenings can bring a Rail Ale Train, a Fish and Chip supper train or even a Murder Mystery on the Pullman dining train. The 'Golden Arrow' Pullman dining services, which operate predominantly for Saturday evening dinner or Sunday lunch also provide a unique combination of luxury silver-service three-course meal on a steam-hauled train and has been hailed as the very best of its type by reviewers. Though often used for birthdays and other celebrations the railway also provides for weddings, where Sheffield Park and Horsted Keynes are both licensed for civil ceremonies and provision for a reception either on the train or in the Birch Grove Suite at Sheffield Park.

As on many of Britain's top heritage lines today, the busiest month of the year is December, when Santa visits the railway, as do his reindeer and other helpers to ensure a magic and memorable day.

So there you have it – steam in the South on London's doorstep. ●

Making Fresh Tracks to the Sunny South and West

Chapter 4

SO MUCH MORE THAN A SEASIDE RAILWAY!

The Romney Hythe & Dymchurch Railway is not just any seaside miniature railway. Not only has it carried generations of happy holidaymakers over its 13½-mile 'main line in miniature' from Hythe to Dungeness, but it has also carried freight, acted as school transport and even became a fully fledged military railway during the Second World War.

It was devised by two men, racing driver, millionaire land owner, former Army officer and miniature-railway fan Captain Jack Howey and Count Louis Zborowski, a wealthy aristocrat famed as a racing driver.

The count dreamed of building a fully working express railway in miniature, with locomotives that would be scale replicas of main line steam locomotives, but running on 15in gauge, not 4ft 8½in standard gauge.

The duo failed to buy the Ravenglass & Eskdale Railway in the Lake District, a 15in gauge line laid on the trackbed of an earlier 3ft gauge freight railway.

Undeterred, Zborowski ordered two Pacific locomotives to be designed by the leading model railway engineer of his day, Henry Greenly, which were built in Colchester by Davey, Paxman and Co, in anticipation of the day the pair would have a railway of their own on which to run them. They were named *Green Goddess*, after the 1921 stage play by William Archer, which Howey enjoyed, and *Northern Chief*.

However, Zborowski was killed while racing at Monza in the Italian Grand Prix before the pair could be delivered.

The captain was left alone with the two locomotives and having to find a line on which to run them. Greenly came up with the idea of building a railway along the coast of Romney Marsh.

A double-track line was laid over the eight miles between Hythe and New Romney, the railway's headquarters, and the official opening took place on July 16, 1927, with another Pacific, *Hercules*, hauling the first train.

Howey extended the double tracks to Dungeness via Greatstone the following year.

The line was billed as the 'Smallest Public Railway in the World' and proved enormously popular. Soon there were nine miniature versions of express Pacific locomotives, just like those on the main line hauling a fleet of luxurious coaches.

At the outbreak of the Second World War, this part of the Kent coast found itself in the front line of Britain's defence, as the English Channel is narrowest around this point.

The little railway suddenly found itself pressed into Army service. The War Department then created the only miniature armoured train in the world as the line was used for Army patrols of the coast, and later in the conflict, it was also used extensively for the building of PLUTO (Pipe Line Under The Ocean), which fuelled the Allied invasion force following the D-Day landings in June 1944.

Making Fresh Tracks to the Sunny South and West

ABOVE: Yorkshire Engine Company duo No. 10 *Dr Syn* and No. 9 *Winston Churchill*, both supplied to the line in 1931, doublehead a special train at the end of the 2014 season. CHRIS KENNEDY/RHDR

LEFT: Davey Paxman 4-6-2 No. 1 *Green Goddess*, one of the first two locomotives on the line. DEREK PRITCHARD/RHDR

ABOVE LEFT: The railway founder is remembered in the name of the Captain Howey Hotel next to the line in New Romney. ROBIN JONES

OPPOSITE: Davey Paxman 4-8-2 No. 6 *Samson* prepares to leave the Dungeness terminus. The new Dungeness lighthouse is in the background. Dungeness is a settlement with houses plonked all over the shingle at random, with no fenced-off gardens and linked only by telegraph poles and wires – a real 'wild west'; outback scenario. ROBIN JONES

The railway was handed back to its owner after the end of the war, and the Hythe to New Romney section re-opened to the public in 1946.

The new Romney to Dungeness section followed a year later – with Laurel and Hardy performing at the official re-opening.

However, the war years had taken their toll on the line, and the New Romney to Dungeness section had been reduced to single line only, as the raw materials to rebuild were scarce and the cost of reinstatement enormous.

The postwar growth of tourism along the Kent coast greatly benefited the railway, but as cheap package holidays abroad became readily available, fewer holidaymakers came and receipts fell.

Howey had hoped to build a railway that would last a lifetime. He died in September 1963 with the lack of investment in the line already evident, a problem that was not fully addressed by subsequent owners. The rolling stock was ageing and giving rough rides, the locomotives were costly to maintain and ridges were in poor condition.

Multi-millionaire enthusiast, Sir William McAlpine, who once owned *Flying Scotsman*, stepped in to reverse the downward trend in 1973, and since then, the railway has gone from strength to strength.

In 1974, a new train shed was erected over the New Romney platforms to give the impression of a major city terminus.

The fleet expanded in 1976 with the arrival German-built locomotive No. 11 *Black Prince*, while all 10 original locomotives remain in service, covering thousands of miles each year.

As well as the nine Pacifics and 4-8-2s, there was Krauss 0-4-0 tender tank locomotive No. 4, which left the railway in 1926 after construction and ran in Belfast with the new name *Jean*. It returned to Romney in the 1970s was restored and is known as *The Bug*. There is now a total of 16 locomotives.

Not only is the line a major tourist attraction, but it also provides a public service between the small towns and villages between Hythe and Dungeness. Indeed, it was originally conceived as a public service, rather than an out-and-out visitor attraction.

The railway is under contract to the local council to transport children to and from The Marsh Academy in New Romney. Local residents are transported to shopping centres and the railway has operated 'shoppers specials'. Holiday camp trains have operated with campers at Romney Sands and St Mary's Bay.

The railway is licensed by the Post Office for rail postal services, and is allowed to issue its own postage stamps. A four-wheel secure postage wagon was built, and several first-day covers have been issued. The railway operates a parcels service, whereby parcels can be ferried from one station to another.

ABOVE: Davey Paxman 4-6-2 No. 3 *Southern Maid* was supplied in 1926. ROBIN JONES

Making Fresh Tracks to the Sunny South and West

ABOVE: Two Pacifics a size apart: *Flying Scotsman*, which went on to become the world's most famous railway locomotive, lines up against the Romney, Hythe & Dymchurch Railway's No. 7 *Typhoon* at King's Cross depot in 1927. ROBIN JONES COLLECTION

LEFT: Davey Paxman No. 7 *Typhoon* of 1926 makes a storming run over the shingle to *Dungeness*. CHRIS KENNEDY/RHDR

BELOW: Davey Paxman 4-8-2 No. 5 *Hercules* in a very different form to that which its builders intended in 1926 – as the centrepiece of a military train defending the Kent coast against the Nazi menace. It is seen passing a bomb crater at Dymchurch. RHDR

ABOVE: This bungalow is said to include a royal saloon used by Queen Victoria. ROBIN JONES

The railway's designers had also envisaged freight being carried, and that is partially why two of the original engines, No. 5 *Hercules* and No. 6 *Samson* were built to the 4-8-2 Mountain wheel arrangement. Despite lacking speed, as such they could haul heavy freight.

In 1937 a quarter-mile branch line was laid to the east of the main line near Dungeness, running to the beach, while Platform 1 at Hythe was extended beside the station buildings and out to the front of the station. The purpose was to move fish from Dungeness to Hythe for onward transportation by road, and the little railway even introduced its own fish wagons, but as a venture it took off in only a small way and was soon withdrawn.

Also in 1937 a subsidiary ballast company was formed, with tipper wagons loaded with shingle from Dungeness beach taken along the fish branch and onwards to Hythe, where the contents were tipped into lorries from a ramp. The service lasted until 1951 when road transport took over.

In the late 1920s, there were plans for a two-mile extension with steep inclines from Hythe to meet the Southern Railway at Sandling Junction: those gradients were another reason why the 4-8-2s were ordered. Those plans came to nothing, but were briefly revisited in the 1980s when fresh surveys were carried out.

From 1982, the line could no longer claim to be the world's smallest public railway. That crown was taken by the 10¼in gauge Wells & Walsingham Light Railway in North Norfolk, laid along 4½ miles of the Great Eastern Railway's Wells-next-the-Sea branch.

Captain Jack's line not only lasted his lifetime as he intended, but it is still a thriving concern in the modern age, long after the full-size steam locomotives, which its engine fleet aimed to replicate, were withdrawn from British Railways' service. He was a Sunny South legend ahead of his time. ●

BELOW: Krauss 0-4-0TT No. 8378 of 1926 No. 4 *The Bug* heads a service train at Dungeness. CHRIS KENNEDY//RHDR

ABOVE: The entire modern-day steam fleet lines up outside the shed at New Romney. RHDR

LEFT: No. 5 *Hercules* at the Southern Railway's Ashford Works alongside Bulleid West Country light Pacific No. 21C119 Bideford in 1946. *Hercules* had been taken there to have its wartime armoured plating removed, and came face to face with one of the Sunny South's newest streamlined locomotives. RHDR

RIGHT AND BELOW RIGHT: The Romney Hythe & Dymchurch Railway is only one of several narrow gauge railways at Dungeness, the site of one of the biggest expanses of shingle in the world. Here the very rich flora and fauna, with more than 600 different types of plant and many rare insects such as moths, bees and beetles, and spiders found nowhere else in Britain, have seen it declared a Site of Special Scientific Interest. A series of ramshackle narrow-gauge tracks with their own bridges, viaducts and embankments have been laid by fishermen from the coastal road to the high shingle ridge overlooking the sea, so they can haul their catch over the stones. Various forms of homemade locomotives were used to haul these trains, and around the year 2000 there were still around eight fish railways in use. However, modern concrete or matting pathways have 'done a Beeching' and since made them redundant. ROBIN JONES

BELOW: The remote village of Dungeness with its two lighthouses and nuclear power station is no Crewe, Derby, Swindon or Eastleigh, but is every bit a 'railway town'. Many of the bungalow homes started out as redundant wooden-bodied carriages bought by local fishermen from the Southern Railway as homes for as little as £10. As well as the Romney, Hythe & Dymchurch Railway, New Romney was served by a standard gauge branch from 1884 until 1967, and it was over this line that the carriage bodies were brought. The one pictured standing in front of Dungeness Old Lighthouse has been extended over the years but still has the old carriage in the middle. Another, a white bungalow opposite the Britannia pub was once a royal saloon for Queen Victoria. Many of them have been expanded and modernised over the decades, and today can sell for hefty six-figure sums. ROBIN JONES

Chapter 5

DOUBLE DEVON DELIGHT!

In the wake of the success of the launch of the Bluebell Railway, a business-minded group decided to set up a counterpart in South Devon, intending it to be a money-making tourist attraction as opposed to a purely enthusiast outfit. A remarkable series of events resulted in two heritage lines serving the area, one offering a superb re-creation of a Great Western country branch line, the other some of the finest coastal views of any railway in Europe.

Around the time that the Bluebell Railway was running its first services, early efforts were being made to see if South Devon could emulate Sussex, and have a heritage steam railway of its own.

On February 28, 1959, Collett 0-4-2T No. 1466 – later preserved at Didcot Railway Centre – hauled the last scheduled passenger train on the GWR Newton Abbot to Moretonhampstead branch.

Railway preservation in South Devon had its roots in a bid to save the GWR. The rector of nearby Teigngrace, Canon OM Jones, and Torquay enthusiast EG Parrott set up the South Devon Railway Society to see if they could follow the Bluebell blueprint and save this branch.

They campaigned for the reintroduction of passenger trains to the Dartmoor town, and on June 6, 1960 a Paignton-Moretonhampstead special, 'The Heart of Devon Rambler', carried more than 200 people. Soon afterwards, the society leased Teigngrace Halt on the branch as its headquarters.

Yet the group achieved no more. The Western Region lifted the northern half of the branch beyond Bovey Tracey, while retaining the southern portion for freight.

The would-be revivalists' efforts were not in vain, for they used the experience that had been gained to investigate other possible lines to be saved in Bluebell fashion.

A prime target here was the GWR Kingsbridge branch, nickamed the Primrose Line, running from South Brent along the valley of the River Avon, serving Gara Bridge, Loddiswell and Avonwick, which closed on September 14, 1963.

The revivalists won the support of Kingsbridge Town Council, but as they left the meeting in the town, to their dismay, they saw contractors already lifting the track, a typical fate of lines closed in the Beeching era and, indeed, before. It was like a team taking the lead in the FA Cup final only to lose 10-1.

Attention then turned to the GWR branch from Totnes to Ashburton. Revivalists Bob Saunders and Peter Stedman brought together a group of businessmen including John Evans to re-open the line to passengers.

However, unlike the Bluebell, any revival here would not be an attempt to re-introduce the public services that had been lost, nor would it be heritage for heritage's sake.

The group's plan was to revive the branch as an unashamedly profit-making tourist attraction. The group saw that very soon, in the wake of British Railways' 1956 Modernisation Plan, which called for diesel and electric trains to consign steam trains to history, there would be people who wanted to remember the good old days and ride on them again, and bring their families along too. They were so right.

The protagonists established the Dart Valley Light Railway Co Ltd to buy the line and acquire suitable locomotives, the first arriving on October 2, 1965 in the form of GWR prairie No. 4555, Collett 0-6-0 No. 3205, and four BR(W) auto trailers.

LEFT: The locomotive that hauled the Dart Valley Railway's official opening train on April 5, 1969, GWR pannier tank No. 6412, heads a South Devon Railway service train past Hood Bridge on February 15, 2016. BRIAN SHARPE

ABOVE: Few scenes in the UK heritage railway portfolio scream 'summer holiday!' like this spot where the Dartmouth Steam Railway passes above the beach huts at Goodrington Sands. The author's family hired one of these for a July fortnight back in 1962, when he was just five! Heading the train towards Kingswear is 1924-built GWR 2-8-0T No. 5239 *Goliath*. Operator Dart Valley Railway plc has long had a policy of naming its locomotives in order to widen their appeal to younger family members. DSRRC

BEECHING RE-OPENS A LINE!

It was on April 5, 1969, the same year that the branch was bought from British Rail, that the axeman himself, Dr Richard Beeching, officially re-opened the section of the branch from Buckfastleigh to Totnes. The first public train was hauled by GWR pannier tank No. 6412 and as the businessmen had predicted, the venture was an overnight success.

Sadly, the last two miles of the line to Ashburton were never re-opened to the public. Neither the company nor the preservation movement as a whole could stop the northernmost section of the branch, from Buckfastleigh to Ashburton, being taken by the Ministry of Transport for use as part of the new A38 trunk road from Exeter to Plymouth.

And in 1971, a year short of the branch's centenary, the line was severed to make way for the widening of the A38, cutting off the beautiful Brunel-style terminus station at Ashburton.

Had the same problem arisen today, it is almost certain that the roadbuilders would have been ordered to provide an alternative route alongside, or amend their plans to avoid the railway. However, despite widespread local opposition to the loss of the line, the heritage sector had yet to develop that kind of muscle back in 1969-70.

As needs must, Buckfastleigh was remodelled from a through station into a terminus.

What did survive, however, was seven miles of quintessential GWR country branch line, its banks filled with bluebells and primroses in the spring, and services run in the traditional way by small tank engines and auto trailers. As such, it blossomed in the years that followed.

One drawback was the lack of an eastern terminus at Totnes, because Dart Valley officials were unable to reach an agreement with British Rail for their trains to run into the town's main line railway station. Initially push-pull trains were used, controlled from an auto-coach at one or both ends and reversing just short of the junction.

However, eventually land near to the junction was acquired, and a run-round loop laid in 1977. A platform was added a few years later but there was no public route between the station and Totnes. At this time the station appeared in the timetable as Totnes Riverside. Visitors to the railway arriving by main line train had to catch a bus from Totnes to Buckfastleigh from where they could ride the train to Totnes and back, then return to Totnes by bus.

To avoid confusion, the station was renamed Littlehempston Riverside in the 1980s. At the same time, the station building from Toller on the Bridport branch, which closed in 1975, was re-erected at Littlehempston.

British Rail finally allowed heritage line trains into the main line Totnes station in 1985, and for three years regular services were run into it. However, the charges imposed on the Dart Valley made such an operation uneconomic, and so the trains eventually returned to using Littlehempston in 1988.

In 1993 a new footbridge was built alongside the existing railway bridge, thus providing public access to the station from Totnes and its main line station. The Dart Valley station was renamed again, to Totnes (Littlehempston). However, long before then, the Dart Valley company found itself with far bigger fish to fry, with transport history to be made.

A SECOND DART VALLEY RAILWAY

The single-track branch from Paignton to Kingswear was long regarded as a 'main line by the back door', being an extension of the doubletrack route to Torquay and Paignton.

Indeed, the line was so busy on summer Saturdays that the Park sidings were opened alongside Paignton station in 1930 to provide room to stable the extra carriages, and the running line was doubled as far as Goodrington Sands Halt.

The 1950s boom in summer holidays saw yet more carriage sidings opened in 1956 at Goodrington, with a turntable installed the following year. Kingswear signalbox was also given a new lever frame in 1960.

While the closure of sparsely used rural lines such as the Ashburton branch could at some stage be begrudgingly understood by the public, nobody in the '60s thought for a moment that the line south of Paignton could be threatened with closure.

While Dr Beeching is often mistakenly blamed for the closure of railway lines, both before and after his time as chairman of British Railways, he didn't list that route for the axe.

The shock closure proposal came while Barbara Castle was Labour transport minister. She spared the St Ives and Looe branches in Cornwall, commenting on their picturesque nature, and won many plaudits for her

ABOVE: Man bites dog! Four years after leaving British Railways, Dr Beeching was back – to re-open the line to Buckfastleigh as the Dart Valley Railway. JOHN BRODRIBB

LEFT: The South Devon Railway celebrated the exact 50th anniversary of the first heritage-era stock movements over the Ashburton branch. On October 2, 1965, GWR prairie No. 4555 hauled two coaches down the line to Buckfastleigh, before Collett 0-6-0 No. 3205 brought two more. Back then, many passengers on the special train took advantage of the chance to ride along the closed Ashburton branch, On October 2, 2015, the train headed by No. 3205 was re-created with the help of Ray Lee and 5542 Ltd. It is seen at Totnes (Littlehempston). SDR

legislation, which paved the way for the establishment of passenger transport authorities in urban areas, and in doing so protected commuter lines.

But there would be no reprieve for Kingswear from her.

The adjoining short branch from Churston to Brixham closed on May 13, 1963, having always suffered the disadvantage of being a station built high above the town.

Kingswear wharf was closed to freight traffic on May 4, 1964 and ordinary goods traffic was withdrawn on June 14, 1965. From April 18, 1966, most trains from Paignton to Kingswear operated as shuttle services, apart from during peak season. Slimming down or running down?

The line lost its Sunday trains from September 24, 1967, although some resumed during the summer of 1968. The crossing loop at Churston was closed on October 20, 1968 along with to the updated signalbox at Kingswear.

When Labour was in opposition before its 1964 election victory, it promised to sack Beeching and reverse all of his cuts if it came to power. Harold Wilson's government not only kept Beeching on for a while, but proceeded to implement more closures over and above those that he had proposed.

The bombshell came in November 1968 when it was formally proposed that the line from Paignton to Kingswear should be closed entirely.

RE-PRIVATISATION!

Yet, closure did not happen immediately, and indeed never really took place at all. For behind the scenes, a series of talks was begun. In 1972, Terry Holder, a former director of The Economist, became managing director of the Dart Valley Railway.

Following the huge success of the Buckfastleigh operation, he saw enormous potential in the Kingswear line.

It may just have been seven miles long, but the first half of the route with its red-sand beaches of Goodrington and Broadsands, the latter viewed from the top of a viaduct giving the impression of floating on air, is unforgettable.

Greenway Tunnel takes the traveller into a very different world: the cliffs and waves give way to the dramatic wooded slopes of the ria estuary of the River Dart, as a flotilla of masts of sailing craft come into view.

On scenery alone, never mind its location in the middle of one of Europe's most popular holiday destinations, the line could do everything that the original Dart Valley directors set out to do, and much more, but if someone else took over it could threaten the Buckfastleigh revenue.

Mega-enthusiast, Sir William McAlpine, one of the early investors in the Dart Valley, with a full-size standard gauge railway in the grounds of his home at Fawley Hill near Henley-on-Thames, paid BR £150 to hire a DMU to ride the length of the line to inspect it to Kingswear. "This was a thing that could not be missed. It was a line that could take the very biggest locomotives, and we were worried that it would compete with the Buckfastleigh line."

Shock waves reverberated through the heritage sector when it was announced that the Dart Valley company had bought the line on December 30, 1972.

Furthermore, the existing daily timetabled services continued without a break, from New Year's Day, 1973.

The Paignton to Kingswear line had become the first operational passenger-carrying section of the national network to be denationalised. The total purchase price of £275,000 included the whole line and most of the Kingswear waterfront including the Royal Dart Hotel. The company subsequently sold off that, and other surplus land assets to recoup much of the purchase price.

The heritage movement was still in comparatively early stages, but down in deepest Devon there was an operator that now owned two magnificent heritage lines.

Yet how many revived lines have been able to run an all-year-round timetabled passenger service as opposed to a tourist line?

The nationalised network was, and still is, hugely subsidised by the Government, and

LEFT: GWR 4-6-0 No. 4920 *Dumbleton Hall* heads past Waterside caravan park en route to Kingswear. BRIAN SHARPE

RIGHT: GWR prairie No. 4555 on a demonstration goods train at Kingswear. BRIAN SHARPE

BELOW: The world's most famous steam locomotive, LNER A3 Pacific No 4472 *Flying Scotsman*, steams over Broadsands viaduct on September 1, 1973 after Sir William McAlpine brought it back from California where it was marooned. BRIAN SHARPE

ABOVE: WR 4-6-0 No. 7827 Lydham Manor climbs away from Goodrington Sands on the Dartmouth Steam Railway on May 29, 2016. KARL HEATH

lossmaking lines were being kept open by the taxpayer. Remove the subsidy, and nothing could make a revived line pay if it tried to offer services identical to those under BR.

As we have seen elsewhere in the Sunny South, any profits from summer-holiday season ticket sales were easily wiped out and worse by low patronage during the rest of the year, during which time the carriages needed to cater for the mid-year boom in traffic had to be stored.

So the Dart Valley's running of local trains through the year quickly came to an end after the first summer season. There would never be another winter timetable from Paignton to Kingswear, as the company from then on adopted the heritage/tourist attraction format of running only in profitable times of the year.

The line was rebranded as the Torbay Steam Railway and later the Paignton & Dartmouth Steam Railway.

The year 1973 saw Sir William McAlpine bring no less than LNER A3 Pacific No. 4472 *Flying Scotsman* to the railway, where it underwent trials during the summer season and provided a major publicity boost.

He had rescued No. 4472 from San Francisco after the failure of Alan Pegler's ill-fated North American tour of 1969-70, which left the locomotive's owner bankrupt. He bought the A3 for £25,000 and after it returned to the UK in February that year, he paid for its overhaul at Derby Works. After the Torbay summer season, it was transferred to Steamtown at Carnforth from where it ran on many main line tours.

Following years of frustration and setbacks for the South Devon Railway's signal and telegraph team, Ashburton Junction signalbox was commissioned on May 21.

Trains on the line are now controlled by electric train token through its entire its length.

The system offers more flexibility and has made the old train staff and ticket working between Bishops Bridge and Totnes redundant.

Further work is still to do to modify the alignment of the track towards the Totnes Riverside station throat, which will then allow new gates for the rare breeds farm crossing to be operated directly from the signalbox and also a new bracket starting signal to be erected closer to the platform end.

CHOOSING BETWEEN THE TWO

The Buckfastleigh line was considered the main concern with the Torbay line of junior importance. However, passenger uptake in a mainstream holiday resort made it inevitable that the roles would soon reverse.

The Buckfastleigh line never improved on the 120,000 passengers carried in that first season, and by the late 1980s was seen as a drag on the company's resources. Trade on the Buckfastleigh line diminished as that on the Paignton route grew from strength to strength.

One idea given consideration at one stage was relocating the Romney, Hythe & Dymchurch Railway to the Buckfastleigh branch, converting it to 15in gauge, but the idea was not taken further.

However, by the end of the '80s, losses on the Buckfastleigh line soared to the point where closure again loomed as a possibility.

Barry Cogar, the now-retired general manager of Dart Valley Railway plc at that time, recalled: "We were concentrating our resources on Buckfastleigh, but it was dragging the whole operation down. Meanwhile, the Paignton & Dartmouth was struggling to cope with loadings."

Eventually, Barry took his concerns to the board, and suggested that the Buckfastleigh line should be closed and sold off. His Beeching-style recommendation was approved but, as might be expected, was greeted with widespread disdain in the enthusiast quarter.

The saviour this time came in the form the Dart Valley Railway Association, the society formed in 1965 to support the company. Its members took over the Buckfastleigh branch and ran it by themselves.

A total of 56,368 passenger journeys were made, and thanks to the use of voluntary

LEFT: An idyllic summer scene on the River Dart sees a dingy user wave to a passing South Devon Railway train headed by 1930-built GWR pannier tank No. 5786. In recent years, this locomotive has carried the maroon livery in which it ran as London Transport No. L92, following its sale by British Railways.

ABOVE: In late March each year, the South Devon Railway offers local residents the chance to travel at half price. On March 22, 2015, GWR 0-6-0PT No. 6412 passes Collett 0-6-0 No. 3205 at Buckfastleigh. When it was previously based at the West Somerset Railway, No. 6412 was the star of the children's TV series The Flockton Flyer, while No. 3205 hauled the first public train on the Severn Valley Railway in 1970. SDR

labour instead of salaried staff, the financial situation improved – but not enough to satisfy Dart Valley Railway plc. Barry Cogar stood at Buckfastleigh station in front of TV cameras and told journalists that the branch was losing £100,000 a year, and was therefore up for sale.

To the rescue came bank manager, Richard Elliott, who had joined the association in 1965 and was representing the society on the company's board.

He remembered that first day of services back in 1969, and was determined not to let 20 years of hard graft disappear. "Dr Beeching had been busy closing down so many stations and lines around the country that the Dart Valley Railway thought it would be fun to get him here and re-open one instead," he said.

"It was a Wednesday and I took the day off work because, although I started as a volunteer at the station in 1965, I was actually working in a bank at the time. I saw and heard Beeching's speech and also worked on the first train."

Richard produced a plan to take over the line and run it as a charitable trust – using a ready-made company at supporters' disposal.

The Dumbleton Hall Locomotive Society, a registered charity, was actively restoring Barry scrapyard hulk GWR 4-6-0 No. 4920 in Buckfastleigh's workshops.

Richard took advantage of a legal loophole, as the Dumbleton Hall group already had the powers to run a railway. It transformed itself into the South Devon Railway Trust, with Richard – who quit his job in the banking sector to run the operation – as general manager and company secretary.

This time round, only a bare minimum of paid staff were employed. To replace them, Richard formed an army of volunteers from the local community, many of whom had never shown an interest in railways before. Many retired people turned out to offer their services and expertise free of charge, their reward being part of the new social circle that the venture generated.

With the Dart Valley fleet having moved to Paignton, the society's main asset was *Dumbleton Hall*, which was too heavy to run on the line that had been built largely to light railway standards, and could generate income only by being hired out.

Nonetheless, a fleet of steam and diesel locomotives was eventually built up.

GOING IT ALONE
Since the second takeover in 1991, mammoth strides were taken to develop the Buckfastleigh line as a major heritage venue, with 450 volunteers.

A signalbox rescued from Bishops Bridge at Athelney in Somerset was installed at Staverton station, where the old passing loop was reinstated, while several miles of track were relaid with concrete sleepers, and repairs to three main bridges, including Nursery Pool Bridge, have been undertaken.

The Buckfastleigh shop and its restaurant were expanded and improved, generating another vital income stream. The railway also owns the adjacent Buckfast Butterflies and Dartmoor Otter Sanctuary, significant and worthwhile visitor attractions in their own right.

While care was taken to retain the ambience of the much-loved 'typical' West Country branch, other strings to the railway's bow have been added. In BR days, the Ashburton branch saw only one example of modern traction in the form of an occasional visit from a Class 03 shunter: today, it is the home of the South Devon Diesel Group with its impressive fleet. While steam was the primary reason for the foundation of virtually all of today's heritage lines, the once widely despised modern traction now has its own following. The Bluebell Railway was from the beginning to recent times religiously anti-diesel: not one example was allowed on to its metals. Now it not only has regular visits by diesel-hauled railtours but holds – horror of all horrors for the hardcore purists – diesel galas!

Eventually, HM Railway Inspectorate raised the South Devon Railway's axle loading for the first time in its history to 23½ tons, allowing *Dumbleton Hall* to run on its 'own' line.

In 2000, the South Devon Railway started negotiations to purchase the freehold of the line from Dart Valley plc for £1.15 million, the money being raised through a share issue, loans, donations and revenue.

In 2002, the Dart Valley plc granted the SDR a 199-year lease on condition of a new Transport & Works Order being granted (a legal requirement), which would allow the final transfer of the freehold title for a nominal £1.

In 2007, the line was named Ian Allan Heritage Railway of the Year in the National Rail Heritage Awards. That year it carried 100,449 passengers, its best season since 1969.

On February 8, 2010, the South Devon Railway bought its freehold from Dart Valley Railway plc, for the nominal £1, after the lengthy statutory Transport & Works Order was finally completed. At last, the railway was master of its own destiny.

The following year, Buckfastleigh changed from being a rural former intermediate station into a major heritage engineering centre, following the acquisition of Roger Pridham's Tavistock boiler works.

RK Pridham Engineering started life in three tin sheds, formerly Pridham's garage in the village of Lamerton in west

LEFT AND ABOVE: While the Paignton to Kingswear line boasts matchless coastal and estuarine scenery, that of the tranquil valley of the Dart followed by the South Devon Railway, famously lined with primroses in spring, presents a dramatic contrast. Ancillary attractions are viewed as important to the railway, which owns Buckfast Butterflies and Dartmoor Otter Sanctuary nextdoor to Buckfastleigh station, and for passengers who take a ride on the seven-mile line to Totnes (Littlehempston), there is also a joint ticketing arrangement with Totnes Rate Breeds Farm, which has the biggest colony of red squirrels in the South West. SDR/ROBIN JONES

ABOVE: The former Cradley Heath signalbox from the West Midlands now guards the South Devon Railway's main line connection at Ashburton Junction. Following years of frustration and setbacks for the line's signal and telegraph team, the signalbox was commissioned on May 21, 2016. Trains on the line are now controlled by electric train token through its entire its length. The system offers more flexibility and has made the old train staff and ticket working between Bishops Bridge and Totnes redundant. SDR

ABOVE: In GWR Brunswick green livery, Dartmouth Steam Railway flagship WR 4-6-0 No. 7827 *Lydham Manor* passes the wide sweep of Goodrington Sands en route to Churston and Kingswear. DSRRC
BELOW: GWR 0-4-2T No. 1450 departs from Buckfastleigh on February 16, 2016. BRIAN SHARPE

ABOVE: In 2011 WR 4-6-0 No. 7827 *Lydham Manor* was briefly repainted as scrapped sister No. 7800 *Torquay Manor*, for its appearance in the Churston 150 celebrations. Here it is seen with GWR 2-8-0T No. 5239 doubleheading a service train past Broadsands en route to Churston. DSRRC

Devon. His involvement in boilers began when he undertook welding jobs for insurance companies.

Run by father-and-son Roger and Paul Pridham, the firm was established in 1975 and earned a reputation second to none for railway and traction-engine boiler repairs.

In 1985, its original site was demolished and further land purchased to make way for a new purpose built 4000 sq ft workshop on the same site.

With space at a premium, in 2005 the firm bought a 2¼-acre site on a new industrial estate near Tavistock, built a new 9500 sq ft unit over 18 months and moved in.

The move was to be short lived. After 35 years in the business, both founder Roger Pridham and his family thought it was time for him to retire.

Roger held talks with the South Devon Railway, ending with both parties signing a formal legal agreement that would not only safeguard the Pridham family's considerable, if not unique, boiler engineering skills and facilities for the future, but also provide the railway with the ability to repair its own 13-strong steam locomotive fleet.

All three of Pridham's full-time expert staff relocated to Buckfastleigh and immediately started work on an SDR locomotive boiler under temporary cover while a new boiler shop was designed by SDR volunteer and retired architect, Clive Pepper, to accommodate them.

After planning permission was obtained, a sizeable new steel-framed and clad structure was swiftly erected to house the press equipment, including the massive 700-ton John Shaw press, which bends boiler plates to shape and is one of only two such specialist machines in the whole of western Europe.

Since then South Devon Railway engineering has undertaken numerous contracts for the heritage movement. What was once the domain of the likes of Swindon and Crewe is now part of Buckfastleigh's daily business, and provides a steady income stream while benefitting heritage traction all over the country.

The Totnes (Littlehempston) eastern terminus is to revert to its Dart Valley Railway-era name of Totnes (Riverside) from the start of the 2017 season following a suggestion from the line's Totnes Group endorsed by the railway's trust board.

■ For details of South Devon Railway services, visit www.southdevonrailway.co.uk or telephone 01364 644370.

TORBAY'S RAIL-BOAT TRANSPORT HUB

Dart Valley Railway plc has, over the years, made strategic improvements to its Torbay line both to improve efficiency and enhance the visitor experience.

Early on, an independent station alongside the main line station at Paignton, known as Queens Park, was opened to serve the Kingswear trains on the site of the old Park Sidings.

A loop was reinstated at Churston in 1979 using colour light signals, and in 1981 the turntable from the British Rail sidings at Goodrington was moved to the north of the station aligned on the formation of the old Brixham branch.

In 1991 the control of all signalling was moved to a new panel at Britannia Crossing near Kingswear.

A locomotive workshop was opened at Churston in 1993 and a carriage shop opened three years later.

In 2007 the passing loop at Goodrington Sands was reinstated, along with the carriage sidings to give more space for storing rolling stock.

In 2011 new offices for the railway and boats were opened at Kingswear in the style of a large GWR-style signalbox, despite some local controversy over its position.

The following year saw the Dartmouth Steam Railway's station at Paignton rebuilt in GWR style at a cost of around £1 million, and a new unstaffed station opened at Greenway Halt to serve novelist Agatha Christie's Greenway Estate.

However, arguably its most dramatic step forward was the purchase of two riverboat companies.

The first issue of *Heritage Railway* in April 1999 reported that the company had bought Dart Pleasure Craft, restoring the Kingswear-Dartmouth passenger ferries to railway ownership.

The railway to Kingswear was built by the Dartmouth & Torbay Railway, opening on August 16, 1864 and while Dartmouth had a railway station, uniquely it never saw any trains. The original aim had been to reach Dartmouth but the station building there, which sold train tickets and processed parcels but lacked platforms, was only ever reached by ferry.

The railway was frustrated in its efforts to build a line across the River Dart and so was forced to terminate its line on the east side of the river. The building survives but has long been out of railway use and is now a restaurant.

ABOVE: Flagship *Lydham Manor* is cleaned for another day's service. DSRRC

ABOVE RIGHT: Busy Kingswear station, the terminus of the line and the embarkation point for the ferry to Dartmouth. DSRRC

RIGHT: The company's ferry *Kingswear Princess* and 300-passenger vessel *Dart Venturer* pass a naval ship moored off Dartmouth. DSRRC

FAR RIGHT: The paddle steamer *Kingswear Castle* is now part of the Dartmouth Steam Railway & River Boat fleet. DSRRC

Soon after the acquisition of Dart Pleasure Craft, the rival Red River Cruises was acquired, and the now-legendary Round Robin trips, train one way, boat up the river to Totnes and return to Paignton by bus, were launched with huge success.

Building on the success of the railway, it emerged as the jewel in the crown of a transport hub. Under the trading name of River Link, it expanded to run boat trips to Teignmouth, Torquay and at one stage, as far afield as Salcombe, as well as trips within the River Dart.

Rebranded as the Dartmouth Steam Railway & River Boat Company, it now promotes itself as more than a heritage railway, offering holidaymakers a range of combined trips giving them a full day to experience some of the best scenery in the area with time to explore towns along their chosen route. In 2016, the railway extended its period of two-train operation to cater for increased demand and to be able to integrate with the expanding trips offered by boat and bus.

Steam trains now run from mid-February right the way through to December. The company has introduced services starting in Torquay by both bus and boat, offering an extension to its popular Round Robin, giving passengers the opportunity to spend time in Totnes, Dartmouth and Paignton. Also growing in popularity is the Sea Train Adventure, which offers passengers the chance to go from Torquay by boat enjoying stunning views of the coastline to Dartmouth, returning by train.

So, the company has become a fully integrated transport provider offering trains, boats and buses, following in the GWR tradition. However, there are no plans to introduce an air service as the GWR did.

The company also runs the ferry service between Torquay and Brixham. Also, coastal cruises from Dartmouth operate six days a week taking visitors outside the estuary and along the coast towards Start Point, viewing the coastal villages of Blackpool Sands, Torcross and Slapton Sands, which were used for training purposes in the Second World War.

For passengers to take full advantage of all the services on offer, the Jubilee Pass was introduced a few years ago. It is a two- to five-day ticket allowing hop-on, hop-off freedom to use any service operated by the company.

The historic paddle steamer *Kingswear Castle* is the last remaining coal-fired paddle steamer in operation in the UK today and, under charter to Dart Valley Railway plc, is running on its home waters of the River Dart once more.

Built in 1924 at Philip & Son of Dartmouth, it plied its trade between Totnes and Dartmouth until 1965. Its engines are even older, dating back to 1904. In its heyday, it could carry almost 500 passengers.

It is listed as part of the National Historic Fleet of ships of Pre-eminent National Significance.

It runs 1¼hr Dartmouth river Cruises and trips between Dartmouth and Totnes so that passengers can now journey aboard as part of the Round Robin excursion.

A huge oak has indeed grown from small acorns sown by a handful of entrepreneurs at Buckfastleigh in the mid-1960s. The fact that the company is a very rare example on a heritage railway that pays annual dividends to its shareholders says so much, and justifies the vision of more than half a century ago.

■ For more details of Dartmouth Steam Railway & River Boat Company services, visit www.dartmouthrailriver.co.uk or telephone 01803 555872.

A RETURN TO ASHBURTON?

Could either, or both, railways capitalise on their marvellous progress and extend their lines?

From time to time, the question of re-laying the Brixham branch is asked. In April 2015 Coun Gordon Oliver, the new mayor of Torbay, called for it to be reinstated and instructed council officers to investigate the opportunities for the reintroduction of trains between Churston station on the Dartmouth Steam Railway and outer Brixham.

Under his proposals, a new light railway would follow the route of the branch that was closed in 1962.

Nowadays it would be impossible to reinstate the entire length of the old branch, as houses have been built over the formation at the Brixham end, and the site of the station has been redeveloped.

LEFT: On July 10, 2016, the 'Torbay Express' ran from Bristol Temple Meads to Kingswear with LMS 4-6-0 No. 46100 *Royal Scot* as power. It is seen leaving Kingswear. DAVID HUNT

Mr Oliver described the light rail plan as, "an ambition fraught with many difficulties."

Adding: "But I do believe it would be good for our fishing port and for Brixham, which is flourishing at the moment.

"Part of the existing track could be used, though that much closer to the residential area is not accessible. It would be for passengers only but I think it would be very popular and good for tourism and business. We would have to negotiate access and look at the right design."

However, one proposal that has already generated significant national support is the extension of the South Devon Railway back into Ashburton station.

The idea of rebuilding the line north of Buckfastleigh on a new formation alongside the A38 trunk road, which swallowed up the original formation was mooted back in the earlier days of the South Devon Railway. However, a decision of the Dartmoor National Park Authority on July 3, 2015 to approve a masterplan for Ashburton's Chuley Road area, in which the former station, its goods shed and locomotive shed stand, gave the would-be revivalists infinitely greater urgency.

The masterplan involves the conversion of the station train shed into a community centre, building a convenience store and then allowing the trackbed to the southern edge of the town to be used for housing. If the trackbed ends up being built over, hopes of ever restoring the GWR branch in its entirety, and bringing a tourist boom to Ashburton, would be scuppered forever.

However, the Friends of Ashburton Station group, which was formed to bring the railway back into the town, at an estimated cost of £20 million, demanded a review of the decision, which was subsequently placed on hold for a year while other options are considered.

The Friends group has drawn up its own proposal, which would not only offer a visitor attraction but also offer a solution to the intended redevelopment of the Chuley Road area.

Rob Kinchin-Smith, from the Friends group, said that other benefits of its blueprint proposal would include car parking in the Chuley Road area for local residents and businesses, a park-and-ride service into Buckfastleigh, the possibility of a safe off-road cycle link between the two towns, and flood mitigation and drainage work necessary for the locality.

The Friends proposal also centres around the use of small tank engines and auto trains, a trademark feature of both the Ashburton branch and the Dart Valley Railway.

Rob said: "Depending on suitable curvature and gradients, Ashburton would be served by normal South Devon Railway service trains were the extension to be built, but we believe that the auto train shuttle service has much to recommend it as a unique selling point for the project.

"For the enthusiasts and the Heritage Lottery Fund it would revive the old Dart Valley Railway vision of 'the quintessential GWR West Country branch line, complete in all respects' and provide a unique experience as a regular timetabled service.

"It would also allow the historic Ashburton terminus to be recreated authentically, smooth any impact of passenger footfall on the community of Ashburton and make the Buckfastleigh-Ashburton service far more useful as a 'park and ride' compared with less frequent, longer trains.

"Following professional engineering and environmental input and the meetings with DNP and statutory consultees, the viability and deliverability of the rail link is now established beyond doubt."

The multiple benefits of having a steam railway in a town, especially one with no other significant tourist magnet, are now well documented all over the UK. Whether the Dartmoor National Park Authority sees the light before the option is lost for all time remains to be seen. ●

RIGHT: Artist Alan Hayward FREng CEng *MICE* MIStructE, a keen amateur watercolourist, and former partner at leading bridge engineers Cass Hayward, has produced this new visualisation of a revived Ashburton station. The Friends of Ashburton Station's main civil/structural advisor, Alan is also civil engineer to the Bodiam-Robertsbridge rail link project on the Kent & East Sussex Railway. FoAS

BELOW: On July 4, 2015, GWR 0-4-2T No. 1420, carrying its former Dart Valley Railway name *Bulliver*, left Buckfastleigh on a Gilpin Demolition low-loader to take part in Ashburton's annual carnival. The low-loader was fitted with track and a ramp built by a team of volunteers and full-time staff from South Devon Railway Engineering. Local town and district councillor, Charlie Dennis, who is also a South Devon Railway driver, sorted out the entry and transport, and went on the footplate with the two young cleaners who had spruced up the locomotive. The float won first prize in its class. No. 1420 then travelled to Newton Abbot for its carnival on July 11. SDR

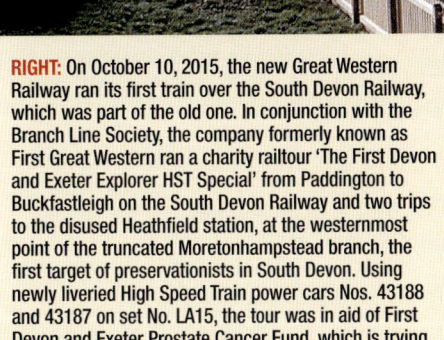

LEFT: An undated view of Churston station from British Railways' days shows GWR 14XX No. 1470 on a Brixham branch train with a 2-6-2T on a Kingswear service. The Association of Train Operating Companies has suggested building a park-and-ride for Brixham at Churston, but not re-opening the Brixham branch. GREAT WESTERN SOCIETY

RIGHT: On October 10, 2015, the new Great Western Railway ran its first train over the South Devon Railway, which was part of the old one. In conjunction with the Branch Line Society, the company formerly known as First Great Western ran a charity railtour 'The First Devon and Exeter Explorer HST Special' from Paddington to Buckfastleigh on the South Devon Railway and two trips to the disused Heathfield station, at the westernmost point of the truncated Moretonhampstead branch, the first target of preservationists in South Devon. Using newly liveried High Speed Train power cars Nos. 43188 and 43187 on set No. LA15, the tour was in aid of First Devon and Exeter Prostate Cancer Fund, which is trying to raise £20,000 for a portable scanner. The special is seen alongside the River Dart. COLIN WALLACE

Chapter 6

BRITAIN'S FIRST ELECTRIC RAILWAY

Brighton seafront's Volk's Electric Railway may appear to be just another seaside tramway, a relic from the resort's Victorian heyday. However, it not only brought electric trains to Britain, but it is the oldest in the world still running, and is now destined for a far brighter future.

In a country where steam reigned supreme, Magnus Volk was a rare example of a man who not only successfully introduced an alternative but sowed the seeds of what would one day be considered a premier form of traction.

The son of a German clockmaker, Magnus Volk was born at 35 (now 40) Western Road, Brighton on October 19, 1851. Locally educated, he became apprenticed to a scientific instrument maker but on the death of his father in 1869 returned home to assist his mother with running the family business.

His real interest, however, lay in the worlds of science and engineering, in particular anything that was powered by electricity.

In 1879, he successfully demonstrated the first telephone link in Brighton. The next year, he connected the first residential fire alarm to the fire station.

In 1880, at the age of 29, he became the first resident of Brighton to fit electric lights to his home at 38 Dyke Road, and over the next four years went on to fit electric incandescent lighting to the Royal Pavilion and its grounds, the Dome, the town museum, art gallery and library. Contacts made during this work proved instrumental in his most famous project of all.

On August 4, 1883, Volk unveiled a quarter-mile-long 2ft gauge electric railway running from a site on the seashore opposite the town's aquarium to the Chain Pier. Brighton Corporation granted Magnus Volk initial permission to run it for three months.

Power was provided by a 2hp Otto gas engine driving a Siemans D5 50v DC generator. A small electric car was fitted with a 1½hp motor giving a top speed of about 6mph.

ABOVE: Magnus Volk: Pioneer of electricity, who also built an electric car in 1888. VERA

ABOVE RIGHT: Cars Nos. 8 and 9 pass at Halfway station. ROBIN JONES

RIGHT: A Volk's Electric Railway two-car service running eastwards. ROBIN JONES

LEFT: Volk's Electric Railway Cars Nos. 7 and 8 in sunshine, newly repainted in the 125th anniversary livery of maroon and cream. IAN GLENHILL/VERA

BELOW LEFT: Poster advertising Magnus Volk's short-lived and decidedly eccentric 'Daddy Long Legs' Brighton & Rottingdean Seaside Electric Railway. A total of 160 passengers could be carried on the single car *Pioneer*. VERA

Volk did not invent electric traction. The first known electric locomotive was built by Scotsman, Robert Davidson, in 1837 and was powered by galvanic cells. Davidson followed it up with a bigger locomotive named *Galvani*, which was exhibited at the Royal Scottish Society of Arts Exhibition four years later.

This second locomotive was tested on the Edinburgh & Glasgow Railway in September 1842, but the limited electric power available from the batteries prevented its general use.

The world's first electric passenger train was demonstrated by Werner von Siemens in Berlin in 1879. Its locomotive was driven by a 2.2kW motor and the train, which consisted of the locomotive and three cars, and reached a maximum speed of 13kmh. Over four months the train carried 90,000 passengers on a 320yd circular track. The electricity, provided by a nearby stationary dynamo, was supplied to the train through a third isolated rail situated between the tracks.

In 1881, the world's first electric tram line, also built by Siemens, opened in Lichterfelde near Berlin, Germany.

While the principle of an electric locomotive may have originated in Scotland, Volk brought it to England in the form of a workable concept.

He soon sought powers to extend his line westwards along the beach to the town boundary, but the council refused. Instead, he obtained permission to extend eastwards from the Aquarium to the Banjo Groyne, and the Arch at Paston Place to provide workshop and power facilities. He also decided to widen the track to 2ft 8½in gauge, and he designed two more powerful and larger passenger cars.

The route followed the seashore, and needed timber trestles to bridge gaps in the shingle, and severe gradients to allow the cars to pass under the Chain Pier.

The new line opened on April 4, 1884 at first using one car. The upgraded power plant in the Arch gave an output of 160v at 40A, more than enough to propel the two new cars along the 1400yd-long railway. A loop complete with halt was provided halfway along the route for the cars to pass.

With the arrival of the second car, a five- or six-minute service was provided daily summer and winter, excepting Sundays until 1903. The service operated until 1940 when the threat of invasion closed the railway during the Second World War.

While local cab drivers and fishermen working from the beach were not impressed with the competition, the railway was a huge hit with the public. Two new cars, Nos. 3 and 4 entered service in 1892, and a fifth car followed in 1897.

RIGHT: An alternative to walking along the seafront, the Volk's Electric Railway is of paramount importance in terms of British transport history. ROBIN JONES

ABOVE: The Brighton terminus of the unique Brighton & Rottingdean Seaside Electric Railway. VERA

LEFT: One of the Siemens & Halske early German electric trains on display inside the Berlin Technical Museum. It ran on what was the world's first electric railway, but Brighton's Volk's Electric Railway is the oldest still operating. ROBIN JONES

In 1890, frustrated at his inability to extend beyond the Banjo Groyne to Rottingdean, Volks produced a scheme for another new kind of railway – one that ran through the sea.

The Brighton & Rottingdean Seashore Electric Railway consisted of two parallel 2ft 8½in gauge tracks, billed as 18ft gauge, the measurement between the outermost rails. The tracks were laid on concrete sleepers mortised into the bedrock.

The single car used on the railway was a 45ft by 22ft pier-like building that stood on four 23ft-long legs and weighed 45 tons. It too was powered by electric motors.

It was officially named *Pioneer*, but many called it 'Daddy Long Legs' and the nickname stuck.

Not only did it need a driver, but a qualified sea captain was on board at all times.

Uniquely in British railways, the car was provided with lifeboats and other safety measures.

Building of the second line began in 1894 and it officially opened on November 28, 1896, only to be severely damaged by a storm a week later.

Volk rebuilt the railway including *Pioneer*, which had been turned on to its side, and it re-opened in July 1897.

The railway, arguably the most eccentric in Britain, also proved popular, but faced physical difficulties, for high tide slowed the car down, and Volk did not have the finance to install more powerful motors.

In 1900, groynes built near the eccentric railway to prevent beach erosion were found to have led to underwater scouring under the sleepers and the line was closed for two months while repairs took place. The council decided to build a beach protection barrier, and ordered Volk to divert his line around it. He could not afford to do so, and so closed his second line down.

The track, car and other structures were sold for scrap, but some of the concrete sleepers can still be seen at low tide.

After the Brighton & Rottingdean Seashore Electric Railway venture failed, Volk obtained permission to extend his first line beyond the Banjo Groyne to Black Rock and opened the extension in September 1901, bringing the total length of the railway to one-and-a-quarter miles.

The longer line needed more cars and three were added; by 1926, the fleet had been brought up to 10. The last car built specifically for the railway was a winter car, which arrived in 1930.

In the same year the redevelopment of Madeira Drive saw the railway cut back at the western end to a site opposite the aquarium. That was a big setback for the line as the terminus was now no longer next to the pier entrance.

Sadly and short-sightedly, the line was also cut back by several hundred yards at the Black Rock end. The council decided to build a new swimming pool on the land currently occupied by the station and so cut the line even shorter.

The new Black Rock station was opened on May 7, 1937 when Volk, then 85, and the deputy mayor took joint control of Car 10 for a journey.

It was Volk's last public appearance as he died peacefully at home 13 days later. He is buried at St Wulfran's churchyard in Ovingdean near Brighton.

Control of the railway passed briefly to his eldest son, Herman. The lease from Brighton Corporation was to expire on April 1, 1939 but it granted an extension to April 1, 1940. On that date the corporation formally took over the line, together with 18 regular employees, under powers invested in it through the 1938 Brighton Corporation (Transport) Act.

By then, Britain was at war again with Germany but a service with eight cars

RIGHT: Beneath a menacing sky, which threatens to evacuate the beaches, a Volk's Electric Railway tramcar heads back to Aquarium station in the shadow of the Brighton Wheel with the passengers guaranteed to stay dry! VERA

56 Making Fresh Tracks to the Sunny South and West

continued until the end of June 1940, thereafter with the threat of an invasion looming the entire beach was closed and the railway ceased to run.

All stations were demolished and the cars stored under the seafront arches, where they remained for five years.

REBUILT AND REOPENED
By good fortune, Brighton Corporation decided to rebuild the railway and work began in 1947.

Three of the cars, including those from 1884, had rotted beyond repair and were scrapped. The rest of the fleet was overhauled and re-varnished in the traditional way.

Services resumed on Saturday, May 15, 1948, initially running throughout the year but since 1954 the railway has operated only during the summer season from Easter to September.

Original cars Nos. 1 and 2 were scrapped and replaced by two Southend Pier Railway trailer cars which, converted to motor cars became Nos. 8 and 9 in the fleet.

An effort was made to 'modernise' the fleet in the early 1960s with a new brown and yellow livery and new 'tram-style' controllers. Cars were also converted to run as pairs, thus reducing the number of drivers required.

During the late 1960s and '70s, Brighton began to be severely hit by competition from cheap Mediterranean package holidays. The Black Rock swimming pool closed in 1978, leading to a further drop in passenger numbers.

Questions were asked as to whether the expense of keeping the railway open was justified, but in the end it was decided to soldier on at least until its centenary in 1983. That event was a huge success, with Volk's youngest son Conrad driving a special train comprising cars Nos. 3 and 4.

Afterwards, it was decided that the railway should remain open.

As stated earlier, Volk's Electric Railway was not the first in the world to run on electricity, but all the earlier ones have long since passed into history. It was the first in Britain, and is therefore of immense national historical importance, rather than a mere local antique.

By bringing the electric railway concept to Britain. Volk paved the way for the creation of the London Underground and electrified overground suburban lines, the third-rail electric Southern Railway/Region, which today dominates the network in the Sunny South and ultimately the inter-city trunk routes such as the East and West Coast Main Lines, which form a backbone of the country's provincial transport system.

The railway's western terminus, Aquarium station, stands opposite the Sealife Centre. However, just like the electric railway, this building is far more important than just another aquarium in a national chain. Dating from 1872, it is nothing less than the world's oldest working aquarium, conceived and designed by Eugenius Birch, the architect responsible for the West Pier, which is awaiting rebuilding after being left to decay and being gutted by fire. The interior of the aquarium has been kitted out to look like something from a Jules Verne submarine theme park, and its ambience dovetails well with the early electric railway that runs outside.

TOP: Car No. 9 passes through the depot where No. 10 is parked up. ROBIN JONES **ABOVE LEFT:** Maintenance of Car No. 7 in progress at the railway's depot. VERA **ABOVE MIDDLE RIGHT:** The entrance to Aquarium station. VERA **ABOVE RIGHT:** Yes, it does snow in the Sunny South! VERA

THE LOTTERY STEPS IN
In 1983, the centenary year, there was grave doubt as to whether the railway could continue but Brighton Borough Council (as it was then) made the decision to maintain the operation on a shoestring budget. This policy continued for another 30 years with the resulting decay in both buildings and the historic fleet... but then, in 2013, an application was made for Heritage Lottery funding.

In September 2015 Brighton & Hove City Council was awarded a Heritage Lottery grant of £1.65 million to build a new depot, new Aquarium Station and visitor centre and restore three cars. Magnus Volk's legacy had been saved.

Volk has also been immortalised in Brighton's own Walk of Fame, the brainchild of local resident David Courtney, the man who discovered singer Leo Sayer in the 1970s. Based on the Hollywood Walk of Fame, it is the only one of its kind in Britain. All the 100 names are laid alongside the resort's waterfront development, and Volk is up there with the likes of Dame Anna Neagle, Rudyard Kipling and Chris Eubank.

In terms of the impact that electric railways had on British transport, maybe he is the greatest Brightonian of them all.

Patronage is reasonably buoyant today, although there are many who have commented that it could be far greater if the line could in some way be re-extended westwards back to the pier entrance, and eastwards beyond Black Rock to Brighton marina.

Since 1995, the tramway has been supported by a growing band of enthusiasts under the banner of the Volk's Electric Railway Association (VERA), who, on occasions, even take over the running of the trains.

If you fancy doing something a little more adventurous than bucket and spading at Brighton, by joining VERA and helping out on the railway visit www.volkselectricrailway.co.uk to find out more. ●

RIGHT: Does Halfway station boast the smallest station building anywhere?

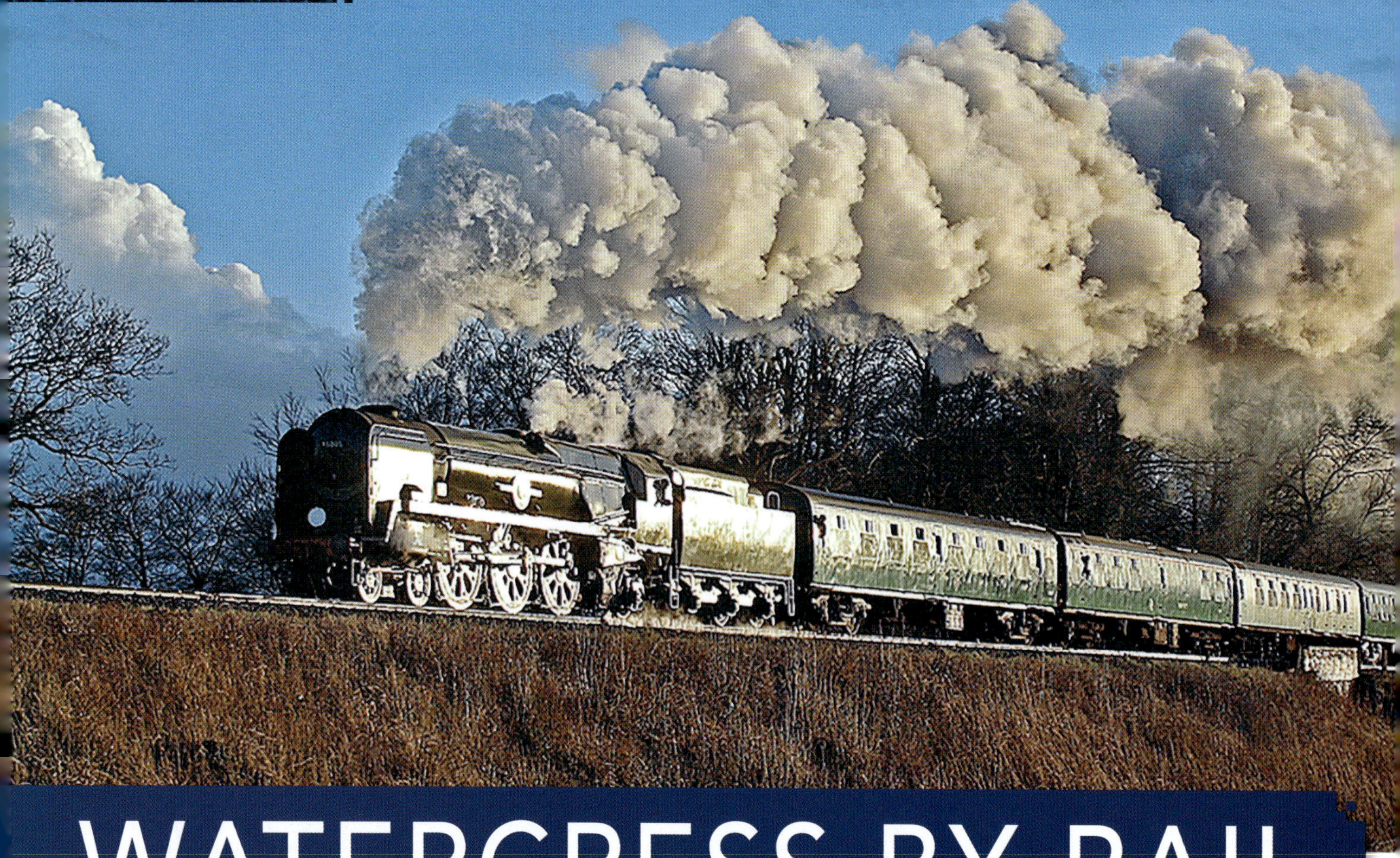

Chapter **7**

WATERCRESS BY RAIL

Closed by British Rail, the surviving section of the Alton to Winchester route was revived and rebuilt as the Mid Hants Railway, one of the major bastions of main line steam in the Sunny South, and a magnificent encapsulation of the Southern Railway and Southern Region of yesteryear.

LEFT: Say it with flowers: the Alresford terminus of the Mid Hants Railway. MHR

The Mid Hants Railway, one of Britain's premier heritage lines, is marketed as the Watercress Line and runs along the edge of the South Downs National Park in Hampshire. The railway was nicknamed for its early role in transporting locally grown watercress to the markets in London and beyond.

In 1861, the Alton, Alresford and Winchester Railway Company was authorised under an Act of Parliament to build a new railway to connect to the existing LSWR lines at Alton and Winchester.

ABOVE: LSWR 700 class 0-6-0 No. 30700 with a short pick-up goods train at Alresford station in British Railways days. Designed by Dugald Drummond and built by Dubs & Co in Glasgow from 1897 onwards, this class of 30 engines was primarily designed for goods traffic, but the locomotives were occasionally to be found on specials and excursion trains. All survived to be taken into British Railways' Southern Region stock. The first to be withdrawn was No. 30688 in September 1957 from Feltham shed after being involved in an accident, and the final seven were all taken out of service in December 1962. This example dated from 1897 and was withdrawn from Exmouth Junction shed on November 30, 1962 and was scrapped two years later. None were preserved. MHR
LEFT: Over 'the Alps': Bulleid Merchant Navy Pacific No. 35005 *Canadian Pacific* catches the glint of the setting sun in Mid Hants Railway service on March 3, 2007. MATT ALLEN/MHR

ABOVE: An early postcard of Medstead station. MHR **ABOVE RIGHT:** LSWR staff at Ropley station in 1891. MHR
RIGHT: Alton station in British Railways days. MHR

Smith & Knight was hired as contractors on February 3, 1863. Its job was to fence off the course of the line, excavate the cuttings and use the spoil from these to build the embankment. The firm also built the 22 underbridges and 20 overbridges.

Priority at this time was given to the section from Alton to Alresford, in hopes of opening this section by autumn 1864. Once the main earthworks and track laying were sufficiently advanced, work could begin on the stations. These were built by Bull & Sons, but all the signalling work was done by Stevens & Sons which was the LSWR's main contractor.

It was opened on October 2, 1865 as the Mid Hants Railway.

Trains comprising four passenger services each weekday were operated by the LSWR, which eventually purchased the Mid Hants Railway Company in 1884. From then on, services increased to six trains each way on weekdays and two on Sundays for the first time.

The line served the population of Alton, Medstead, Ropley, Alresford, Itchen Abbas and the surrounding areas.

Alton is the largest town on the line. It was a centre for brewing, with Crowley and Halls breweries forming a crucial local industry.

Medstead station is the only one that was not built before the opening of the line: local residents had to wait until August 1868. On October 1, 1937, Medstead was renamed Medstead & Four Marks because of its proximity to the village of Four Marks.

At 644ft above sea level, it is currently the highest operational standard gauge railway station in southern England. It is also one of the most delightful 'typical' country stations you will find anywhere in Britain's portfolio of heritage railways.

Ropley station is a good distance from the village of Ropley. The station is known for its elegant topiary on the Down platform.

Alresford station was just 59 miles from London and sited in a comparatively rural location and built on the southern side of the town. From here, the watercress trade began to use the railway for the transport of its crops to London and much further afield.

Itchen Abbas is the fifth station on the line and no longer exists. It was the last stop before Winchester.

ABOVE: Clipping the topiary at Ropley in the steam era. MHR
RIGHT: Track restoration underway in 1976. MICHAEL PEARSON
LEFT: British Rail's closure notice for the line. ROBIN JONES

During its lifetime passenger traffic on the line increased but as elsewhere, post-Second World War freight went into decline because of soaring competition from road transport. All freight traffic was withdrawn from the line between 1960 and 1964. It then became primarily a passenger line and was used as a diversion route between Southampton and London.

The general decline during the 1960s saw the removal of staff from Itchen Abbas, Ropley and Medstead & Four Marks leaving Alresford as the only manned station.

The longevity of the railway was called into question when Dr Beeching declared war on the line in his 1963 plans. Once the electrification to Bournemouth was complete it was considered unnecessary to keep the Mid Hants operable.

Closure notices were issued by British Railways in 1967 and drew much opposition, resulting in five years of objections and consultations that merely resulted in staying its closure. The last day of service was on February 4, 1973.

However, all was not lost. The present company was formed in 1973 with the original objective of running a commuter service during the week with steam trains at weekends, but multiple factors prevented this ambition from being realised.

The section between Alresford and Alton was bought from British Railways and steam trains commenced operating on the three-mile stretch from Alresford to Ropley on April 30, 1977. However, British Railways had already torn up the tracks and even removed the ballast over the remaining seven miles

ABOVE: Bulleid West Country light Pacific No. 34007 *Wadebridge* heads 'The Cunarder' on October 27, 2005. BRIAN SHARPE

ABOVE: National Collection locomotive Southern Railway LN class 4-6-0 No. 850 *Lord Nelson* simmers at Medstead & Four Marks on June 7, 2011. The four-cylinder class was designed by Richard Maunsell in 1926, for Continental boat trains between London (Victoria) and Dover harbour, but were also later used for express passenger work to the South West. Sixteen of them were constructed, representing the most powerful (although not the most successful) Southern 4-6-0 design. They were all named after famous admirals. ROBIN JONES

ABOVE: Visiting BR Pacific No. 70000 *Britannia* stands alongside resident No. 34007 *Wadebridge* at Ropley shed, as *Lord Nelson* passes with a service train on June 14, 2004. PETER TRIMMING*

ABOVE AND BELOW LEFT: On June 11, 2013, former *Flying Scotsman* owner Sir William McAlpine officially re-opened the Handyside footbridge, which had been relocated from King's Cross – where it starred in Warner Brothers' Harry Potter blockbuster movies – to Ropley. ROBIN JONES

to Alton and, as at Swanage, this had to be relaid by an army of volunteers.

The section to Medstead & Four Marks opened in 1983 and the last section to Alton in 1985. The line now runs all 10 miles from Alresford to Alton where there is an interchange with the national network, allowing passengers to transfer between the two. Locomotives and incoming and outbound charters run on and off the main line.

THE RAILWAY TODAY

It has been a very long time since watercress was carried over the Mid Hants Railway, but the line has many, many delights to offer the visitor today, not least of all a wonderful Sunny South ambience.

You can relax and travel through the heart of the leafy Hampshire countryside with fares offering all-day unlimited travel so you can alight at each of the four stations.

At Ropley station you can enjoy a stroll on the elevated picnic area, from where you

LEFT: On May 8, 2012, the National Collection's Southern Railway V or Schools class 4-4-0 No. 925 *Cheltenham* moved under its own power for the first time in 30 years, at Eastleigh Works, as a result of a collaboration between the Mid Hants Railway and the National Railway Museum. The restoration of the engine was undertaken by a team led by Mid Hants locomotive director, Chris Smith, and it went on to enter regular Watercress Line traffic as well as visit other heritage railways. ARLE IMAGES

Making Fresh Tracks to the Sunny South and West

RIGHT: The new LSWR-style Up side waiting shelter at Ropley was erected over 50 weeks by volunteers and includes Victorian decorative cast-iron canopy columns from Ringwood station, which closed in 1967. South West Trains donated an original double-faced clock from Aldershot station. It includes a table that was originally in the waiting room at Bentley station and a freestanding solid-fuel stove typical of the type used in the 1920s. Opened by the LSWR in October 1865, the main station buildings at Ropley are situated on the Down side. Until the 1930s, when it was demolished, there was only a small waiting room provided on the Up side. In the National Railway Heritage Awards 2015, the Mid Hants won the Stagecoach Volunteers Award for the construction of the shelter. ROBIN JONES

can walk in Harry Potter's footsteps over the iron Handyside footbridge where he received his Hogwarts Express ticket. This famous bridge was originally sited at King's Cross station but was moved to Ropley during the award-winning £500 million redevelopment of London's Great Northern Railway terminus.

Handyside bridge takes you into Ropley locomotive yard; here you can get up close to the engines and see behind the scenes in the impressive engineering workshops.

The steep gradient of the line to Medstead & Four Marks means this station requires a fleet of large, powerful steam locomotives capable of hauling heavy trains 'over the Alps'; a spectacular sight and sound at any time of the year.

At the peaceful country station of the highest station in southern England, you can relax and watch the world go by.

At the Alton end of the line you can also join the mainline as the station is just an hour from London Waterloo. This bustling market town has a delightful mix of historic buildings

ABOVE LEFT: Resident LMS 'Black five' 4-6-0 No. 45379 on footplate experience duties. PETER TRIMMING*

LEFT: The luxury wooden chalets overlooking the railway are painted in matching Southern Region corporate livery. ROBIN JONES

and modern shops, and links to Jane Austen's house in nearby Chawton.

Ropley station has also mushroomed into a holiday village Southern Region style. The station, including the new Up platform waiting room is immaculately turned out in Southern green and cream livery.

Immediately alongside the station on the northern side is a new chalet park – which is painted in exactly the same colours.

Enterprising neighbouring farmer, Chris Graham, who opened six of the luxury wooden lodges overlooking the railway in 2014, built the holiday village named Watercress Lodges.

The venture proved so successful he has expanded it with campsite facilities. A separate charity, which organises holidays for disabled people has just opened a seventh purpose-built chalet on the site.

A footpath directly from the chalet site accesses the railway, and holidaymakers can take advantage of special cut-price travel on it. Chalet park users can buy a week's rover ticket for the cost of two days' travel, allowing them to ride between Alton and Alresford as often as they wish.

Despite their close proximity and similarity, the railway and the chalet park are totally separate businesses.

CANADIAN PACIFIC: ENGINEERING A FUTURE FROM THE PAST

The Mid Hants Railway is now home to Bulleid Merchant Navy Pacific No. 35005, which is the centre of a £1.5-million rebuilding project backed by the Heritage Lottery Fund.

No. 35005 was built in 1941 at Eastleigh Works and entered traffic in January 1942. It was the fifth of the first 10 Merchant Navy class locomotives to be built at the works.

With its 4-6-2 configuration and 6ft 2in driving wheels, the class was most suitable for hauling express passenger trains, but was officially designated as mixed traffic. During the Second World War it was not uncommon to see Merchant Navies hauling freight and military trains.

Although fantastic performers, the class had numerous reliability issues, as a result, there was a major rebuilding scheme to RG Jarvis' conventional design minus the air-smoothed casing. *Canadian Pacific* was rebuilt in Eastleigh Works in 1959.

However, the reign of steam was soon to come to an end. Not long before its withdrawal in October 1965 *Canadian Pacific* became a record holder. On May 15, 1965, Dave Wilson (fireman) was rostered to work the 9.20pm from Waterloo with Gordon Hooper (driver). During this run, No. 35005 reached 105mph on the descent to Winchester from Basingstoke. The run from Waterloo to Basingstoke was achieved in 43 minutes 48 seconds.

This was not the fastest speed recorded by a Merchant Navy. On June 26, 1967, No. 35003 *Royal Mail* recorded the highest speed ever for the class. Hauling a train comprising three carriages and two parcels vans (164 tons tare, 180 tons gross) between Weymouth and Waterloo, the mile between milepost 38 and milepost 37 (between Winchfield and Fleet) was covered in 34 seconds, at a speed of 105.88 mph. This feat was also the last authenticated speed in excess of 100mph achieved by a steam locomotive in the UK.

Sadly, *Royal Mail* was scrapped after the end of Southern steam. So *Canadian Pacific* is the fastest and oldest-surviving Merchant Navy Class locomotive on a heritage railway. In 1966 it was sold to Woodham Brothers' scrapyard in Barry.

In 1973 it was bought by the now-closed Steamtown museum in Carnforth, Lancashire. It was then sold to Andrew Naish in 1990 and was restored to working condition and the main line, briefly running in blue livery.

In 2001 it was acquired by Steam Dreams and formed the backbone of the 'Cathedrals Express' excursions. During this time, it made frequent visits to the Watercress Line.

ABOVE: Bulleid Merchant Navy Pacific No. 35005 *Canadian Pacific* at Eastleigh in 1960. DAVID HEYES

RIGHT: Volunteers working on *Canadian Pacific*. MHR

However, on October 19, 2002 during a 'Cathedrals Express' from London to Canterbury it blew a small tube near the firebox crown, filling the cab with steam. This incident resulted in *Canadian Pacific* being withdrawn for 2½ years to be fixed and confined to preserved railway operation only.

Bought by the Mid Hants Railway in 2006 for £300,000, it will become the line's flagship steam locomotive once its restoration back to working order is complete.

The Canadian Pacific Project is divided into two aspects. Firstly, the restoration of No. 35005 in Eastleigh Works and two wooden-framed carriages in Ropley. Secondly, there is a large outreach programme with the aim of increasing people's knowledge about the locomotive, engineering works and the railway; providing activities to encourage more women to choose a career in Science Technology Engineering or Mathematics (STEM), as well as teaching a younger generation the skills to restore a steam locomotive and its carriages.

The railway has six new apprentices based at Ropley and provides work placements for college students and unemployed people. It has a number of mini projects including Women's Work (which centres on the role of women on the railway during the 1940s-1960s, especially the possibility that *Canadian Pacific* was built by a mainly female workforce); the Oral History Project (looking to collect memories including from those working on and using the railway during the Second World War to the 1960s); women's roles on the railway, Eastleigh

Works; *Canadian Pacific* and immigration, and the 'A Different Eye' Media Project (a film documentary on the restoration process and events surrounding the Canadian Pacific Project to be undertaken by local schools and higher education institutions).

The line is also offering several tours (at Ropley and Eastleigh Works) and providing talks to increase people's knowledge of the locomotives, the Watercress Line, and the social history of steam and railways between 1940 and 1960. This includes creating links with communities and schools in London, where *Canadian Pacific* visited during its service for Southern and British Railways.

In 2015 the project was awarded £895,000 from the Lottery Fund to aid in the total project cost of £1.5 million. Some of the funding gap is being made up by volunteer input, but donations are still needed to complete the project. To find out how to donate and other ways you can support the project, visit www.watercressline.co.uk/canpac •

Chapter 8

30 YEARS OF MOORS VALLEY MARVELS

Seaside miniature railways were once a standard feature of all mainstream resorts, as youngsters who were taken on holiday by train wanted to ride on one that was more their size. The Sunny South is home to the Moors Valley Railway, a complete system operated on main line principles that is more akin to narrow gauge running on miniature railway track. Not only that, it also builds its own locomotives.

Based at Ashley Heath in Dorset near the Hampshire boundary to the north of Bournemouth is the unique Moors Valley Railway, which in 2016 celebrated its 30th anniversary.

Situated within the Moors Valley Country Park near Ringwood, this 7¼in gauge ran its first train on July 26, 1986 using equipment moved from the owner's previous railway at Tucktonia, a small theme park at Tuckton in Christchurch, Dorset.

The railway boasts two signalboxes, track circuiting, as well as a mixture of colour, light, and semaphore signals all linked by a lineside emergency telephone system.

Its infrastructure includes two stations, a waiting room, a turntable, engine shed, two carriage sheds, several signal gantries, three gated level crossings, four footbridges, four tunnels, and perhaps its main feature, a spiral.

Engineer Jim Haylock, who conceived and built the mile-long line, first became seriously involved in locomotive design and construction as a member of the Malden Model Engineering Club in Thames Ditton.

He was inspired when former Romney Hythe & Dymchurch Railway chief engineer, Roger Marsh, built a 0-4-2T in 1968 that he named *Tinkerbell*, and wanted one for his own garden railway. *Tinkerbell* is widely considered the first 'sit in' 7¼in gauge locomotive and now has a popular class of locomotives named after it.

Operating with *Tinkerbell* and another Marsh 0-4-2T No. 3 *Talos*, work began building 4-6-0 No. 5 *Sapper* (rebuilt 1993), 0-4-4T No. 7 *Aelfred*, 0-6-2T *Medea* and a privately owned 2-4-0 No. 1 *Sir Goss*.

When the Tuckton site was sold for building development, Jim's railway was moved to its present location, where it carries more than 100,000 passengers each year.

ABOVE: The King's Cross of the miniature railway world: the Kingsmere terminus of the Moors Valley Railway. MVR

LEFT: Based on East African Railway's Class 24 locomotives, Couling-built No.19 *Athelstan* is a development of No.12 *Pioneer*, but with a 2-8-0 wheel arrangement. Painted in EAR maroon, *Athelstan* is fitted with vacuum disc brakes on the tender and has the cylinders inclined at approximately 10º. *Athelstan* is named after the first king of England, the grandson of Alfred the Great. MVR

Over the past 30 years, the fleet has grown into a collection of 21 locomotives that can be seen running today.

The 7¼in gauge is one that can offer a reasonable-sized engine with the power to pull a reasonable-sized train. However, when a narrow gauge prototype is followed, a much larger outline emerges. If, in addition, a narrow gauge engine is based on a freelance design as they are at Moors Valley Railway, an even larger proportion is possible. Its locomotives have a height of 48in, width of 26in, lengths of up to 17ft and a weight of up to two tons.

The railway was the first attraction to open in the Moors Valley Country Park, which was built on the site of Kings Farm with the main station now occupying the cow sheds.

Since opening, the railway has evolved to provide a picturesque mile-long journey alongside the manmade lake and around the play areas.

The layout enables various different routes including reverse operation of the railway allowing for many interesting train movements, especially on gala days. There is also a model railway and gift shop, refreshment kiosk and two ice-cream outlets.

Known in railway circles as 'Dorset's Steam Factory', the Moors Valley Railway's workshop has seen the construction of more than 20 steam locomotives and two diesel locomotives, ranging from 2-4-4T No. 9 *Jason*, built in 1989, to three 2-6-2s No. 10 *Offa*, No.11 *Zeus* and No. 12 *Pioneer*.

Unique in the world of 7¼in gauge railways, No. 15 *William Rufus* was

BELOW: It's not Clapham Junction, but at times it seems as busy! MVR

ABOVE: A line-up of steam locomotives outside the Kingsmere East signalbox. MVR
BELOW: A woodland ride behind 4-6-2 No. 12 *Pioneer*. MVR

outshopped as a 2-4-0+0-4-2 Garratt in 1997.

Several locomotives have been built for private owner-drivers, such as 0-4-4T No. 16 *Robert Fooks*, 0-4-4T No. 17 *Hartfield*, 4-6-2 No. 18 *Thor*, 2-8-0 No. 19 *Athelstan* and 0-4-2T No. 24 *Perseus*.

As we saw in Chapter Two, the railway has also built a freelance 0-4-0T *Emmet*, which has visited other heritage lines.

The workshops are responsible for the everyday maintenance of the railway, locomotives, rolling stock and infrastructure along with the construction of new equipment.

Much of what you see in and around the railway has been constructed on site, in the workshops. The fleet of 40 coaches enables the railway to carry more than 100,000 passengers a year, while the large collection of private owner wagons and maintenance vehicles add to the impression of a full-size narrow gauge railway.

The railway prides itself on being a commercial enterprise, run with a large number of volunteer staff helping a small

RIGHT: A doubleheaded works train passes a packed passenger service. MVR

BELOW: Outshopped in 1999, 2-4-4T *Hartfield* is pictured in the Moors Valley Railway's Kingsmere loco yard. CEDRIC JOHNS

ABOVE: Lakeside station on a summer's day. MVR

ABOVE LEFT: Pictured on September 9, 2015, *Hestia* was completed that year and is an updated version of the original Tinkerbell class steam locomotive built by Roger Marsh in 1968. The locomotive was started back in 2003 by Joe Nemeth in Bristol for the now-closed Oldown Miniature Railway. The loco, no more than a boiler and a kit of parts, was purchased in 2008 by the present owner and took seven years to reach completion. Sharing the same overall dimensions and looks of the original *Tinkerbell*, the loco features a locomotive type boiler and bearings on all motion work ensuring efficient and reliable operation. ANDY WEBB

LEFT: Styled on South African Railways' locomotive design, 2-6-2 No 11 *Zeus* is one of three similar types built in the Moors Valley Railway workshop for heavy passenger traffic. CEDRIC JOHNS

BELOW: Fun for all not only on the Moors Valley Railway but on either side of it too: is it the epitome of the classic seaside miniature railway? MVR

team of dedicated full-time employees.

There are many areas where volunteers can get involved, including locomotive staff, guards, signalmen and railway maintenance. All volunteers are fully trained to professional standards and are committed to providing an enjoyable experience for passengers.

Having established itself as a busy tourist attraction with its nostalgic and enthusiastic approach, the railway considers itself to be part of the uniquely British heritage of miniature steam railways and is a founder member of Britain's Great Little Railways.

The park has developed over the past 30 years and has become a great day out for families with adventure playgrounds, cycle hire, forest play trail, Go Ape high wire course, Segway tours, a visitor centre, restaurant and golf course.

The railway is celebrating its 30th anniversary with a whole year of special events including more Santa Special dates than ever before.

The railway is open weekends and school holidays, then daily from June to mid-September, 10.45am to 5pm (10.45am to 4.30pm November to February).

Driver Experience courses are available at £110 per person with a 10% discount for two people booking together. The instructor-led course on how to prepare and drive a steam engine requires no previous knowledge or experience.

For more information visit www.moorsvalleyrailway.co.uk •

Chapter 9

SEA CHANGE IN THE SUNNY SOUTH!

Several seaside resorts in the Sunny South went into decline when the railway branch lines that had placed them on the tourist map in Victorian times closed down. This was primarily because of a lack of patronage out of season, but it was also at a time when the huge rise in car ownership gave holidaymakers more flexibility and choice. However, one Southern seaside branch refused to lie down and die – and instead was reborn in part as a tramway!

Exmouth, Budleigh Salterton, Sidmouth, Seaton, Lyme Regis… all classic seaside resorts that found themselves served by the Southern Railway, but only the first of these retained its branch line after the Beeching Axe.

In an ideal world, it would have been marvellous if they had all been linked together by a main line railway, like pearls on a necklace.

However, the hilly terrain of east Devon and west Dorset meant that was never to be, although I often wonder what might have happened if the great Isambard Kingdom Brunel, who created the nature-defying but still problematic Dawlish sea wall route for his South Devon atmospheric railway, had been engaged by the London & South Western Railway in these parts. As it was, the LSWR main line from London via Yeovil to Exeter ran a few miles inland and relied on branches to serve resorts that started out as ancient ports and small fishing settlements – Exmouth,

ABOVE: LSWR M7 0-4-4T No. 30046 at Seaton in June 1958. The terminus seems busy enough with passenger and freight workings, but within eight years it would be closed.

68 Making Fresh Tracks to the Sunny South and West

ABOVE: The Western Region took over the former LSWR branches in East Devon during a boundary shift in the latter days of steam. Owing to a diesel shortage for a few weeks from February 1965, Collett 14XX auto tank No. 1442 was sent to work the Seaton branch. This locomotive was famous for being a regular on the Tiverton branch, where it acquired the nickname the 'Tivvy Bumper'. It is now the centrepiece of the Tiverton Museum. SEATON TRAMWAY

ABOVE: LSWR M7 0-4-4T No. 30048, an example of the class best associated with the Seaton branch in its postwar years, at Colyton in 1960. COLOUR-RAIL

BELOW: The Sunny South here we come! Happy holidaymakers, some of whom will have travelled from Waterloo, disembark at Seaton ready to start their summer vacations, in this early 1960s scene. SEATON TRAMWAY

ABOVE: GWR 64XX pannier tank No. 6430 at Colyton station. Two members of the 64XX class, Nos. 6400 and 6430, were allocated to the former Southern Railway shed at Exmouth Junction in March 1963, after it fell into Western Region hands. From there, they worked the Seaton branch, and were briefly joined by No. 6412 before the line's services were dieselised. SEATON TRAMWAY

Budleigh Salterton, Sidmouth, Lyme Regis, and Seaton.

It was the arrival of the Seaton & Beer Railway in 1868 that turned Seaton into a busy holiday resort. After the LSWR opened its main line to Exeter in 1860, local people saw that a rail connection might reinvigorate their town, then a port used only by small fishing boats.

Locals obtained an Act of Parliament for their proposed line on July 13, 1863, empowering it to build it from the LSWR's Colyton station (later Seaton Junction) to a terminus to the east of the town.

The branch line opened for traffic on March 16, 1868, with five trains each way each weekday, with mixed operation for two Up trains and one Down.

The line was 4¼ miles long with two intermediate stations, at Colyton Town and Colyford.

It was bought outright by the LSWR on January 1, 1888.

The line was worked at first by Beattie 2-2-2 well tanks, beginning with No. 12 *Jupiter* and No. 3 *Phoenix* being in use at the beginning. Class O2 and T1 class 0-4-4Ts replaced the Beattie engines in the 1890s, occasionally supported by an Adams radial 4-4-2T.

From 1930, auto trains were introduced on the branch.

Most associated with the Seaton branch in its postwar years were LSWR Drummond M7 0-4-4Ts, even Bulleid light Pacifics were reported to have run on the branch.

On summer Saturdays after 1949 there was considerable extra traffic on the line, with two locomotives together operating nine-coach trains with through coaches to and from London. However, from 1962 through working to and from the branch ceased.

Diesel multiple unit working took over the branch from November 4, 1963, but as elsewhere, the savings promised by modern traction on loss-making branches with the associated reduction in overstaffing failed to save it.

The line was closed on March 7, 1966. While such seaside branches were well patronised in the holiday season, often trains were empty through much of the rest of the year, and British Railways did not deem it cost effective to store rakes of carriages for just six weeks' use a year.

While around 1200 passengers rode on the Seaton branch on summer Saturdays, less than a dozen were there to make the final trip that late winter.

THE EASTBOURNE ELECTRIC TRAMWAY LOOKS WEST

The route of the old branch railway still reverberates to the sound of steel wheels. However, they do not belong to trains in the conventional sense, but traditional British trams, a typical sight in city streets throughout the country in the first half of the 20th century.

What's more, there is something very unusual about these trams. Several of them are indeed genuine trams from the last century, but they have been dismantled and reduced both in scale and size, to make them about two thirds as big as the originals.

No longer do these trams ply their trade through urban roads, but alongside the beautiful unspoilt estuary of the River Axe.

Here is the single feature that makes Seaton different from anywhere else in Britain today.

The Seaton Tramway has its origins in a manufacturer of milk floats and other battery-electric vehicles.

Claude Lane, owner of the Lancaster Electrical Company in Barnet, north London, had a passion for trams and at his factory in 1949 he had built a 15in gauge tram based on ex-Darwen Car 23, then running on the Llandudno & Colwyn Bay system.

ABOVE: Headed by Drummond M7 No. 30048, the push-pull train for Seaton is waiting for passengers on a damp day. RICHARD GREEN*

ABOVE: A watery scene photographed after prolonged rain during the Seaton branch's three years of diesel operation. SEATON TRAMWAY

TOP LEFT: The design of the Southern Railway's now-demolished Seaton terminus had much in common with London suburban or even Underground stations. SEATON TRAMWAY

Hugely popular as an attraction at fetes, Claude was surprised by its popularity. He ran it for a summer season at St Leonards, Sussex in 1951 and for five seasons at Rhyl from 1952.

He decided to lease a permanent site much further to the east along the Sunny South, at Eastbourne in 1953, and set up Modern Electric Tramways Ltd to operate it.

His 2ft gauge Eastbourne Electric Tramway ran for two-thirds of a mile between Princes Park and the Crumbles and his factory made a larger open-top tram, Car 6, also based on the open-top design of Llandudno & Colwyn Bay vehicles, to run on it.

It was followed in 1958 by the similar Car 8, in 1961 by Car 4, which was based on a Blackpool Tramways 'open boat' design, and in 1964 by Car 2, based on a London Metropolitan Tramways' design.

The growth of Eastbourne's road system began to squeeze the tramway out and Claude began looking for a freehold site.

He became aware of the imminent closure of the Seaton branch, and eventually British

ABOVE: One of Claude Lane's first 2ft gauge miniature trams on his line at Eastbourne. SEATON TRAMWAY
ABOVE RIGHT: And the dogs came too! Alsatians to all stations on the Eastbourne Electric Tramway. SEATON TRAMWAY
RIGHT: A busman's holiday for this Eastbourne Electric Tramway crew lapping up the sunshine on the Sunny South! SEATON TRAMWAY

ABOVE: Superb views of the delightful Axe Valley are relished from open-top Car 12, which was built in 1966 and based on a London Feltham-type tram. SEATON TRAMWAY

ABOVE RIGHT: Based on design elements from Plymouth and Blackburn tramcars, Car 11, the 'pink tram', runs alongside the beautiful Axe estuary. SEATON TRAMWAY

RIGHT: Cars 2 and 8 alongside each other at Colyton. ROBIN JONES

Railways agreed to sell the trackbed to him, on the condition that he obtained a Transfer Order as well as a Light Railway Order.

Some local residents who objected to his plans told a public enquiry that trams would create unacceptable noise and harm the natural beauty of the Axe Valley. However, Seaton Town Council argued that the tramway would become a major asset to the area, and after assurances were given about safety at Colyford level crossing, Claude won the day.

SEATON'S SECOND COMING

Full fathom five thy father lies.
Of his bones are coral made.
Those are pearls that were his eyes.
Nothing of him that doth fade,
But doth suffer a sea-change
Into something rich and strange.

So runs Ariel's ethereal song from Shakespeare's The Tempest. This is what happened here: like so many others in the Beeching era, the little seaside branch was ripped up, and rather than left to be reclaimed by nature or developers, the rails returned, not as a heritage line in the classic sense

BELOW: The company's 25th anniversary at Seaton saw an Edwardian-style terminus built in the town, seen here with three trams in service. SEATON TRAMWAY

BELOW: Two-tone blue 2002-built Car 9 waits to depart from Colyton. SEATON TRAMWAY

Making Fresh Tracks to the Sunny South and West

ABOVE: Two attractions in one: not only do you get to ride in an open-top tram on the Sunny South, but you can watch the rich variety of birdlife too.
ABOVE RIGHT: The restored but reduced Exeter Car 19 in Riverside Depot. A veteran of this part of the Sunny South, it was rebuilt into its current format in 1998. ROBIN JONES

of the word as epitomised by the Swanage Railway, but as a tramway running through the countryside and estuarine meadows giving unrivalled views of the abundant wading bird life that surrounds it.

The new line was built to a gauge of 2ft 9in. In 1969, Claude had built Car 8 to larger proportions than its predecessors in readiness for the wider track.

From September 1969, the complete Eastbourne system was dismantled, transported 100 miles westwards and reassembled before the 1970 holiday season ended.

Claude and his assistant, Allan Gardner, made 36 return lorry journeys between Eastbourne and Seaton.

On August 28, 1970, Car 8 became the first tram to run in passenger service on the Seaton branch, taking power from a battery car as overhead wires had yet to be installed.

A depot at Riverside just north of the original Seaton branch station, which was demolished following closure, was installed so that in winter the existing trams could be regauged.

The line reached Colyford, the midway point, but before the first full season could start, Claude died from a heart attack on April 2, 1971.

Allan Gardner took over as managing director to complete the project with the aid of volunteers. A 'train' returned to the Seaton branch in the shape of a diesel shunter bought to assist works Car 02 in hauling equipment.

Passing loops were installed at Axmouth and Swan's Nest, allowing trams to operate simultaneously. During 1973, overhead wire and fittings were installed, and the first tram powered from the overhead lines ran that September.

However, with the original Seaton station site lost, a town centre presence was urgently needed, and land was bought to lay a new trackbed to a fresh terminus site next to Harbour Road car park, the work being finished in May 1975.

Flood damage in 1978 and subsequent remedial work delayed the final extension to Colyton until 1980.

Attention then switched to expanding the fleet to cope with demand.

Metropolitan Tramways Car 94, which was obtained by Claude in 1962, was reduced in size by cutting the body length ways in half and narrowing it by 2ft. It entered service in 1984 as enclosed single-deck saloon Car 14, and was launched into traffic by the late comedian Larry Grayson.

Likewise, original Bournemouth Tramways Car 106 was reduced in scale and re-emerged from the workshops in 1992 as Car 16.

In 1998, former Exeter Tramways Car 19, which ran in the city from 1906 until the system closed in 1931, was reduced in size and restored from derelict condition to become the third enclosed saloon.

More new trams followed in the 21st century in the form of Cars 9, 10 and 11, all of a hybrid design based on the old Plymouth and Blackburn full-size versions.

The tramway now has an exceptional variety of vehicle from open double-deckers and basic wooden seats to luxuriously upholstered wood-panelled cars, and has sufficient trams to run a service every few minutes in the high season.

Today, the tramway carries more than 100,000 visitors a year, numbers that compare very favourably with the patronage of the old steam branch. The journey takes approximately half an hour to travel from end to end.

Special services are often run so that visitors can view the rich variety of bird life along the estuary.

The original station building at Colyton survives, and has been tastefully adapted into a continental-style terminus complete with a souvenir shop and restaurant facilities. The Tramstop Cafe at Colyton station offers an extensive menu of hot meals and snacks, to eat in or take away.

Offering an amazing array of exciting and educational experiences and special events; the tramway also hosts children's birthday parties, weddings and more!

No attempt has been made to extend the tramway further north along the rest of the old branch to Seaton Junction on the Waterloo-Exeter main line, a question frequently raised by visitors.

However, it is set to move closer to the centre of the resort from which it takes its name.

TOP RIGHT: Passengers boarding at Colyton. ROBIN JONES
TOP LEFT: Waitress service at Colyton station. SEATON TRAMWAY
LEFT: Pointwork at the line's Riverside Depot, set into brick paving street-tram style. ROBIN JONES
BELOW: An artist's impression of the planned new Seaton terminus. RAY HOLE ARCHITECTS

Plans have been passed for a new state-of-the-art terminus, a modern, all-weather facility which will enhance visitor comfort, offer the usual facilities expected of a leading visitor attraction, and improve the interpretation of the tramway's history and operations to ensure that even more visitors can enjoy the magic of the trams and the Axe Valley for decades to come.

The new station will replace the existing Edwardian-style ticket office built in 1996, which has been somewhat outgrown as visitor numbers have increased in recent years. It will be built to a new contemporary design focusing on the tramway's remarkable heritage. •

BELOW: Car 9 passing Riverside tram depot at Seaton. ROBIN JONES
BELOW RIGHT: All that remains of Colyford station from the railway age is the Victorian cast-iron gents' toilet. ROBIN JONES

LIFETIME LOYALTY

You can become a lifetime loyalty card member at the Seaton Tramway and receive a one third discount off standard headline fares, including all-day explorer tickets for yourself and one other guest. The cost is a one-off payment of £10 per adult, and £5 per child (3-15).

In addition you will save 10% on the special days out programme and special events, and also receive 10% off at the Seaton Tramway shops and Tramstop Cafe.

Loyalty cards can be purchased at the Seaton terminus and Colyton station ticket offices, by telephone on 01297 20375 or online at www.tram.co.uk

Making Fresh Tracks to the Sunny South and West

Chapter 10

THE RETURN OF THE HAYLING BILLY

The legendary and much-loved Hayling Island branch was closed by British Railways more than half a century ago despite making a profit, yet you can still catch a steam train along the Hampshire resort's beach.

A branch indelibly etched into the romanticism of the Sunny South was the Hayling Island line, famous as the haunt of London, Brighton & South coast Railway A1X 'Terrier' 0-6-0Ts from Victorian times right up until its demise.

Hayling Island lies between the ria estuaries, or drowned river valleys, of Langstone Harbour and Chichester Harbour, and is four miles long and four miles wide at the southern end. A single bridge takes the island's spine road, the A3023, over the quarter-mile channel that divides it from the mainland.

The branch, which linked Hayling Island to the mainland at Havant, with intermediate stations at Langston (the final 'e' of the nearby village was never used) and North Hayling, was affectionately known as the 'Hayling Billy', a name now carried by the footpath along the old track.

The line was opened by the LBSCR for goods on January 19, 1865, and for passengers on July 16, 1867.

In so many ways it was a classic holiday branch. Heavily used during the summer months as people from the south coast would travel down to the beach, but patronage was sparse during the winter months.

Its main engineering feature was an embankment over the mudflats in the sheltered waters of Langstone Harbour and the associated wooden swing bridge that linked it to the mainland.

This bridge proved the downfall of the branch. While British Railways closed other Sunny South seaside branches for reasons of economy owing to poor patronage outside the summer season, here it was the need to replace the rotting swing bridge.

When the Southern Region decided over the winter of 1962 to close the branch, it was, unlike counterparts elsewhere, making a small profit. Yet a replacement bridge was considered an investment too far.

The last timetabled service train ran on the evening of November 2, 1963. To clear the remaining goods stock away, it was a mixed train hauled by A1X No. 32650.

The day after closure, a special was run, hauled by 'Terriers' Nos. 32636 and 32670 and this was the last-ever train on the branch. All three 'Terriers' survive in preservation, on the Spa Valley, Bluebell and Kent & East Sussex railways respectively, as do three others that worked on the Hayling Island branch: No. 72 (32636) *Fenchurch*, the famous No. 32655 *Stepney* on the Bluebell, No. 32662 *Martello*, at Bressingham Steam Museum in Norfolk, and No. 32646 (originally *Newington*, now *Freshwater*), No. 32650 on the Isle of Wight Steam Railway, and No. 32678 on the Kent & East Sussex Railway.

After closure, the latter was sold to the Sadler Railcar Company, which later sold it on to Brickwoods Brewery, using it as the Hayling Billy pub sign where it remained for 13 years. In 1979 the next owners of the brewery donated the locomotive to the Wight Locomotive Society.

There was a second seaside life for No. 32640 (originally named *Brighton and Newport*). Scheduled for scrapping, it was one of several main line engines bought by Butlin's, in this case for display at its Pwllheli holiday camp in North Wales. The Wight Locomotive Society later purchased it.

After closure, an attempt was made to re-open the island branch, using a former Blackpool Marton Vambac single-deck tram,

ABOVE: LBSCR Stroudley A1X 0-6-0T 'Terrier' No. 32661 was one of several class members that worked the Hayling Island branch to the end. Dating from Victorian times, the 'Terriers' were the only engines light enough to cross Langston Bridge. Built in 1875 as No. 61 *Sutton*, it is seen in 1958 being coaled ready for its return to Havant. It survived until April 1963. BEN BROOKSBANK*

74 Making Fresh Tracks to the Sunny South and West

ABOVE: LBSCR A1X 'Terrier' No. 32678 crosses Langstone Bridge in June 1962, the last summer of operation on the Hayling Island branch. The locomotive is now reserved on the Kent & East Sussex Railway. COLOUR-RAIL

No. 11. The tram was stored in the goods yard at Havant, and later, on Hayling Island itself.

However, with no support from the local authorities forthcoming, the re-opening venture came to nothing and the tram never ran on the line yet it survived, and is now running at the East Anglia Transport Museum.

The attempted re-opening delayed the lifting of the track, which took place in the spring of 1966, and included the demolition of most of the structure of the bridge at Langstone Harbour.

Today, the area where the tracks once stood on the Havant side of the line is a local nature reserve and footpath, over which it is possible to walk from Havant station all the way to where the bridge was located, by Langston station.

The Hayling Island side of the line is now a combined footpath, bridleway and cycleway, part of Route 2 of the National Cycle Network.

The goods shed at Hayling Island station is now a theatre.

THE SECOND COMING

Yet, steam has returned to Hayling Island, which claims to be the place where windsurfing began – a British Malibu!

In 1985, British courts ruled in favour of one-time Hayling resident, Peter Chilvers, who claimed to have invented the sport in 1958, when at the age of 12, he innovatively attached a sail to a board.

Admittedly it was a basic affair, with a straight split boom rather than the curved

ABOVE: The spirit of the old 'Hayling Billy' is invoked into this local pub sign. ROBIN JONES

ABOVE Although it currently has none of its own, steam locomotives are regular visitors to the Hayling Seaside Railway. Enthusiasts young and old enjoy Statfold Barn's new-build Quarry Hunslet 0-4-0ST *Jack Lane* as it waits to leave Beachlands on Remembrance Day 2015. HSR

Making Fresh Tracks to the Sunny South and West 75

ABOVE: Alan Keef steam outline 0-4-0DM No. 3 *Jack* still carries the 'historic' livery of the old East Hayling Light Railway as it approaches Eastoke Corner with a train from Beachlands. HSR

BELOW: No. 3 *Jack* heads out of Beachlands across the shingle. ROBIN JONES

TOP: The Moors Valley Railway's visiting freelance new-build 0-4-0T *Emmet* at Beachlands station on September 11, 2010. ZABDIEL*

ABOVE: A flashback to 2002 as heavily modified Simplex No. 1 *Alan B* works a Hayling Seaside Railway construction train to the then 'head of steel' near Beachlands. HSR

wishbone booms of modern windsurfers, but the court upheld his claim based on film footage, saying that later modifications by other designers were just "obvious extensions".

Chilvers went on to become a successful engineer for Lotus cars and set up his own sailing and windsurfing centre in London. The sport is hugely popular back in Hayling, where participants use the open beach and Channel breezes to maximum effect.

When not windsurfing local people never forgot the Hayling Billy, and in the mid-80s, a group was formed with the aim of reinstating the branch.

But Havant Borough Council had already decided to turn the trackbed into a cycleway and footpath, leaving no room for a standard gauge line.

Group members suggested a narrow gauge line on the old formation, but were outvoted by committee officials who said that it had to be standard gauge or nothing.

One of the members, Bob Haddock, who by then had become convinced that there would be a demand for a narrow gauge tourist line on the island, founded the East Hayling Light Railway.

After being thwarted in bids to lay a track on various local sites, a home was found at the Mill Rythe Holiday Camp, where the 2ft gauge EHLR ran successfully for several years.

The council was impressed, and included a railway in its draft plan for Hayling's popular Pleasure Beach.

Bob was delighted at the prospect of moving his line to a far more lucrative location only for the council to refuse planning permission for a scheme it had itself proposed! It transpired that several local residents had objected to the loss of their favourite seats on the beach.

As the owner of a local attraction said, "If someone wanted to build a sandcastle on Hayling Beach 10 people would complain about it".

Bob campaigned for more than 12 years before the Department of the Environment overturned the council's decision and gave him permission to build the railway along the beach.

Following closure of the EHLR at Mill Rythe work started in October 2001 on the building of Beachlands station on land leased from the neighbouring Funland Amusement Park.

The relocated line finally opened to passengers on July 5, 2003, rebranded as the Hayling Seaside Railway, and eventually linked the coastal village of Eastoke Corner to the funfairs at Beachlands.

In early 2015, after a lengthy period of campaigning to the local authority work started on a new depot at Eastoke Corner as the lease on its depot at Beachlands had expired.

Operating on Saturdays, Sundays and bank holidays throughout the year, and daily during school holidays, trains are formed of traditional enclosed wooden-bodied bogie carriages, constructed by volunteers in the line's own workshops.

Most trains are hauled by 1988 Alan Keef 0-4-0 steam outline diesel hydraulic No. 3 *Jack*, assisted by a small collection of historic industrial Ruston and Simplex diesels.

On special occasions steam locomotives are hired in, driven and maintained by the line's own footplatemen, many of whom also volunteer with the Hampshire Narrow Gauge Railway Society and the private Statfold Barn Railway at Tamworth in Staffordshire.

Visiting locomotives have included *Emmet* from the Moors Valley Railway at Ringwood, Bagnall 0-4-0ST *Wendy* from the HNGRS, which is normally based at Bursledon Brickworks, and most recently Statfold's new-build Quarry Hunslet *Jack Lane*.

The privately owned railway is always on the lookout for new volunteers, with two stations to rebuild and a popular service to run throughout the rebuilding.

For more details of how to come on board, visit www.haylingrailway.com

ABOVE: The goods shed at the former Hayling Island branch terminus is now a theatre. ROBIN JONES

ABOVE: The new Hayling Seaside Railway depot at the Eastoke Corner eastern terminus takes shape. ROBIN JONES
LEFT: The other form of public transport on Hayling Island's beach. ROBIN JONES

Making Fresh Tracks to the Sunny South and West

Chapter 11

SECONDHAND ROSE O

At 148 square miles, the Isle of Wight is the biggest and second most populous island in England and has several resorts that have been holiday destinations since Victorian times. It also once had a 55½-mile railway network, famed for its use of obsolete locomotives and stock cascaded down from lines on the mainland. That still holds true for both of the island's railways today.

The first railway on the Isle of Wight appeared in 1832 in the form of the two-mile-long narrow gauge horse-worked Hamstead Tramway. It was constructed to carry goods by royal architect John Nash serving his estate, connecting Hamstead Quay and brickworks with surrounding farmland and Hamstead House.

When Nash's fortunes declined, so did the tramway.

The first conventional railway line to open on the island was the Cowes & Newport Railway, which opened to passengers in June 1862.

It was followed by the Isle of Wight Railway, which opened its initial line from Ryde to Shanklin in 1864, the same year that horse-drawn trams began running along Ryde Pier, connecting ferry services to the town.

The IWR reached Ventnor in 1866, and five years later, the Ryde tramway was also extended to meet the railway at Ryde St John's Road.

The Ryde & Newport Railway opened in December 1875, with operations controlled by the Cowes & Newport Railway.

In 1875, the Isle of Wight (Newport Junction) Railway opened the main part of its 10-mile Sandown to Newport line, but it took until 1879 to reach Newport, leaving debts soaring and the company going into receivership in 1880. It was the bought by the Cowes & Newport/Ryde & Newport company, which became the Isle of Wight Central Railway.

In 1877 the LBSCR and LSWR were granted powers to extend Ryde Pier and lay a railway from the pier head to St John's Road. It was completed in 1880, when the Ryde tramway was shortened to run only along the pier.

In 1882, the IWR opened its branch line from Brading to Bembridge, from where a short-lived train ferry linked to the Hayling Island branch.

In 1889, the Freshwater, Yarmouth & Newport Railway opened its 12-mile line

ABOVE: LBSCR 'Terrier' No. W8 *Freshwater* on a service train on October 13, 2012. IoWSR/JOHN FAULKNER

78 Making Fresh Tracks to the Sunny South and West

THE SUNNY SOUTH

ABOVE: Sunset special: LSWR O2 No. W24 Calbourne heads an Isle of Wight Steam Railway train in November 2010. IoWSR

from Newport to Freshwater, with services operated by the IWCR.

The island was more or less, in railway terms, a microcosm of what had happened on the mainland, with independent companies linking firstly the major cities and then towns.

Completing the island portfolio was the Newport, Godshill & St Lawrence Railway's Ventnor West branch line from Merstone, on the Sandown-Newport line, to St Lawrence on the south coast, which opened in 1897 and extended to Ventnor West in June 1900.

In 1903, statutory powers were obtained for the South West & Isle of Wight Junction Railway to build a fixed railway from the island to the Hampshire mainland across the Solent, via a tunnel. It was a joint project between the LSWR and the Freshwater, Yarmouth & Newport Railway, but the outbreak of the First World War scuppered the 2½-mile tunnel project.

At the Grouping of 1921, all island lines passed into the ownership of the Southern Railway, which made considerable efforts to invest in them. However, this took the form of relocating rolling stock, which had been superseded elsewhere, such as 23 William Adams LSWR O2 0-4-4Ts cascaded from London suburban services. 'New' coaches came from the LBSCR and SECR.

The locomotives were given numbers under an unusual system where each number was individual only on the island. Each locomotive officially carried its number with a W prefix to indicate this, and given a nameplate relating to a place on the island.

As elsewhere, Nationalisation in 1948 brought the writing on the wall for many rural routes, even before anyone had heard the name Beeching.

The Freshwater, Yarmouth & Newport, Ventnor West line, Bembridge branch and Sandown to Newport line had gone by the end of 1956.

Beeching nonetheless made his mark, and in 1966 services were withdrawn on the Ryde to Newport and Cowes lines, and between Shanklin and Ventnor.

Beeching also wanted rid of the Ryde to Shanklin line, but the Southern Region instead came up with a novel idea. Electrify it.

The only problem was Ryde Tunnel which, following the closure of the line in its steam-operated form, had the trackbed in Ryde Tunnel raised to reduce flooding and decrease gradients. The lower clearance that resulted precluded the use of mainland third-rail stock, but another Secondhand Rose solution was at hand. Obsolete London Underground stock, which had a lower height, could fit under the bridge, and so 10 Northern Line cars dating from 1938 were bought. The new electric service began in March 1967.

A NEW RAILWAY COMPANY FOR WIGHT

Steam traction had established itself as a much-loved tradition on the island, and there were those who looked to the mainland and saw what outfits such as the Bluebell, Dart Valley and Severn Valley railways had achieved. So in 1971, the Isle

ABOVE: LSWR O2 0-4-4T No. W17 *Seaview* running over what is now the Isle of Wight Steam Railway in British Railways days. MIKE ESAU/ IoWSR

RIGHT: A 1914 Railway Clearing House map of the Isle of Wight railways.

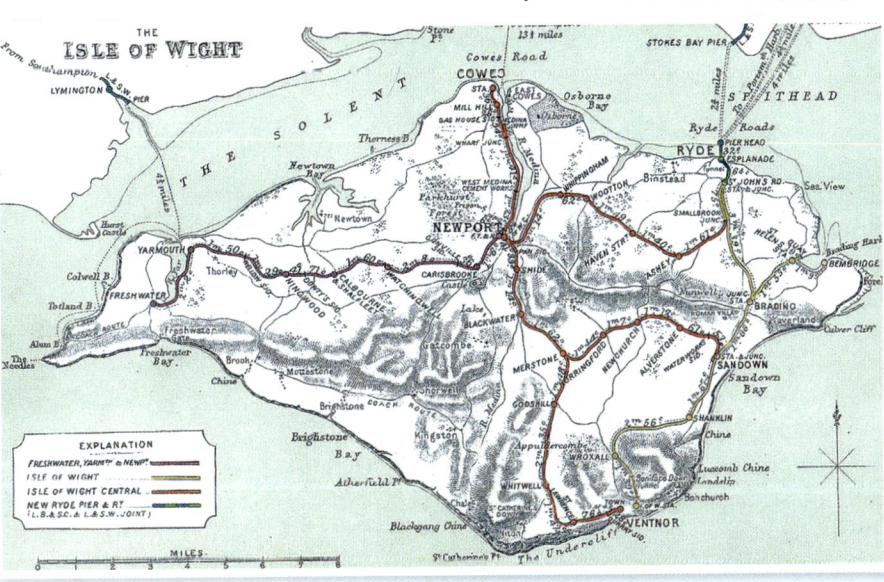

Making Fresh Tracks to the Sunny South and West

ABOVE: No. 24 *Calbourne* shunting stock at the Isle of Wight Steam Railway's original base at Newport in 1970. IoWSR

LEFT: Supporters and volunteers welcome the fledgling heritage line's rolling stock into Havenstreet station on January 24, 1971, following the enforced move from Newport. IoWSR

of Wight Railway Co Ltd was formed to buy the 1½-miles of track between Wootton and Havenstreet.

However, the revival had its origins in the 60s, when teenager, Ron Strutt, failed in his bid to buy an old island engine from British Railways.

Ron and friend, Iain Whitlam, called a meeting in south London during late 1965 to see if others were interested in preserving something of the old island lines. The Wight Locomotive Society was formed with the aim of buying at least one O2 class engine and possibly some carriages. That was achieved in 1966 with the help of wildlife artist, David Shepherd, who later bought two former main line engines of his own and founded the East Somerset Railway on which to run them.

So 1891-built No. 24 *Calbourne* was bought along with two SECR carriages and three LBSCR vehicles.

At first, the stock was based at Newport station, but on January 18, 1971, the society was given a week's notice to quit. An all-out effort by enthusiasts saw the collection moved by rail to Havenstreet before the tracks at Newport were lifted.

The Isle of Wight Steam Railway opened for business on Easter Monday, 1971, with *Calbourne* hauling its rake of three LBSCR carriages 1000yds to Woodhouse and back.

From that small beginning, the heritage line, which has Wootton as its western terminus, has been gradually extended eastwards from Havenstreet towards Ryde.

In 1991, it opened its 3½-mile extension to Ashey and Smallbrook Junction on the Ryde-Shanklin line, where a new interchange station was built, allowing passengers to interchange with the electric trains.

ABOVE: LBSCR E1 0-6-0T *Burgundy* at Cranmore – now destined to assume the identity of No. 2 *Yarmouth*. IoWSR

LEFT: Ivatt 2-6-2T No. 41298 heading to Wootton from Havenstreet with the first train of the day on March 31, 2016. IoWSR/TERRY SMITH

THE RETURN OF 'TERRIERS'

The IoWSR has two LBSCR William Stroudley 'Terriers' – once a mainstay of island motive power – in its fleet.

No. 8 *Freshwater*, built in 1876 at Brighton Works was originally numbered 46, carried the name *Newington* and was based at Battersea. In 1903 it was purchased by the LSWR to operate on the Lyme Regis branch, and a decade later, was hired by the Freshwater, Yarmouth & Newport Railway. It arrived on the Isle of Wight on June 25, 1913, with seven carriages.

The FYN bought the locomotive in 1917 and gave it the number 2. Under Southern Railway ownership, it was renumbered No. 8 and given the name *Freshwater*.

British Railways transferred it back to the mainland on May 4, 1949. It mainly worked the Hayling Island branch until withdrawal on November 9, 1963. It was then acquired by the Sadler Railcar Co and for three years was based at Droxford, Hampshire on the former Meon Valley line. It was then bought by Portsmouth brewer Brickwoods and used as a pub sign outside the Hayling Billy public house on Hayling Island.

In 1979 the Wight Locomotive Society reached agreement with Brickwoods' successors, Whitbread Wessex Ltd for No. 8 to return to the island, which it did on June 25 that year. It returned to steam on June 21, 1981, and in 1998 a new boiler costing £35,000 was ordered.

ISRAEL NEWTON OF BRADFORD

Sister No. 11 *Newport* was built in 1878 and was originally numbered 40 and named *Brighton*. Its designer Stroudley chose it to represent the LBSCR at the Paris exhibition of that year. It made many trial runs in the Paris area in order to demonstrate the effectiveness of its Westinghouse air brake system, and was awarded a gold medal for its design, workmanship and finish.

Originally working in London, in 1901 it was bought by the Isle of Wight Central Railway, and arrived on the island on January 8 the following year.

The Southern Railway renumbered it No. 11 and in 1930 gave it the name *Newport*.

Under British Railways, it worked on the Hayling Island branch, the Kent & East Sussex Railway and had spells at Brighton, St Leonard's and Newhaven.

It was withdrawn from service on September 27, 1963 and was bought by Sir Billy Butlin for display at his Pwllheli holiday camp.

Sir Peter Allen, then president of the Wight Locomotive Society, wanted to see a 'Terrier', back on the island and agreed a 10-year loan, *Newport* arriving on January 27, 1973. Bought outright from Butlin's in July 1976, its overhaul was completed in 1989.

Withdrawn from service in 2002 for overhaul, it too received a new boiler from Israel Newton, at a cost of £70,000. And passed its steam test in March 2014.

The railway has built up a fleet of steam locomotives and diesel shunters, but has excelled itself in mirroring the Bluebell Railway in retrieving Victorian and Edwardian wooden carriage bodies, restoring them to pristine condition and mounting them on a chassis. In terms of vintage carriage restoration, the IoWSR is a world leader. In 2004, it was awarded £499,000 by the Heritage Lottery Fund towards its project for a carriage shed and works at Havenstreet station as well as a rolling programme for the restoration of further bodies recovered from various locations around the island.

The railway is unique in offering travel exclusively in wooden-bodied carriages all of which formerly ran on the island system. It offers a rare chance to experience authentic Sunny South branch line travel not just of yesterday, but also of the day before that!

THE LINE TODAY

The IoWSR passes through five miles of unspoiled island countryside between Wootton, Havenstreet, Ashey and Smallbrook, recapturing the days of the branch line railway

Brought to life again are those perky tank engines and quaint, wooden-bodied carriages, which were once such a familiar sight all over the island until the mid-1950s.

However, it is not just the trains that are preserved, for here too is all the associated infrastructure, from traditional operating practices and equipment through to old railway buildings recovered from long-closed lines.

The railway is owned and operated by the Isle of Wight Railway Co Ltd. Services are operated on most days from June to September, together with selected days in April, May, and October and public holidays.

It stages more than 20 special events each year, including wine and real ale festivals, the 1940s Experience, steam galas, Fright Night, the Island Steam Show and Santa specials.

ABOVE: Queen Elizabeth II flags off a train from Havenstreet on May 19, 2004, when she visited the station to officially open its Lottery-funded carriage and wagon workshop. IoWSR **LEFT:** Isle of Wight Steam Railway flagship No. 24 *Calbourne* celebrated its 125th birthday in 2016. IoWSR

ABOVE: LBSCR 'Terrier' No. 11 *Newport* in the Havenstreet platform, with Ivatt 2-6-2T No. 41298 and O2 No. 24 *Calbourne* on shed on March 28, 2016. IoWSR/JOHN FAULKNER

Operated by a dedicated team of volunteers backed by a full-time workforce of 25, the railway has received several prestigious regional and national awards including Independent Railway of the Year on no fewer than three occasions, despite fierce competition from more than 100 lines on the mainland.

In 2010, the railway was named the UK's Best Heritage Project in the National Lottery Awards, while in 2012 the railway was honoured with The Queen's Award for Voluntary Service – the MBE for volunteer-orientated organisations.

More recently the railway has received the Tourism South East Best Large Visitor attraction award and the Visit England Visitor Attraction Quality Scheme Gold Accolade – the first heritage line in the country to receive this award.

One of the island's top five attractions, the IoWSR is visited by approximately 110,000 people each year. Additionally, film and television crews have used the line extensively for programmes ranging from period dramas to documentaries.

IVATTS ARRIVE ON ISLAND 50 YEARS LATE!

In 2009, the railway took delivery of three locomotives donated by The Ivatt Trust.

Formerly based at the Buckinghamshire Railway Centre, the trio were 1951-built Ivatt 2-6-2T No. 41298, which had been largely restored, with boiler work and major running gear completed; 1952-built sister No. 41313, a longer-term project, and 1950-built Ivatt 2MT 2-6-0 No. 46447, which will donate spare parts for both tank engines, while being restored cosmetically for static display.

Ironically, the 2-6-2Ts represented a type that had been earmarked by the Southern Region for 'Secondhand Rose' use on the island, and would have been shipped across the Solent had Southern steam not ended in 1967.

No. 41298 ran under its own power again in September 2015, and on March 17 the following year, hauled its first passenger train in half a century.

Meanwhile, the IoWSR agreed to exchange one of the Ivatts with the East Somerset Railway for a locomotive representative of an island type. Unrestored Ivatt 2-6-0 No. 46447 has gone to Cranmore to be restored to running order, and will then run on the ESR for 10 years under a loan agreement.

Coming the other way across the Solent was LBSCR E1 0-6-0T *Burgundy* – one of the 'forgotten' engines of preservation. Under the arrangement, the IoWSR acquired *Burgundy* from owner Richard Bellchambers, and will restore it to running order. A generous bequest to the IoWSR funded the purchase and restoration project.

E1s worked on the Isle of Wight alongside the famous O2s, but none of the class that worked on the island survived into preservation. *Burgundy* is not a true island engine but is the last survivor of its type, having been sold out of service by the Southern Railway into industry in the 1920s. The 1877-built E1 will assume the identity of No. 2 *Yarmouth*.

Ivatt 2-6-0s worked along the Cheddar Valley line and therefore it is appropriate to have a representative of the class at the ESR.

TRAIN STORY

A new £1.2-million visitor, conservation and education facility at Havenstreet was officially opened on June 6, 2015.

Named the Train Story Discovery Centre the ceremonial ribbon cutting was conducted by Paul Hudson, chairman of the Heritage Lottery Fund's South East England Committee, who signed off the £970,000 grant assisted by the youngest of the facility's volunteers, interpreter guide, Kathryn Lockyer, who lives in Havenstreet.

The name reflects the building's contents, aims and ambitions as its four covered roads house the vintage Victorian and Edwardian traction and rolling stock that makes the line unique. A sheltered fifth line is alongside the main building under a lean-to shelter providing a partially protected stabling facility.

Paul Hudson said that the new building would protect the IoWSR's vintage railway collection, now deemed to be of national importance. The facility, which provides another major attraction, was partially opened in March 2014 and fully opened a year later attracting excellent reviews from visitors: 60% of passengers that year visited the centre.

A ribbon-cutting event saw flagship locomotive *Calbourne* steamed light engine into Train Story for the occasion, coupled to a vintage carriage.

On February 6, 2016, the IoWSR was announced as a joint winner of the Heritage Railway Association's Annual Award (Large Groups), along with the Severn Valley Railway, which had just celebrated its 50th anniversary year.

The IoWSR carried off the accolade for its Train Story visitor centre. The award citation read: "An ambitious and imaginative project that has created an interesting and well-interpreted museum as well as providing secure and covered accommodation for the railway's operational fleet of historic Isle of Wight carriages."

THE ISLAND LINE

While it is part of the national network, the electric line from Ryde Pier to Shanklin could easily be considered a heritage railway by the back door, in view of its continued use of London Underground tube trains of yesteryear.

During sectorisation of British Rail in the 80s, the line became part of the Network SouthEast sector, and its services were rebranded as Ryde Rail.

British Rail opened two new stations on the line, Lake in 1987 and Smallbrook Junction in 1991, in co-operation with the steam railway.

The double track between Sandown and Brading, along with the Brading passing loop, were removed in 1988. The following year,

ABOVE: The Train Story building at Havenstreet. PHIL MARSH **LEFT:** The official opening of Train Story by the Heritage Lottery Fund's Paul Hudson and railway volunteer Kathryn Lockyer on June 6, 2015. PHIL MARSH

the passenger service was branded as Island Line for the first time.

After the privatisation of British Rail, the rights to run Island Line services on the line were offered for tender as a franchise. Uniquely on the national network, the franchise agreement also required the successful bidder to maintain the railway line in addition to the stations and trains. Stagecoach Group won the franchise and took over from October 1996.

The Department for Transport designated the line as a community railway in March 2006, under reforms to help boost use of rural and branch lines.

From February 2007 the Island Line franchise was merged with the mainland South Western franchise, which Stagecoach also won. The company now runs Island Line under its South West Trains subsidiary, but as Island Line Trains. Stations have been painted in a heritage scheme of cream and green.

In the mid-1990s it was planned to re-open the line south of Shanklin, to the original terminus at Ventnor, reached by a tunnel above the resort. However, the scheme was shelved because of the high costs.

In 2015, fears were sounded that the 8½-mile electric line could be closed, half a century after Beeching, because of the need to spend up to £40 million on the pier, new trains and track.

The IoWSR firmly ruled out suggestions that its volunteers could take over the line. The steam railway had hoped to one day be able to run into Ryde on the vacant trackbed alongside the electric line, but that was a very different matter to taking it over outright.

IoWSR general manager, Peter Vail, said: "We have a business and desire to extend the IoWSR to Ryde, but the thought that we share the line with Island Line has never been discussed with us and it is neither practical or permissible. The IoWSR aspiration would be only be possible if the two railways remain separate, running on parallel and not shared tracks."

He said that while the thought the heritage railway could run Island Line was flattering, the business reality was that to take on such responsibility would be beyond its resources.

In February 2016, a report into the future of the line, by transport expert, Christopher Garnett, who was brought in by the Isle of Wight Council to take a look at the options available, unveiled proposals to convert the electric line into a tramway.

Under those proposals the line would be singled, with passing places, in order to reduce costs, and the third rail replaced by overhead lines. It was reported that 10 15-year-old T-69 trams, which were built in 1999, and had previously operated on the Midland Metro, could be purchased secondhand – what else on Wight? – and reused for this scheme.

Garnett said that it would cost too much to import a new generation of secondhand London Underground Bakerloo Line tube trains, because they might not be available for another 11 years. Also, by the time they reached the island, they would be four decades old and costly to maintain because of their age. He noted that a single-line tram system would be more suitable, because it could be expanded to run over town streets.

He added: "It is considered that converting to a single-line tram operation, with passing places and 'line of sight' running would greatly simplify the railway, reduce costs and allow for a 15-minute frequency.

"Under this proposal, the IoWSR would be given the released section of double track between Smallbrook Junction and Ryde St John's station where they would be given access to the western platform.

"This would bring direct economic/tourist benefits to the island and Ryde in particular. It would also clearly benefit IoWSR, which in return has offered to provide its technical and engineering support, including constructing the passing loop and other changes required."

A RETURN TO NEWPORT?

An extension of the line westwards from Wootton to Newport has long been suggested in the past. However, it is unlikely that the full extent of the original line into the town will ever be restored as there is now a road on the site of Newport station and houses have been built on another part of the former line.

The best hope here lies with a stretch of trackbed running from Wootton to the outskirts of Newport at Halberry Lane, which is still free from development.

Everywhere on the mainland, the economies of towns have benefited greatly from the arrival of a heritage railway: Minehead on the West Somerset and East Grinstead on the Bluebell are two of many shining examples. Wareham has all the promise of another when the Swanage Railway reaches it.

Far more often than not, the required capital investment for major extensions is out of reach of heritage railways. Yet local authorities are nowadays more tuned in than ever before to the benefits of a steam railway in their midst, and can help unlock the sizeable grant aid funding required.

Imagine the attraction of steam running from Ryde to Newport, and passengers being able to jump on board soon after crossing the Solent on a ferry. Such a scheme, if it ever happens, will be years in the future, but would surely elevate the IoWSR into the Premier League of heritage lines. Local traders and hoteliers would undoubtedly reap big dividends in a true win-win situation. ●

BELOW: An Island Line former London Underground tube train crossing Ryde Pier on July 28, 2008. FRED BONIFACE*

Chapter 12

THE HOP-PICKERS' LINE

The Kent & East Sussex Railway is a classic example of a line that was built 'on the cheap' under the provisions of the 1896 Light Railways Act to link sparsely populated rural backwaters to the national network. It eventually became part of the light railway empire of the legendary Colonel Holman F Stephens, to whom a museum at the line's Tenterden Town station is dedicated.

TOP: The December Santa season on the Kent & East Sussex brings with it the opportunity to photograph in stunning winter light. The late-running 2.58pm from Northiam, hauled by USA tank No. 65 catches a very lucky burst of sunshine as it climbs Wittersham Bank en route to Tenterden. KESR

LEFT: A splendid archetypal Colonel Stephens' empire light railway summer scene: LBSCR A1X 'Terrier' 0-6-0T No. 32678 hauls a rake of vintage wooden-bodied carriages along the Kent & East Sussex Railway. Originally outshopped from Brighton Works in 1880 as No. 78 *Knowle*, this locomotive holds a key place in Sunny South railway folklore, because it was the last 'Terrier' in BR service, hauling the final train over the lightly laid West Quay lines at Newhaven and the severely weight-restricted swing bridge over the River Ouse on August 10, 1963. Bought for static display at the Butlin's Minehead holiday camp where it was displayed alongside LMS Pacific No. 46229 *Duchess of Hamilton* before being purchased by the KESR in 1975, it is now owned by the Terrier Trust. KESR

LEFT: Hawthorn Leslie 2-4-0T No. 1 *Tenterden* was bought new for the opening of the Rother Valley Railway in 1899. It was withdrawn for overhaul in 1938 and scrapped in 1941.

The earliest plans for a railway for Tenterden were made in the 1850s. The South Eastern Railway proposed that its Ashford to Hastings line should pass through Tenterden but a more southerly route through Appledore and Rye was chosen in 1851, largely through military influence.

In 1855, 1864, 1872, 1876, 1882 and 1895 plans to build a line to Tenterden from either Headcorn or Paddock Wood were proposed but all failed to materialise.

In 1896, new proposals were put forward to construct a railway from Robertsbridge on the Tonbridge-Hastings line to Tenterden. These were authorised under the 1896 Light Railways Act, which permitted the building of lines to a lower standard than the main line, but limited speed to 25mph. The provisions of the Act govern most of today's heritage railways.

Holman Fred Stephens was appointed to engineer the line as a light railway. The Rother Valley Railway, as it was initially known, was the first line to be built under the new legislation that encouraged the building of cheaply constructed lines in remote rural areas that main line railway companies deemed not worthy of attention.

Such cheap construction was known to have a limited life but reconstruction from eventual profits was thought possible.

The first section of the Rother Valley was opened for freight between Robertsbridge and a station at Tenterden, now known as Rolvenden on March 26, 1900, and to passenger traffic on April 2 that year.

Stephens was appointed general manager in 1899 and managing director in 1900. He attained the rank of Lieutenant-Colonel in the Territorial Army in 1916 and was subsequently known as Col Stephens.

The initial success of the Rother Valley Railway caused the directors to obtain powers for, and plan extensions to Cranbrook, Appledore, Pevensey and Rye. None of these was built but an extension up the hill to the present Tenterden Town station was opened in 1903 with an extension to Headcorn opened in 1905. A further extension to Maidstone was authorised but funds were not forthcoming to complete this.

The now-renamed Kent & East Sussex Railway enjoyed a modest prosperity, albeit with a subsidy for its northern extension from its neighbouring South Eastern & Chatham Railway, but sank into increased losses and bankruptcy in 1931.

ABOVE: LBSCR A1X 'Terrier' 0-6-T No. 32670 arrives at Tenterden Town. Built as No. 70 *Poplar*, it entered service on December 4, 1972, and was sold to the Rother Valley Railway in May 1901. It withdrawn in 1931 but restored to service in 1933 using parts from sister No. 5 *Rolvenden* and a new boiler was fitted in 1943. It later worked on the Hayling Island branch and was withdrawn in November 1963. Purchased privately, it arrived back on the KESR on April 10, 1964, giving the heritage line an authentic item of motive power from its earlier history. KESR

Unlike most railways it didn't lose its independence in the Grouping of 1923 and Col Stephens needed to use great ingenuity to maintain some sort of financial balance during the 1920s.

He introduced a new form of train in 1923 with two Ford road buses linked back-to-back and fitted with metal rail wheels. This was financially successful but not particularly popular with passengers who were, by this time, deserting the line for more convenient road buses. Nevertheless the railway continued to provide an essential service for the rural community, particularly for farmers that it was designed to serve.

Good management after Col Stephens' death in 1931 by his successor, William Austen, ensured the line's survival through the 1930s and the Second World War until the line finally lost its independence when all of Britain's railways were nationalised from January 1, 1948. It then became part of the Southern Region.

Nationalisation brought many material benefits to the railway as improvements were made, but traffic was increasingly lost to roads. During a typical week in 1953, only 118 passengers travelled on 90 trains, many of which ran empty. The inevitable result was that the line was closed to passengers on January 2, 1954: the Tenterden to Headcorn northern section lost all traffic and was lifted.

Goods continued to be hauled on the original section and the occasional passenger train, particularly for hop-pickers and ramblers, appeared in the summer. By 1961, however, nearly all traffic had gone and the railway was closed.

During the period of the railway's independence and insolvency in the 1920s and 1930s, railway enthusiasts and others had become attracted to the railway's eccentricities and uniqueness. In 1948 the

Making Fresh Tracks to the Sunny South and West

ABOVE: Heading across a level crossing east of Bodiam en route to Tenterden Town on September 9, 2014, is Hunslet Austerity 0-6-0ST No. 3791 of 1952 *Holman F Stephens*. One of a batch of 14 built as war reserve stock, and originally numbered WD191, it entered service at Bicester Military Railway where it carried the name *Black Knight*. Placed into store in 1962, it was withdrawn from service in August 1968. Sold out of Army service, it arrived on the KESR in February 1972. ROBIN JONES

LEFT: At the crossroads: The location of the proposed new level crossing on the A21 Robertsbridge bypass in East Sussex, the biggest hurdle to reconnecting the Kent & East Sussex Railway to the main line. GEOFF COURTNEY

magazine Punch was sufficiently moved by the loss of independence to commission a poem illustrated by the eminent cartoonist, Roland Emmett, called The Farmers' Train. Such sentiment showed how the railway had become a local, indeed a national, institution and soon after closure a society was formed with the object of preserving the line.

The founders had a 13-year-struggle ahead of them before the first trains were run. Protracted legal battles with the then Minister of Transport saved the line from demolition but the line was only saved when the society agreed to drop the Bodiam-Robertsbridge section with three road crossings from its restoration plans.

Negotiations then proceeded quickly and the present registered charity took over the line in 1973. Years of neglect and the original lightly engineered nature of the railway meant that the task had to be tackled in stages.

The first two miles at Tenterden were opened on February 3, 1974. A major renewal of a river bridge enabled an extension by 1977 to Wittersham Road. Further consolidation was then necessary but Northiam was finally reached in 1990 and Bodiam in 2000, a century after the line first opened.

EXTENDING BACK TO ROBERTSBRIDGE

Thousands more visitors could come to Tenterden when a planned extension to the light railway is completed.

Work on restoring the missing link between Bodiam and Robertsbridge is well underway, under the banner of a modern Rother Valley Railway.

When finished, it will link the Kent & East Sussex Railway with mainline connections to London and Hastings, enabling tourists to visit Tenterden by train: currently Tenterden is the largest town in Kent without a railway connected to the main line.

The Rother Valley Railway Ltd is carrying out the work to extend the line by 3½ miles, which will eventually allow passengers to travel a total of 14 miles between Tenterden and Robertsbridge.

ALONG THE LINE TODAY

Tenterden is one of the most picturesque towns in Kent. Its broad tree-lined high street offers a selection of shopping facilities and is dominated by the pinnacle tower of St Mildred's Church.

Tenterden first rose to affluence as a ship-building port when the surrounding marshes were under the sea and ships docked at Smallhythe. The train journey takes visitors across these marshes, making it one of the lowest sections of railway in the country, as part of the route is below sea level.

Tenterden Town station is the headquarters of the railway and contains some of its principal buildings including carriage and wagon workshops. Facilities for visitors include a shop, refreshment rooms, a children's playground and the excellent award-winning Colonel Stephens Museum.

The museum houses many, many exhibits ranging from full-size locomotives and rolling stock to a wax dummy of the Colonel, telling the story of the man and his 16 railways.

The collection was begun in the 1960s by Philip Shaw, present chairman of the museum committee, who began setting aside items donated by former employees of the Stephens' empire.

A large number of personal relics of the Colonel have survived, including nearly all the furniture and paraphernalia of his office, a representation of which may be seen in the museum.

The collection was first displayed in the town museum in Station Road, Tenterden, which was opened in 1977, in what were once the railway stables. The opening of a new display in a building in premises adjacent to the station at Tenterden took place in stages between 1996 and 1998.

Although the museum directly owns most of the collection, a few items are on loan from the National Railway Museum and a few individuals. In 2014, the museum won the Heritage Railway Association's *Heritage Railway* magazine Interpretation Award.

As the train leaves Tenterden, the line falls steeply away towards the marshes at an average gradient of 1-in-50 for more than a mile (the train has to work very hard on its return). The Wealden scenery across the valley is particularly fine as the line crosses the Cranbrook road about halfway down. The descent continues and the line curves sharply

LEFT: USA class 0-6-0T No. 30065 attacks the 1-in-50 bank from Rolvenden to Tenterden at 'Wet Cutting' with a short goods train on a Martin Creese photo charter. KESR

The next station, Wittersham Road, is reached through marshlands collectively known as the Rother Levels. To the right a series of channels dug at right angles to the railway were used to farm crayfish and on the left, in the woodland, if you are lucky you may see wild boar, which are also farmed. The terrain generally is very wet and until comparatively recently was subject to frequent flooding. The most characteristic trees along the lineside are willows.

The trains cross over the New Mill Channel, a tributary of the River Rother, which now runs alongside for several hundred yards. There are always many swans here, particularly in the winter months.

The line curves gently into Wittersham Road, a station apparently in the middle of nowhere, which actually handled quite heavy agricultural traffic. However, Wittersham itself is nearly three miles away and Rolvenden Layne is the nearest village, being a long mile the other way. The station had an exciting time during the Second World War when it was the depot site for a large rail-mounted gun that fired at France. The ammunition store for this is still to be seen on the corner of the picnic site.

The sidings here are used by the permanent way department and house a growing collection of track maintenance machines.

Starting from Wittersham Road, the train is faced with a steep but short climb as, following the light railway tenets under which the railway was built, the line follows the contours of the land rather than cutting through it.

Over the summit the line now falls towards the Hexden Channel and the River Rother whose valley is very wide and open at this point. Romney sheep dot the landscape and you will often see turf cutting as you cross this area. To the left the Hexden Channel and the Rother join and sweep out past the Isle of Oxney on which Wittersham stands towards

to the left at Orpin's Farm where the track levels out and crosses the main road before running into Rolvenden station, 1½ miles from Tenterden Town.

Rolvenden was always the headquarters of the locomotive works, which remain on the site. However, the original buildings have long since gone. The village of Rolvenden is 1½ miles away, and contains some attractive cottages and a church that is pleasantly situated. Lovers of historic vehicles will find the CM Booth collection in the centre of the village of great interest and a short distance outside the town is the oldest post mill in Kent.

RIGHT: Taking pride of place inside the Colonel Stephens Museum is Alfred Dodman & Co. 0-4-2T No. 1 *Gazelle*, which ran on the Shropshire & Montgomeryshire Light Railway and has been claimed to be the smallest standard gauge steam locomotive in the UK. Built in King's Lynn in 1893 as a 2-2-2 well tank, it was converted to 0-4-2WT in 1911 by the Colonel. The S&MR was taken over by the War Department in 1941 but abandoned a few years later. *Gazelle* was transferred to the Longmoor Military Railway and displayed outside the camp. ROBIN JONES

BELOW: The wax dummy of Col Stephens at work in his re-created office. ROBIN JONES

ABOVE AND LEFT: Tenterden Town station, the headquarters of today's Kent & East Sussex Railway. ROBIN JONES

Romney Marsh and the sea at Rye. As we turn slowly up the valley, Northiam station is reached after crossing the main A28 road.

Northiam station was for 10 years the terminus of the revived line and has extensive parking facilities. Parking is encouraged here for a trip to Bodiam for there are no parking facilities at the terminus station.

The village that you can see on the other side of the valley is actually Newenden with Northiam one mile up the hill in the other direction. It contains a very interesting church, and on the outskirts of the village is Great Dixter, a marvellous medieval house restored by Sir Edward Lutyens and surrounded by magnificent gardens.

The next three miles see the railway sweep up the valley between the flood plain and the rich farmland on the hillsides, demonstrating the skills of the engineer, Col Stephens. As you look ahead to your right, you will see nestled under the hill the magnificent medieval castle at Bodiam that was built to defend the highest navigable point of the Rother.

Trains pass through fields that were covered with the typical hop gardens that once brought so much traffic, and finally terminate in the immaculately restored Bodiam station, so characteristic of the Victorian light railway.

Today the station building houses a booking office and seasonal gift and refreshment outlet. Across the yard are visitor toilets, housed in a building constructed in the style of a period coal merchant's office. Adjacent is a waiting room, which houses memorabilia from the hop-picking era with which Bodiam station was so associated.

At the rear of the station reconstructed hoppers' huts are complemented by a small hop garden. The Cavell Van is berthed in a siding at the station and is open on most days that trains operate. Built as No .132 in 1919 at Ashford Works by the South Eastern & Chatham Railway; this van was the prototype of a family of similar designs built by the SECR and its successor Southern Railway, with production eventually exceeding 1600 vehicles.

In May 1919, the vehicle was chosen to convey the body of nurse Edith Cavell, who had been shot by the Germans for treating British soldiers in Belgium, from Dover to London with full military honours.

The subsequent production vehicles were consequently known by railwaymen as Cavell Vans.

Later in July 1919, the same vehicle carried the body of another national hero of the time, Cpt Fryatt, from Dover to London (Charing Cross) for a memorial service at St Paul's. He too had been shot by the Germans, for using his merchant ship to try to ram a U-Boat in defence.

On November 20, 1920, No. 132 conveyed the body of the Unknown Warrior, with full military ceremony, from Dover to London. On arrival, the coffin stood overnight in the London Brighton & South Coast Railway station's Platform 8 (now 18) under honour guard. The next day, November 11, the coffin was placed on a gun carriage and with ceremony fit for a field marshal was taken to the unveiling of the Cenotaph by King George V.

The king placed a wreath of red roses and bay leaves on the coffin and then followed the gun carriage to Westminster Abbey for the burial. A plaque on Victoria station commemorates the arrival of this train. No. 132 has been returned to running order so that it may be used in special trains and as a national educational asset for schools. The vehicle has been returned to its funeral-train appearance and has a display inside outlining its history with a replica of the Unknown Warrior's coffin mounted on a central catafalque and draped in a large union flag.

Bodiam Castle is a 10-minute walk away across the valley. Visitors can step back in history as they explore the impressive battlements and towers, which offer breath-taking views across the countryside. Visitors presenting a valid Kent & East Sussex Railway ticket receive discounted castle admission. •

ABOVE LEFT: Restored South Eastern & Chatham Railway PMV No. 132 carried the coffins of two of Britain's greatest First World War heroes and also that of the Unknown Soldier. KESR **ABOVE RIGHT:** British Thomson-Houston diesel electric locomotive No. 40 is the surviving member of a class of three built in 1931 for the internal system at the Ford plant in Dagenham, where it was numbered 1. Withdrawn on July 5, 1966, it arrived at Tenterden two days later. It was hired to James Hodson & Sons, Robertsbridge Flour Mills in 1967. It hauled the last train from Robertsbridge to Bodiam in February 1972 before the track was lifted on that section. MANHATTAN RESEARCH INC
BELOW: Transport of delight: Former London Transport No. L92 climbs the 1-in-50 bank towards Tenterden on the Kent & East Sussex Railway with the 2.20pm from Bodiam on August 8. The 0-6-0PT entered service with the GWR as No. 5786 in 1930 and after withdrawal by BR in 1958 was bought by LT, remaining on its active fleet until 1969. Based on the South Devon Railway, it was a guest locomotive on the KESR throughout August 2015. GEOFF COURTNEY

Chapter 13

BIG HERITAGE, SMALL LOCOMOTIVES!

Eastleigh is a name indelibly inscribed in Southern Railway history, heritage and folklore. It was the site of one of the company's main locomotive-building workshops and one of its biggest engine sheds. Nowadays, a much more modest concern keeps steam alive in this part of the Sunny South – the Eastleigh Lakeside Steam Railway.

In 1838 the London & South Western Railway built its line from Southampton to Winchester with a station serving the village of Barton.

It was at first named Bishopstoke Junction, but in 1868 the villages of Barton and Eastly were combined into one parish.

A parish church, the Church of the Resurrection, was built in the same year. Local novelist, Charlotte Yonge, donated £500 towards the £2300 cost of the church and was asked to choose a name for the 'new' parish; either Barton or Eastly.

She chose Eastly, but with the new modern spelling of Eastleigh. It would become one of Britain's greatest railway towns.

The LSWR opened its carriage and wagon works at Eastleigh in 1891. Twelve years later, Chief Mechanical Engineer, Dugald Drummond, oversaw the building of a large motive power depot in the town,

ABOVE: Three full-size Bulleid Pacifics line up at an open day at Eastleigh Works on May 23, 2009. Left to right are Merchant Navy No. 35005 *Canadian Pacific*, Battle of Britain No. 34070 *Manston* and West Country No. 34028 *Eddystone*. ROBIN JONES

superseding the maintenance and repair shops at Northam in Southampton.

January 1910 saw locomotive building likewise transferred to the new workshops at Eastleigh from Nine Elms in London.

Among the locomotives turned out under Drummond at Eastleigh, were the S14 0-4-0 and M7 0-4-4 tank engines, the P14 and T14 4-6-0, and D15 4-4-0 classes.

Following the appointment of Robert Urie as Chief Mechanical Engineer in 1912, the works was responsible for the construction of the H15, S15, and N15 King Arthur 4-6-0 classes as well as the G16 4-8-0 and H16 4-6-0 tank engines.

After the Grouping of 1923, Eastleigh became the principal works for the new Southern Railway. New Chief Mechanical Engineer, Richard Maunsell, reorganised the works and directed the design and construction of various new classes including the Lord Nelson 4-6-0s, the Schools 4-4-0s, U1 2-6-0s, W class 2-6-4Ts, and Q class 0-6-0s.

After 1937 under Oliver Bulleid, Eastleigh built all 30 of his Merchant Navy Pacifics and six West Country 4-6-2s. During the Second World War, Eastleigh Works built 23 LMS Stanier 8F 2-8-0s. Steam locomotive building ceased in 1950, but the works was kept fully occupied between 1956-61 in rebuilding more than 90 Bulleid 4-6-2s.

In 1962, Eastleigh built the first six Class 73 electro-diesels.

After a management buyout from British Rail Engineering Ltd, the 42-acre works became Wessex Traincare Ltd: later bought by Alstom, it was renamed Alstom Wessex Traincare. The site was closed in 2006 owing to lack of work, but the following year, it was occupied by Knights Rail Services, which began operations on site, using it to store off-lease rolling stock, as well as undertake repairs and refurbishments.

At its height, the works and shed were by far the biggest employer in the town. However, today steam is being kept alive in the town by a much smaller concern.

Eastleigh Lakeside Steam Railway has been operating for nearly 25 years as a miniature railway within the confines of Eastleigh Lakeside Country Park.

The railway began life in 1991 as the brainchild of Clive Upton, and a number of associates. It was known simply as Eastleigh Lakeside Railway using a short piece of temporary 7¼in gauge track, one steam locomotive – Baldwin type 2-4-2 *Sandy River* – and a few carriages, in part of the then-undeveloped country park.

Initially, one shipping container was used as a locomotive shed and storage facility. In 1992, the railway was officially opened with local dignitaries in attendance and the line adopted a more permanent position with the acquisition of a further container and more rolling stock.

As the railway became better known, and an increasingly popular tourist attraction, plans

LEFT: Baldwin-style 2-4-2 *Sandy River* on the opening day in 1991. ELSR

BELOW: The construction of the new station at Parkway in 1998. ELSR

ABOVE: *Sandy River* emerging from the tunnel on March 20, 2016. LIONEL KAY

LEFT: Classics in miniature: 10¼in gauge LNER A4 Pacific No: 4498 *Sir Nigel Gresley*, 7¼in gauge 2-6-2 No. 10 *Sir Arthur Heywood* and 7¼in gauge Lynton & Barnstaple Railway 2-6-2 No. 761 *Taw*. LIONEL KAY

were submitted for a building to be used as a station, workshop, offices and shop, and in 1998 construction was started and shortly after, brought into service.

During the early years, the number of steam locomotives at the railway increased. One of the more important residents, and perhaps the one that signified the start of a particular direction of the railway, was 4-6-2 Pacific No. 1001 *The Monarch*. This engine was built by HCS Bullock, of Farnborough in 1932 as a 10¼in gauge locomotive although it had been re-gauged to 7¼in gauge long before its arrival at Eastleigh.

Following further expansion of the running line, a decision was taken to lay some dual gauge, 10¼in and 7¼in gauge track, which allowed for the operation, by 2000, of larger engines. Eventually, the whole line was relaid as dual gauge, and much of the aluminium rail replaced with steel.

Since that time, the railway has become the home of further Bullock-built locomotives, No. 1002 *The Empress*, No. 2006 *Edward VIII* and, on long-term loan from Kerr's Miniature Railway in Arbroath, No. 2005 *Silver Jubilee*.

There is now a running line of a mile and a quarter that has all the features to be found on the standard gauge from an operational signal gantry, a tunnel – thought to be the longest tunnel on a miniature railway in Britain – a very well-equipped workshop and steep gradients that test not only the locomotives but also the drivers.

With the increasing number of steam locomotives in use – the railway boasts a superb fleet of more than 20 locomotives of which only two are diesel and one is a battery electric.

Eastleigh Lakeside Steam Railway is also very pleased to be at the vanguard of miniature locomotive engineering having had an unrebuilt Merchant Navy No. 21CI

Channel Packet built by engineer, Jesse Moody, for use on the line, and is in the process of having another Bulleid Pacific, a rebuilt Merchant Navy No. 35004 *Cunard White Star* constructed.

Each year, the railway operates services every weekend and daily throughout the school holidays and also has a full programme of special events including Day Out With Thomas events, a summer steam gala and several other steam weekends.

As with all independent railways, it relies heavily on a volunteer workforce to carry out all the functions associated with operating a railway.

There is a nucleus of regular volunteers who supplement the small permanent workforce and assist in the regular maintenance of track, signalling, locomotives and rolling stock. Being a small organisation, promotion through the ranks, as it were, can be quite rapid and all volunteers are given the chance, after a short probationary period, to drive the locomotives starting initially on the battery electric and moving progressively through diesel and on to steam. Of course, not all volunteers want to be drivers and everyone is encouraged to find their own niche within the organisation be it in the gift shop or guarding on the trains.

The railway is always looking for new people to join a friendly gang of regular volunteers and each new recruit is shadowed, for a short period of time, by the volunteer co-ordinator or a senior member of the workforce.

For more information, contact the railway on 02380 612020, visit www.steamtrain.co.uk or email elr@steamtrain.co.uk

■ Thanks to Lionel Kay for helping to compile this chapter. ●

RIGHT: Atlantic No. 1908 *Ernest Henry Upton*, 4-6-0 No. 850 *Lord Nelson* and unrebuilt Bulleid Merchant Navy Pacific No. 21CI *Channel Packet*, all 10¼in gauge, at Eastleigh Parkway station on June 26, 2012. LIONEL KAY

Chapter 14

'SLIM JIM' FROM THE SUNNY SOUTH!

While the term Sunny South had its roots in the steam era, a form of bespoke diesel traction designed for a seaside main line route has become a firm favourite with enthusiasts.

ABOVE: Hastings DEMU No. 1001 comprising Nos. 60116, 60529, 70262, 69337, 60501 and 60118 forms the 'Olympia Express charter' from Hastings to Kensington Olympia on December 21, 2013. TRAIN PHOTOS*

The Sunny South was a prime advertising slogan from the steam era. However, part and parcel of today's Southern heritage sector are examples of modern traction that steam fans have come to love. A standout example here is Hastings Diesels' green Class 201 'Thumper' DEMU set No. 1001, designed specifically for the Hastings to Tonbridge line, but now seen all over the national network.

Hastings Diesels Ltd was founded in 1987 by a group of preservationists who sought to rescue the popular 'Hastings' diesel-electric six-carriage trains – fondly known as 'Thumpers' – following their decommissioning in 1986 after 30 years' active duty with British Rail.

Several tunnels between Tonbridge and Hastings had been built 'on the cheap' by the South Eastern Railway in the early 1850s.

Supervision of the building of the line was lax, enabling contractors to skimp on the lining of the tunnels. Extra layers of brick lining had been required, making those tunnels too small for standard trains.

The line to Bopeep Junction finally opened in 1853, and almost immediately it was discovered that the tunnels had been bored to the minimum possible dimensions and lined so poorly that there was danger of collapse.

Rectifications led to a restricted loading gauge along the line, requiring the use of bespoke rolling stock.

Electrification of the Hastings line was considered as early as 1921, but a succession of proposals never got further than the drawing board.

The Southern Railway started electrifying its main routes in the 1930s, including those to Brighton, Portsmouth and Eastbourne. The Eastbourne scheme included the 'Coastway' route to Hastings, therefore lowering the priority of the Hastings Line.

Steam locomotives served the route from opening until the late 1950s, when it had been decided to build modern 'slimmed down' carriages to fit the notorious clearances.

While the first underframes were under construction at Ashford the idea of diesel electrification was conceived by the Southern Region's then Chief Mechanical and Electrical Engineer, WJ Arnold Sykes, and his deputy, Hugh Smyth.

Plans were hastily made to build the new carriages essentially as electric trains with a big difference: they would carry their own electrical power supply. Instead of taking current from a third rail, they would draw it from an on-board dynamo driven by a diesel engine.

These extra-narrow DEMUs with flat bodysides, affectionately known as 'Slim Jims', were designed to have as much equipment being as possible in common with the Electric Multiple Units, then being built for use throughout the Southern Region, which they closely resembled. The concept would lead to cost-saving and ease of maintenance through standardisation.

The anticipated 10-year lifespan of the DEMUs was expected to keep the Hastings service running until the long-term goal of electrification could be realised, with the offending double-track tunnels converted to single track.

Twenty-three six-coach DEMUs, each consisting of a motor coach at either end of a rake of four trailers, were introduced between January 1957 and June 1958, the bodies being built at Eastleigh.

The DEMUs' first revenue service was on May 6, 1957, and operation to Charing Cross began on June 17, 1957. The DEMUs replaced life-expired steam-hauled stock on all services from London to Hastings via Battle, and they were based at a new purpose-built depot at St Leonards-on-Sea near Hastings.

Pullmans they weren't, but what they lacked in glamour and style, they more than made up for in versatility and reliability, and they lasted in service way beyond their expected lifespan, and far beyond their intended route.

Most sets were refurbished internally during the mid-1960s, and their sycamore-veneer internal panelling was covered with laminate.

The DEMUs were also used on many special workings and railtours in addition to working the Hastings service. They were also used for a regular Saturdays-only Brighton to Exeter diagram during 1972-1977, using a 12-car set in summer and a six-car in winter, incorporating a buffet car.

An outstanding feature of the DEMUs, which contributed to their long service life, was the English Electric 4SRKT engine, which had already been tried and tested on the Egyptian State Railways. This version of the 4K, coupled with an English Electric Type 824 generator, formed the power unit for all of the DEMU stock on the Southern and on the Northern Irish Railways.

ABOVE: Hastings unit No. 1001 with the 'Channel Two' railtour at Bristol Temple Meads on July 7, 2012. RICHARD GRIFFIN/HDL

HASTINGS UNIT IN THE HITHER GREEN DISASTER

DEMU vehicles were also used in 'mix and match' hybrid formations of different classes after their Hastings sets were disbanded. They were used in the three-car Class 206 'Tadpole' units that worked the Reading-Tonbridge service in the 1960s and 1970s, and also in the closely related Hampshire and Oxted units.

Some units were disbanded to reform other Hastings sets after the Hither Green rail crash of Sunday, November 5, 1967.

On that day, the 12-coach 7.43pm Hastings to Charing Cross service, formed by two six-car DEMUs travelling at around 70mph derailed at 9.16pm, just before the St Mildred's Road railway bridge between Hither Green and Grove Park stations near the Southern Region Continental goods depot.

The leading pair of wheels of the third coach were derailed by a broken rail and ran on for a quarter of a mile before striking points,

RIGHT: No. 1001 stands alongside GWR 2-8-0 No. 3850 at Bishops Lydeard with a railtour to the West Somerset Railway on June 19, 2010. DAVID STAINES/HDL

BOTTOM: Hastings DEMU No. 1003 passes Factory Junction, Battersea on its delivery trip from Eastleigh Works to St Leonards Depot on February 27, 1957. HDL COLLECTION

Making Fresh Tracks to the Sunny South and West

ABOVE: The 'Dorset Diadem' crosses over the border from Dorset to Hampshire. HEC TATE*

LEFT: 'Slim Jim' No. 1001 has visited several heritage railways. On May 14, 2011, it visited the Buckinghamshire Railway Centre at Quainton Road with the 'Metrolander' railtour. ROBERT STEWART/HDL

causing 11 coaches to be derailed and four of those to turn on to their sides.

The train came to rest after 250yds, apart from the leading coach that detached and ran on for a further 220yds.

Forty-nine passengers were killed and 78 injured, 27 being detained in hospital. Most of the casualties had been travelling in the overturned coaches. The driver and guard escaped unharmed, but remained in a state of shock.

Among the survivors were 17-year-old singer Robin Gibb of the Bee Gees and his wife-to-be Molly Hullis. He later claimed that travelling in a first-class coach – which he could afford after the band had just had a smash UK hit with Massachusetts – may have saved his life.

The subsequent investigation found that a broken rail at a rail joint had caused the accident.

After the derailment, the line was inspected and a temporary speed restriction of 60mph imposed.

The Ministry of Transport report into the accident criticised the maintenance of the line, especially following a recent increase of the maximum speed of trains over the route.

Inspector Col D McMullen recommended that on main lines and heavily trafficked commuter lines the premature replacement of jointed track by continuous welded rail should be speeded up.

As a result, maintenance of the line was improved inspection techniques and jointing methods were revised, and more significantly, plans for replacing jointed track by continuous welded rail were accelerated. Concrete sleepers were banned at rail joints on the Southern Region.

REDUNDANCY AT ELECTRIFICATION

The Hastings DEMUs eventually succumbed to corrosion of their bodywork, made much worse by the proximity of salt-laden sea air, their St Leonards depot standing right beside the beach.

It was not considered cost effective to carry out extensive repairs to the whole fleet, as they were earmarked for withdrawal once electrification of their home route could be undertaken.

With the usage they were getting it would have been impractical to repair the damage on a fleet-wide scale, and in any case the next major round of investment had long been earmarked for electrification of the route.

In 1983, British Rail announced a £23 million upgrading of the Hastings line. It was to include single-tracking of the substandard tunnels, with remotely operated turnouts, along with electrification and complete resignalling of the whole route.

Spring 1986 saw the London to Hastings service slowly taken over by standard EMUs.

The last 'slimline' Hastings DEMUs ran on Sunday, May 11, 1986. The final trip under BR was the last leg of the 'farewell' railtour, which left Charing Cross at 10.45pm, packed with enthusiasts.

That night, the entire remaining fleet was withdrawn, apart from two units, which were briefly reprieved and shortened for use on the Ashford-Hastings and Oxted-Uckfield/East Grinstead routes.

Used carriages were left to await their fate at various localities including Ashford, Sevenoaks, Ore, and Mountfield sidings. Most units were scrapped.

Nonetheless, the Hastings units had proudly lasted in service for 30 years, three times the length of time for which they had been built.

In that time, they had built up an enthusiast following, despite the heritage sector still being all but dominated by steam.

THE HASTINGS REVIVAL

In July 1986, a group of enthusiasts formed the Hastings Diesel Group to preserve one or more Hastings DEMU coaches.

A year later, buoyed by flurries of interest, the group set up a limited company, Hastings

St. Leonards on Sea looking West.

Diesel Preservation Ltd, to buy a complete six-car unit.

In March 1989, the company bought two-car units, Nos. 1001 and 1013. A total of 15 Hastings DEMU cars were acquired, including five motor-coaches and three corridor firsts.

BR gave the group access to its by-then-closed home depot at St Leonards. In 1990, an associated but separate company, St Leonards Railway Engineering Ltd, was established to take on the lease of the depot. The initial group was wound up, and Hastings Diesel Preservation Limited became Hastings Diesels Ltd.

Eventually, members restored three vehicles, Nos. 60116, 60527 and 60118, which saw use on the Swanage Railway from 1990-93 – fitting as the last BR trains over that branch comprised DEMUs.

Motor coach No. 60116 was named *Mountfield* by the late railway-publishing magnate, Ian Allan, in a ceremony at Swanage on June 30, 1990.

Sister motor coach No. 60000 was named *Hastings* by the mayoress of Hastings on September 28, 1991. The vehicle also won the Association of Railway Preservation Societies Best Restored Coach award in 1992.

The Kent & East Sussex Railway hired a three-car unit comprising Nos. 60000, 60529 and 60116, from 1993-96.

Motor coach No. 60118 was named *Tunbridge Wells* at a ceremony in that town by its mayor on May 12, 1995.

Hastings Diesels' ambition lay beyond running its sets on heritage railways, where the maximum speed is 25mph. It wanted to have a set running on the national network again.

Motor coaches *Hastings* and *Tunbridge Wells* as well as trailer cars Nos. 60501 and 60529 were taken to Eastleigh Works where their axles and running gear were checked and overhauled as necessary. Door locks were changed, Automatic Warning System apparatus was fitted, and many other tasks completed.

The four-coach set passed its inspection, and numbered 1001, was certified for use again on the main line.

Ten years after the fleet was withdrawn, No. 1001 operated its first railtour on Saturday May 11, 1996, taking in routes around Kent, including the Folkestone Harbour branch, before running to London for a replay of the final non-stop run from Charing Cross to Hastings.

The trip was so successful that centre trailer No. 70262 from a 4CEP EMU was added. Buffer car No. 69337 from a 4BIG EMU was altered to fit the set, added in June 2000.

Mountfield gained its certification for main line running in October 2002, giving the operator more flexibility.

No. 1001 has been continuously upgraded to meet current regulatory and health and safety standards. With its centralised door locking, Train Protection & Warning System apparatus, on-train data recorders, buckeye lower shelf brackets and GSM-R radios, it is able to operate anywhere on the national rail network.

The unit has since run more than 500,000 miles on railtours or on hire to Train Operating Companies.

On August 11, 1999, it was used on a 24-hour sell-out railtour that ran to Devon to witness a total eclipse of the sun.

It has been hired on several occasions for use between Portsmouth and Cardiff, for rugby traffic and also for the Glastonbury music festival.

At one stage, TOC Connex hired it for six weeks to run on its original route from London to Charing Cross.

Connex South Central (later Southern) hired No. 1001 for more than four years for 'Marsh Link' services between Ashford and Hastings and Eastbourne.

It has also run more than 60 day trips from the Sunny South to popular destinations such as Weymouth, Cardiff, Boston, Norwich, Weybourne and Salisbury, and on to heritage lines such as the West Somerset, Severn Valley, Bluebell and Great Central (Nottingham) railways.

In July 2015, a crash-damaged Southeastern Class 375 Electrostar EMU was dragged very slowly at 5mph by two Hastings Diesels' motor coaches from Canterbury West to Ramsgate Depot using a special Dellner coupling-adapter, having collided into a herd of cattle that had strayed on to the line between Wye and Chilham.

In August 2015, the two motor coaches spent a week at Thameslink's new depot in Three Bridges shunting some of the new-built Class 700 Desiro City trains.

Motor coach No. 60118 *Tunbridge Wells* had clocked up 632,144 miles in preservation as of March 5, 2016.

Hastings Diesels Ltd also owns 13 non-mainline certified vehicles, which are in various states of readiness.

■ For details of Hastings Diesel Limited trips featuring No. 1001, visit www.hastingsdiesels.co.uk ●

ABOVE: The 'Nene Machine' trip of May 12, 2012, to the Nene Valley Railway saw No. 1001 pass Woolmer Green on the East Coast Main Line. GREGORY BEECROFT/HDL

BELOW: Unit No. 1001 at Reading with the 'Channel Two' tour of July 7, 2012. RICHARD GRIFFIN/HDL

Chapter 15

STEAMING TO THE SEVERN SEA

British Rail closed the GWR Taunton to Minehead branch in 1971, because it could no longer pay its way. However, revivalists turned Britain's longest standard gauge heritage line into a mainstay of the local seaside tourist economy.

It was 1856 when the railway arrived in the old harbour town of Watchet on the erstwhile West Somerset Mineral Railway, bringing down the iron ore from the Brendon Hills to the harbour for onward shipping to the furnaces of the Ebbw Vale Company in South Wales.

Yet while the mineral railway also carried passengers and general goods, it did not form a link with the developing national railway network.

Watchet townsfolk became increasingly concerned at the way rival trading ports along the Bristol Channel were acquiring connections to Isambard Kingdom Brunel's Bristol & Exeter Railway and the far wider world beyond.

The fears led to the original West Somerset Railway being founded, with Brunel nominally its engineer. It opened between Watchet and a junction with the B&ER at Norton Fitzwarren in 1862.

It was a Brunel line although at the time the great man was involved in work on the Royal Albert Bridge across the Tamar estuary at Saltash as well as the *Great Eastern* steam ship, so construction of a routine branch line railway was left to an assistant, Mr Burke, who completed the work after Brunel died in 1859.

The West Somerset was built to Brunel's 7ft 0¼in broad gauge, while the earlier mineral railway had been built to the nationally adopted standard gauge of 4ft 8½in.

It was on July 16, 1874 that the line was extended to Minehead, which was being developed as a seaside holiday destination. This extension was completed by the independent Minehead Railway. The styles of station buildings between Bishops Lydeard and Watchet are of different architectural design to those at Washford, Dunster and Minehead. However, the whole was worked from the start as a branch of the B&ER.

In 1882 the line was converted to standard gauge, when, over one weekend, May 21-23, 1892, the entire Paddington to Penzance main line was narrowed.

The B&ER had already become officially part of the Great Western Railway rather than a de facto extension of its empire and business on the line grew, along with the shorter working week, paid holidays and the idea of leisure time reinforcing local business, as social conditions for the working classes improved. To accommodate the extra passenger traffic, branch station facilities grew, particularly platform lengths, with the final work being done in 1934.

At that stage it was assumed that the railway line and the steam trains would be there forever,

BELOW: Somerset & Dorset Joint Railway 7F 2-8-0 No. 53809, which is based at the Midland Railway-Butterley, powers away from Blue Anchor on November 3, 2015.
BRIAN SHARPE

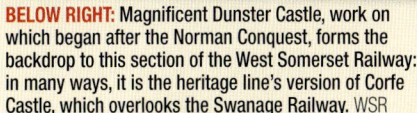

BELOW RIGHT: Magnificent Dunster Castle, work on which began after the Norman Conquest, forms the backdrop to this section of the West Somerset Railway: in many ways, it is the heritage line's version of Corfe Castle, which overlooks the Swanage Railway. WSR

even if the mineral line had gone out of business at the start of the 20th century as cheaper overseas ores displaced the Brendon's output.

However, because of the impetus of the First World War motor vehicle transport was becoming much more efficient and there were plenty of ex-War Department lorries about for ex-servicemen, who had learned to drive during the conflict, to purchase. Lorry chassis could also be fitted with bus bodies by other entrepreneurs looking to start their own transport business.

The greater versatility of road transport highlighted one of the biggest problems with country branches – the tendency for stations to be at a distance from the places they served.

On the Minehead branch Bishops Lydeard was at the edge of the village while the Quantock Hills, Crowcombe and Stogumber were remote enough spots for a bus company to be established for a while in the latter village (it was later absorbed by Western National). The best-placed stations were Watchet and Minehead.

A reliable bus service running through the centre of towns and villages was likely to look more attractive than, say, walking along Long Street and Station Road in Williton to catch a train on a wet December day. Similarly lorries could take small loads directly from supplier to recipient without transhipment en route. Slowly business began to move away and although the trains still ran they were less busy as each year went by.

The trend continued after Nationalisation in 1948 when British Railways inherited a system and stock ravaged by the neglect of six years of war. By the 1960s BR was making annual losses large enough to upset the Treasury and so ICI executive Dr Richard Beeching was appointed as its chairman with a remit to make the railways pay. His solution was a wholesale ending of stations, services and certain types of freight traffic. Of the four branch lines that had once radiated from Taunton, passenger trains to Chard ended in 1962 (freight lingered a while longer), the Yeovil line went in 1964 and the line across Exmoor through Wiveliscombe and Dulverton in 1966.

What sustained the Minehead line longer was the seasonal holiday traffic, boosted by the opening of a Butlin's holiday camp a short walk from the terminus.

Indeed, during 1964-65, more than 27,000 people travelled to the holiday camp by train – but far more arrived by car. Beeching's report pointed to the allegedly huge round-the-year cost of stabling extra coaches for use during peak summer months only.

A massive local campaign was launched in a bid to save the branch, with Exmoor dwellers angry that they would be the furthest people in Britain from a railhead once the line had gone.

The Transport Users' Consultative Committee claimed that considerable hardship would result, and the economy of Minehead would be adversely affected.

The TUCC managed to win the branch a short reprieve, but cutbacks continued. Pick-up goods services ceased from Blue Anchor on August 19, 1963, with freight withdrawn from the whole branch from August 6 the following year. The siding into the paper mill at Watchet was disconnected on February 2, 1965 and the short Watchet harbour branch was closed on May 19, 1965, enabling further savings. Taunton became the freight railhead with goods delivered by lorry, and the expansive sidings at Minehead were lifted with the engine shed demolished and the turntable removed.

The mid-1960s saw signalboxes at Minehead, Crowcombe, Leigh Wood and Kentford Crossing, plus the ground frames at Watchet and Stogumber closed.

Staff were withdrawn from Washford, Crowcombe and Bishops Lydeard in succession and from February 1968, all tickets from intermediate stations were issued by conductor-guards.

ABOVE: A branch train at Minehead in 1902. WSR
LEFT: An Edwardian postcard view of the railway taken from Cleeve Hill at Dunster. ROBIN JONES COLLECTION

Making Fresh Tracks to the Sunny South and West 97

ABOVE: The end is nigh: Minehead station on May 5, 1970.

In 1964, worldwide cinema audiences saw the branch when Crowcombe Heathfield station was used for location filming of the Beatles' first film A Hard Day's Night. It was at the station where Ringo rode a bicycle along the Minehead-bound platform.

By 1970, the line was pared to the bone, with Bishops Lydeard signalbox closing on March 1 and the line from there to Norton Fitzwarren being singled. Locomotive-hauled trains ended with the summer season on September 26, 1970 with DMUs handling the nine daily return trips until the end finally came on January 2, 1971.

Several 'last' trains were run on that day, including one by members of the Great Western Society, which issued special 'last day' covers for stamp collectors. As someone pulled the communication cord on the last outbound service to Minehead, the final timetabled train back from the resort did not leave until 11.40pm – and did not arrive at Taunton until 12.40am on January 3, 1971.

It was also the end of a great tradition at Williton, revived after 35 years for just one day. The GWR had granted what was believed to be a unique concession to a local family, the Martins – the right to sell fruit on the station platform. Ten-year-old Edward Martin who lived in Highbridge House next to the station ran along the platform with a basket yelling "fruit ripe, ripe fruit" following in the footsteps of his father and grandfather.

The holiday camp trade was by then far from offsetting the loss of local passenger business and on January 4, 1971 the line officially closed despite persistent local protests.

REVIVALISTS FINDING THEIR FEET

With the line under threat for such a long period and railway preservation by then established as something that private and volunteer-based organisations could achieve, plans were in place to revive the Minehead branch.

On February 5, 1971, a Minehead Railway Preservation Society organised a meeting in Taunton, and a working party headed by Douglas Fear, a local businessman, was tasked with investigating how the line could be re-opened as a privately owned railway.

That May, a new West Somerset Railway Company was formed to acquire the line and operate a year-round commuter service from Minehead to Taunton alongside which a limited summer steam service could also run.

A deal was agreed with British Rail to purchase the line with the support of Somerset County Council, which helped to secure the line and infrastructure and so no tracks were torn up or bridges demolished. However, the local authority was wary of the lucrative seafront Minehead station site falling into private hands should the railway fail. Instead, the council bought the line itself in 1973 and leased back the operational land to the revivalist company.

The proposed commuter service never materialised, owing to traffic restrictions between the newly installed Taunton Cider Company sidings at Norton Fitzwarren and Taunton, but the line was slowly re-opened as a heritage railway.

Minehead to Blue Anchor was the first section to see trains restored, opening on March 28, 1976 and services were extended to Williton on August 28 the same year. Trains returned to Stogumber on May 7, 1978 reaching Bishops Lydeard on June 9, 1979. The big advantage over the Swanage project here was, of course, the track was still in place, and sections did not have to be relaid by volunteers to get trains running again.

Among other things, that allowed the towed removal of LMS Princess Coronation Pacific No. 6233 *Duchess of Hamilton* from Butlin's by rail in 1975. It was one of several classic locomotives bought by Billy Butlin for display at his holiday camps throughout the country, to amuse youngsters many of whom had travelled there by steam. Often a former driver would be hired to explain the workings of a steam locomotive. However, they were sold off to preservation venues as interest waned after the passing of steam on the main line, and cosmetic maintenance in the salty sea air became a costly affair.

Today, *Duchess of Hamilton* stands on static display in the National Railway Museum at York, its original 1930s streamlined casing having been restored after a lengthy spell back on the main line and running on preserved railways.

Re-opening of the Minehead branch to passenger trains began on March 28, 1976 when Lord Montague flagged away a steam train between Minehead and Blue Anchor. By 1979 trains were running between Minehead and Bishops Lydeard and at 20 miles, the West Somerset Railway had become Britain's longest heritage line. That title has now gone to the 2ft gauge Welsh Highland Railway in Snowdonia with the WSR in second place.

However, matters were not at all well. The original business plan revolved around services running in and out of Taunton operated by diesel railcars with steam operations on a limited scale to appeal to tourists.

For many and various reasons the Taunton link has never come to pass and the year-round local diesel services were less and less used. Reliability of trains also became a problem to

LEFT: BR Standard 9F 2-10-0 No. 92214, visiting from the Great Central Railway, makes a storming run out of Minehead during the annual spring steam gala in March 2016. BRIAN SHARPE
BELOW: The West Somerset Railway is renowned for its coastal views, but also offers a variety of superb unspoiled countryside in the lee of the Quantock Hills. Here SDJR 7F 2-8-0 No. 53808 passes Bicknoller. BRIAN SHARPE

ABOVE: Summer blooms: WR 4-6-0 No. 7828 *Odney Manor* pulls into Crowcombe Heathfield station, where the Beatles once filmed scenes for A Hard Day's Night. IAN SMITH/WSR
RIGHT: GWR 4-6-0 No. 4936 *Kinlet Hall* heads past Doniford Bay, an excellent beach for fossil hunting.
BELOW RIGHT: Inside the signalbox at Blue Anchor. WSR

the point where a local joke went that WSR stood for 'will something run?'

By 1981, the railway was to all intents bankrupt. Paid staff had to be laid off and matters looked grim.

However, the county council was supportive and the volunteers (who included many of the former paid staff) were determined that the line should survive. There were some grim years to come but by 1985 the corner was being turned.

MOVING FORWARDS

A new station at Doniford Halt was opened on the coast east of Watchet on June 27, 1987 to serve a holiday camp at Helwell Bay.

In 1989 the WSR was able to hire BR Standard 9F No. 92220 *Evening Star*, which in 1960 became the last steam engine to be built for British Railways, and later a veteran of the Somerset & Dorset main line, and matters were really progressing with improvements taking place on all fronts.

Since the 1990s progress has continued to be made and the railway is well established as one of the leading tourism attractions in south-west England, carrying around 200,000 passengers per year. In turn, visitor numbers make the line a considerable contributor to the economy of both Taunton Deane and West Somerset as the vast majority are members of the general public using the WSR as part of a day out. Special events such as galas bring many visitors who stay in local accommodation.

Bookings from coach and holiday companies and group organisers are an important part of the business of the West Somerset Railway and discounted travel, plus reserved seating is available for pre-booked groups of 16 or more adults and or seniors.

In 2004, work started on constructing a new triangle at Norton Fitzwarren, which included a part of the old Devon and Somerset line to Barnstaple, and a ballast reclamation depot serving the national network opened there in 2006.

In 2008, a new turntable was brought into use at Minehead. A new station opened on August 12, 2009 at Norton Fitzwarren on a new site a short distance north of the main line. During special events some trains continue a further two miles beyond Bishops Lydeard to Norton Fitzwarren.

During 2007 a regular service ran from Minehead to Taunton and Bristol Temple Meads on two days each week. Known as the 'Minehead Express', it was aimed at holidaymakers travelling to Butlin's at Minehead. It left Minehead at 11.10am and Bristol at 2.06pm with Victa Westlink's Class 31s No. 31452 and 31454 powering the five coaches. These services first ran on July 20 and operated on a total of 18 days, finishing on August 27.

The availability of the main line connection at Norton Fitzwarren has also made Minehead a choice destination for both steam and diesel-hauled charter trains from all over the country.

Maybe, just as the Swanage Railway will re-enter Wareham in 2017, one day West Somerset services will run into Taunton station again.

Not only does the railway have a very impressive fleet of former GWR and BR main line steam locomotives, but it has an excellent heritage diesel fleet too. Included in the diesel fleet, under the auspices of the Diesel and Electric Preservation Group based at Williton, are examples of the Class 14, 35 and 52 diesel hydraulics that ruled the roost on the Western Region following the demise of steam.

SOMERSET & DORSET IN EXILE

The GWR branch was never part of the neighbouring Somerset & Dorset Joint Railway system. However, it has given a bolthole to part of the legacy of that line.

The Somerset and Dorset Railway Trust is based 'in exile' at Washford station.

Its origins lay in an early attempt to preserve part of the S&D based at Radstock from 1969, when the S&D Railway Circle established a base in the station and engine shed with also several items of rolling stock.

Steam open days were held at Radstock to generate funds, a small museum set up and in 1973 the Somerset & Dorset Railway Museum Trust was granted charitable status.

The S&D associated Light Railway Company made plans to re-open half a mile of the S&D from Radstock to Writhlington where it was proposed to construct a mining museum. However, lack of support and finance saw it fizzle out.

During the winter of 1974-75, the museum at Radstock was disbanded, and most of the

rolling stock at was moved to the West Somerset Railway.

The trust owns S&DJR 7F 2-8-0 No. 53808, which is part of the WSR's regular operational fleet under a separate lease agreement. It is one of only two survivors of the class and indeed one of only two surviving S&D locomotives.

At Washford, there's a workshop and yard, where it houses and restores a number of former S&D goods wagons and coaches, as well as former Kilmersdon Colliery Peckett 0-4-0ST *Kilmersdon*, which ran on a system attached to the S&D. The associated museum also features a signalling display based around the small signalbox from Burnham-on-Sea.

SEASIDE SPECIALS

The West Somerset Railway not only operates a standard passenger timetable but offers many special services.

The 'Dunster Castle Express' is a popular combined day out package whereby on Wednesdays and Saturdays, passengers travel by train from Bishops Lydeard to Dunster station where they are met by a coach for the journey to the Grade I listed medieval castle, which towers over Dunster village and is now in the care of the National Trust.

On Wednesdays from May to the end of September, the 'Hestercombe Express' leaves Minehead at 10.15am for Bishops Lydeard,

ABOVE: LMS Stanier 8F No. 48624, visiting from the Great Central Railway for the Somerset & Dorset-themed spring steam gala in March 2016, carries a 'Pines Express' headboard as it makes a storming departure from Minehead. BRIAN SHARPE

ABOVE: BR corporate blue livery beneath a Minehead blue sky: Class 35 Hymek D7017 is one of five Western Region diesel hydraulics in the care of the Diesel and Electric Preservation Group. ROBIN JONES

from where a coach takes passengers to and from Hestercombe with the return being by the 4.20pm steam train from Bishops Lydeard.

The railway also runs a free bus link from Dunster station to Dunster Country Fair at the end of July and Dunster Show in mid-August.

The 'Lynton And Lynmouth Explorer' is another of the combined days out that the railway offers whereby passengers travel by the 10.25am train from Bishops Lydeard as far as Minehead for a connecting coach, which takes them across the northern part of Exmoor National Park to the twin villages of Lynton and Lynmouth. After time for exploration the coach brings the passengers back to Minehead for the 4.25pm back to Bishops Lydeard.

The 'Watchet Afternoon Explorer' offers an afternoon round trip at a discounted price between Bishops Lydeard and Watchet.

The railway also runs fish and chip, cheese and cider as well as murder mystery specials.

The first weekend in August is a big day in the railway's calendar. The West Somerset Railway Association holds its Steam Fayre and Vintage Vehicle Rally at Norton Fitzwarren. It is one of the biggest events of its kind in the west of England with a wide range of traction engines, buses, cars, two-wheelers, tractors, military vehicles and much else besides. The Fayre is held on a site on land acquired by the West Somerset Railway Association within the turning triangle.

Specials are also run in conjunction with the popular Dunster By Candlelight event on the first weekend in December. The village is softly lit, there are parades and street entertainment, and shops, pubs, restaurants and cafes are open.

December also sees carol trains and the staple feature of heritage lines everywhere nowadays, Santa specials.

Yes, British Rail could not make the branch pay, but if the West Somerset Railway, which today brings multiple year-round benefits to the local economy, ever closed, the impact on the locality would be devastating. That begs a question about Beeching's approach: how often was the wider picture taken into account by a railway network in public ownership, over and above losses made by country routes? ●

ABOVE: The former Pwllheli turntable installed at Minehead in 2008 has become a draw for seaside sightseers in its own right. Here, Jeremy Hosking's Sunny South veteran Bulleid West Country light Pacific No. 34046 *Braunton*, which was restored from scrapyard condition at Williton, is turned to the delight of crowds. ROBIN JONES

ABOVE: Visting GWR 4-6-0 No. 4936 *Kinlet Hall* and WR 4-6-0 No. 7828 *Odney Manor* cross Ker Moor. STEPHEN EDGE/WSR
BELOW: GWR 4-6-0 No. 4936 *Kinlet Hall* heads past the great expanse and low-tide shingle to the east of Minehead. The Bristol Channel has the second-highest tidal range in the world after the Bay of Fundy in Newfoundland, and its trademark brown waters are caused by the Atlantic surge pushing back the silt-laden waters of the Severn estuary. Incidentally, *Kinlet Hall* has a very unhappy memory of the not-so-sunny South West. In 1941, it nearly toppled into a bomb crater following a Nazi air raid on Plymouth after sister No. 4911 became the first of the class to become extinct when it was blown up. WSR

Chapter 16

HOLLYCOMBE STEAM IN THE COUNTRY

Steam engines which once hauled slate trains in North Wales are now entertaining visitors to the Sunny South.

Back in the late 1940s Commander John Baldock decided to preserve some of the steam traction engines that were rapidly disappearing from British life.

He had enjoyed a lifelong association with steam. A midshipman at 18, one of his first jobs was running one of a battleship's 30ft-long picket boats with a crew of seven. All of the ships that he served in were driven by steam turbines.

At the end of the 1940s, John became aware that traction engines and steam road vehicles were disappearing into scrapyards and decided to preserve examples.

He advertised in the personal column of The Times and bought his first item, Burrell Gold Medal Tractor No. 3815 of 1919 Sunset No. 2, which is still at Hollycombe.

In 1951, he bought Hollycombe House and an estate of 200 acres. By the early 1960s he had acquired a significant collection of road vehicles and then, realising that no preservation movement for fairground rides and organs existed, acquired examples of these.

In the late 1960s, he extended his interests again, this time into preserving railway equipment.

His collection was eventually opened to the public and, based at Iron Hill in Liphook, became a major Hampshire tourist attraction.

Eventually, what was billed as the Hollycombe collection grew so large it became impossible for one person to maintain, and by 1984 Cdr Baldock decided he would have to close the operation.

Volunteers formed a society to operate the collection, which continued to expand, and in 1998 it passed into the care of the Hollycombe Working Steam Museum Ltd, a charitable trust formed to protect the interests of the assembled collection, which has since benefited from several Heritage Lottery Fund grants.

The venue's narrow gauge railway dates from 1967 and includes used equipment purchased from the Dinorwic slate quarry in Snowdonia, which had recently abandoned its extensive internal rail system. Early engineering help came in the form of weekend volunteers from the nearby Longmoor Military Railway.

Cdr Baldock acquired Quarry Hunslet 0-4-0ST No. 638 of 1895 *Jerry M* along with a quantity of track and several wagons.

Construction of the 2ft gauge line started in 1968 and reached the sandstone quarry by 1971, using some rails from the Longmoor line after it closed.

The Quarry Railway, as it became known, was later extended to include a loop, which brought the running length to its present 1½ miles, running through woodland and fields.

A second ex-Dinorwic engine Barclay 0-4-4 well tank No. 1995 of 1931 *Caledonia* was purchased in 1968.

Four of the five passenger coaches were bought from the Ramsgate Cliff Railway when it closed and a fifth coach was built at Hollycombe to the same design.

The venue has been rebranded as Hollycombe Steam in the Country.

A programme of renewal in recent years is seeing the old track gradually replaced with a heavier, ballasted one that will last longer and reduce maintenance.

A new station, Birch Piece Halt, was opened in June 2011 to serve special events held in the field inside the loop of the railway and to enable extra trains to be run during major railway events.

For many, the highlights of the railway journey are the views over the South Downs and the Sussex Weald; wide sweeping vistas looking down from Hollycombe's location on Iron Hill.

Evening railway rides are very popular on Hollycombe's Halloween Fairground at Night events in October.

ABOVE: Hollycombe's *Jerry M* in action. NIGEL PHILPOTT/HSITC
BELOW: *Jerry M* celebrated its 125th anniversary on September 20, 2015. NIGEL PHILPOTT/HSITC

A third-of-a-mile standard gauge line was also added to the venue, running between the sawmill and the farm, passing the fairground along the way, with one steam locomotive, former Chatham Dockyard Hawthorn Leslie 0-4-0ST No. 2450 of 1899 *Commander B*, named after the collection's founder. It has been out of use for several years.

The venue also has a 7¼in gauge miniature railway with four steam locomotives.

Cdr Baldock moved to a smaller house within the estate in 1990, in his eighties and died following a fall in the grounds of his home at the Hollycombe estate on October 3, 2003.

■ More details of the collection and opening times can be found at www.hollycombe.co.uk, telephone 01428 724900. ●

Chapter 17

ABOVE: *Mariloo* carrying the royal headcode on May 26, 2011. EXBURY

ROYAL STEAM THROUGH THE RHODODENDRONS

Leopold David de Rothschild, a member of the Rothschild banking family, as might be expected had a distinguished career in finance. However, his greatest passions were classical music... and steam trains.

Leopold was born in London on May 12, 1927, the fourth and youngest child and second son of Lionel Nathan de Rothschild, and a great-great-grandson of Nathan Mayer Rothschild, who established the English branch of the family – and the bank – in the early 19th century.

Leo, as he was always known, was brought up mostly at Exbury House, on the estate that his father had acquired in late 1918, which is bounded by the New Forest, the Solent and the Beaulieu River. It was here that his father created the 250-acre woodland garden, famous for its rhododendrons and azaleas.

And it was here that, at the dawn of the 21st century, Leo created a 12¼in gauge railway for visitors to ride on through the stunningly beautiful grounds.

As a young boy Leo had witnessed the construction of Exbury's rock garden in the 1930s. Thought to be the largest manmade rock garden in Europe with rocks brought in from Pembrokeshire, a small railway and steam cranes were used to lift the stones into position.

Leo often joked that he was never given the train set he wanted as a boy; his father's passions were very much for rhododendrons and azaleas. Leo's brother, Eddy, took over the running of the gardens following the death of their father in 1942, and opened them to the public for the first time in 1955.

One of Leo's earliest memories was of the visit to the gardens of King George V and Queen Mary in 1931. Told to bow to the King – "who has a beard" – he duly bowed to everybody who might fit the description till His Majesty kindly stopped him with: "You carry on doing that my boy, and you'll be sick!"

Buoyed by a visit to Lord Braybrooke's railway at Audley End near Saffron Walden, Leo was encouraged to meet locomotive builder Trevor Stirland at Exmoor Steam Railway.

The pair discussed his plans for a railway at Exbury.

Leo's ambitions for a 2ft gauge railway around the historic gardens fell foul of the planners at the local district council, but he persevered with his steam dream.

Scaling down his plans to 12¼in gauge, and taking in a route that skirted the north-east corner of the gardens, which opened up previously unseen areas to visitors, he finally won council approval.

With a station (modelled on Aviemore) and engine shed designed by Dunbar-Nasmith, the railway eventually opened to the public in August 2001, with The Exmoor Steam Railway building its first steam engine, 0-6-2T *Rosemary*, and supplying a second, *Naomi*, in 2002. The pair were named after Leo's sisters.

Exmoor also built a four-wheeled diesel hydraulic locomotive, *Eddy*, for the garden line.

Sussex may have the Bluebell Railway, but Hampshire now had the Rhododendron Line.

The railway boosted Exbury's visitor numbers, which increased from less than 100,000 to close to 130,000 in 2002, its first full year of opening.

Leo was often found driving the steam engine, much to the enjoyment of Exbury's visitors. He had, he said, been 'bitten by the railway bug as a young boy – a disease for which there is no known cure.'

ROYAL SEALS OF APPROVAL

In 2004, Queen Elizabeth II visited the gardens and planted a yew tree. Four years later, she returned – to launch Exbury's third steam engine.

On Saturday, May 3, 2008, a woman among the visitors disguised by a grey raincoat and a headscarf turned out to be none other than Her Majesty.

The 82-year-old monarch was there to ride on the most unusual Royal Train of them all – in the cab of Exmoor-built 2-6-0 *Mariloo*, named after Leo's mother Marie-Louise.

In front of astonished onlookers, she sat in the fireman's seat alongside 80-year-old Leo, a personal friend, dressed in his Exbury Gardens Railway boiler suit and cap, as he drove the engine.

Exbury spokesman, Annie Bullen, said: "Members of the public were around at the time but it seems they didn't bat an eyelid at the Queen."

ABOVE: The Prince of Wales takes his seat in the cab of *Mariloo*, wearing an Exbury Garden Railway cap, during his visit on May 26, 2011. EXBURY

ABOVE: The Queen rides in the fireman's seat of *Mariloo* in 2008. EXBURY

LEFT: *Mariloo* runs through Exbury's American Garden with railway foreman, Ian Wilson, driving. EXBURY

ABOVE: *Mariloo*, with Prince Charles on the footplate, rounds the bend. EXBURY **BELOW MIDDLE:** *Rosemary* on the turntable. EXBURY **BELOW RIGHT:** A fallen Scots pine, which came down in gales, blocked the railway in Summer Lane Garden in early 2014. The wettest January in a century saw parts of the 2ft gauge line track underwater for the first time since its construction in 2001. EXBURY

ABOVE: Leopold de Rothschild names visiting new Exmoor Steam Railway engine *Black Beauty* on August 13, 2011.

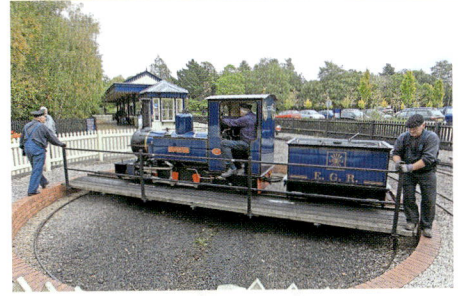

"She came with very few people and was dressed very anonymously. It was certainly as if she was travelling incognito and didn't want to be recognised."

Locomotive builder, Trevor Stirland, who rode on the coal tender behind *Mariloo* to check everything went according to plan, said: "She was very into it, very interested. She rode in the fireman's seat. She was very pleasant."

During her earlier visit in 2004, the monarch had ridden on the footplate of *Rosemary*.

In the year of the railway's 10th anniversary, her son Prince Charles, a renowned steam buff, and Camilla, Duchess of Cornwall, visited the line on May 25, 2011.

An anniversary gala over the weekend of August 13-14 included a re creation of the inaugural steaming of the railway back in 2001.

The anniversary celebrations were opened when the royal couple visited and met long-serving members of staff together with local schoolchildren, who had made collages with colourful flowers.

The Prince unveiled a plaque at Exbury Central Station before sitting in the driver's cab of *Mariloo* for a 20-minute journey over the Rhododendron Line. Again Leo drove the locomotive, with the Prince at his side.

The celebrations also saw Leo name a new 2-6-2 built by the Exmoor Steam Railway.

Black Beauty was accompanied by Exmoor shedmate 0-4-2T *Lorna Doone*. Visitors rode behind rare 'quintuple-heading' runs, when all three Exbury engines together with the two made journeys along the line.

Award-winning actresses Dames Judi Dench and Maggie Smith have also travelled on the 'Exbury Express'.

Leo, who never married, passed away at the age of 84 on April 19, 2012. However, the little railway that he dreamed building steams on, to entertain many more generations of visitors to this most colourful part of the Sunny South.

In summer 2016, Exbury Gardens applied to the New Forest National Park Authority for permission to extend the line by a quarter of a mile. •

RIGHT: Quintuple-header engines *Rosemary, Lorna Doone, Mariloo, Black Beauty* and *Naomi* provide a great spectacle as they pass along the Rhododendron Line on its 10th anniversary in 2011. EXBURY

Chapter 18

EXMOUTH GOES TO WAR!

Set in a tranquil East Devon valley of rare trees and immaculate formal gardens, Bicton Park might seem an unlikely setting for a railway of any sort, let alone one that used locomotives and carriages from a munitions factory. Yet stock from the Royal Arsenal at Woolwich was used to create a railway in this most beautiful of Sunny South settings.

The gardens at Bicton Park were once part of the much – larger Bicton Estate, and home to one of the most influential and wealthy families in Devon. On the death of Mark Rolle in 1907, the estate went to his nephew, Charles, the 21st Baron Clinton and shortly afterwards, Bicton's long era as a private retreat came to an end.

The manor was used during both world wars, firstly as a military hospital and later as a girls' school for evacuees from Sussex. Faced with postwar austerity, Lord Clinton decided it was no longer possible to run such a large place as a family home. He rented, and later sold, Bicton House and Home Farm to Devon County Council for use as an agricultural college.

However, the gardens were not included in the lease and it was more than 20 years later, at the end of the 1950s that Charles's great-grandson inherited Bicton Park and he restored the gardens to their prewar splendour, before opening them to the public in 1963.

At that time it was unusual to open gardens to the public without the assumption there would also be a grand house, but it was never going to be the case at Bicton, so in October 1961, it was decided that an additional attraction would be needed to woo visitors, and a passenger-carrying miniature railway seemed the perfect solution since it would appeal to young and old alike and allow less-able visitors to explore the outer reaches of the park with ease.

The original aim was to build a line in excess of a mile in length, but it was then realised that what appeared to be fairly innocuous gradients would be more than a match for any available 'miniature' locomotive. It was decided instead to look at the possibility of installing a narrow gauge railway – if a suitable locomotive and rolling stock could be found.

Around this time the vast Royal Arsenal munitions factory at Woolwich in east London was being downsized. Once the largest armaments factory in the world and the biggest ever factory in Britain, at its height during the First World War it employed 79,000 personnel, and covering almost 1300 acres, it had its own 70-mile 18in gauge system. This gauge was adopted by the military for dockyards, storage depots, factories and even temporary installations for moving men and supplies on battlefields. The Woolwich site alone had 64 narrow gauge locomotives, 2500 wagons, and 22 carriages.

NDG James, an engineer working on the survey of Bicton Park to determine possible routes, heard about an 18in gauge locomotive residing in the yard of EL Pitt & Co Ltd, in Brackley, Northamptonshire that might still be serviceable. Until its arrival there in 1960, the engine had worked at Woolwich Arsenal. When James visited Brackley in November 1961, he noted that it still carried the nameplate *Woolwich* as testimony to its illustrious but inglorious past.

Woolwich was a rather forlorn sight. It still sports an overtly large spark-arresting chimney of the sort characteristic of trains in early Western movies but obligatory for working in an explosives environment. It was not on rails and weeds entangled its wheels and coupling rods. But with a 0-4-0 wheel classification, a wheelbase of just 3ft 3in able to negotiate tight curves, and every indication of the ability to deliver adequate power to conquer Bicton's gradients, *Woolwich* seemed perfect for the job.

Confident that *Woolwich* could be returned to steam rails were ordered and sleepers were cut in the Bicton Estate sawmills from timber grown on the estate. The very first lengths of rails of the Bicton Woodland Railway were laid at the site of Bicton Gardens station on May 3, 1962.

ABOVE: Steam outline diesel *Sir Walter Raleigh* in action on the Bicton Woodlands Railway in 2016. BWR

104   Making Fresh Tracks to the Sunny South and West

ABOVE: Former Royal Arsenal pair *Woolwich* and *Carnegie* on the Bicton Woodlands Railway in December 1969. BWR
TOP MIDDLE: *Carnegie* in service at Bicton Park. BWR **TOP RIGHT:** *Woolwich* at Brackley around December 1961. BWR
ABOVE MIDDLE: *Woolwich* makes its first run at Bicton in May 1962. BWR
ABOVE RIGHT: *Woolwich* at the Royal Gunpowder Mills at Waltham Abbey in August 2008. ROBIN JONES

Meanwhile, *Woolwich* passed its steam trials at Brackley. Gone was the spark-arrester chimney replaced by something far more elegant and traditional. A few days after delivery to Bicton it was being driven on the short track at the hands of experienced railwayman, George Clarke.

Clarke had spent the whole of his working life on the railways, first with the Southern Railway and, following Nationalisation, on the Southern Region, completing almost 50 years of service. His in-depth knowledge and expertise was invaluable for a novice railway venture such as Bicton.

The search was now on for rolling stock. The unusual gauge meant choices were always going to be limited, but an approach made to WJK Davies who penned a monthly 'Light Railways Notes' feature in Railway World magazine revealed there might be surplus rolling stock at the Royal Arsenal.

Enquiries confirmed there was a number of trucks available, comprising some covered wagons and an open truck that had been used exclusively for transporting hay. However, under strict Royal Arsenal regulations any wagons used for transporting explosives would have to have their timber bodies burnt off before being offered for sale by tender. This would leave just the frames and bogies of the covered wagons, but the open truck that had not carried explosives could be delivered intact.

All the rolling stock had the same bogie, buffer and coupling patterns as Woolwich and that was to prove hugely convenient. In late June 1962 the open truck and six burned-out wagons arrived at Bicton.

It was also decided to add further interest and authenticity to the railway by adding a simple signalling system. Items including signal posts, levers, signal wire and point rods were purchased directly from the Southern Region when the Lympstone signalbox on the Exmouth branch closed in September 1962.

Although its performance exceeded expectations, *Woolwich* was of 'mature age' even in 1963, having been built in 1916, so it was agreed that at least one additional locomotive should be sourced to share the workload. In the first full season of operation, *Woolwich* clocked up more than 1500 miles. For its valiant efforts, the engine was rewarded with not one but three companions, all diesel locomotives from ex-War Department or Ministry of Works stock.

The first of these was a small 0-4-0 Ruston and Hornsby engine, rather utilitarian in appearance. It was given a makeover including a new engine casing and cab, together with a chimney to give the impression of being a steam locomotive, and appropriately named *Bicton*. Built in 1942 for the War Department, it saw service at Lion Brickworks in Scalford, near Melton Mowbray.

Next to arrive was an articulated diesel locomotive with an 0-4-0 + 0-4-0 wheel arrangement. Built in 1954 by Hunslet of Leeds and bearing the nameplate *Carnegie*, this 13¼-ton engine was affectionately referred to as 'the Beast'. With a similar background to *Woolwich*, *Carnegie* had come from the Royal Arsenal where it was named after the then Chief Superintendent. It was also the very last locomotive of any type to be delivered new to the arsenal.

Unlike *Bicton* no attempt was made to dress *Carnegie* to look like a steam locomotive. Its sheer size and presence as a true diesel-powered workhorse was sufficient to make it a new attraction on the line. It arguably provided more power (88hp) than was needed, despite the gradients, but because of the rarity of 18in gauge engines in serviceable condition, the opportunity to acquire it was just too good to miss.

Woolwich, *Bicton* and *Carnegie* would spend the next decade working the line together until engine number four arrived in 1974.

This too was a Ruston and Hornsby that began life as 24in gauge engine built in 1945 for the Ministry of Works. In 1959 it was acquired by the Fairy Glen Miniature Railway at New Brighton near Liverpool, which regauged it to 18in. On arrival at Bicton it was named *Budley*, but spent its latter years as a static display in a car park near the station.

It is unlikely that when the Bicton Woodland Railway was being conceived anyone would have imagined the legacy it would create in the history of narrow-gauge industrial railways. Without doubt, had the line not purchased the likes of Woolwich and Carnegie, these rare examples of 18in gauge workhorses would have been lost forever.

When Bicton Park Botanical Gardens was acquired by its present owners in 1998 the historical significance of what they had inherited was not underestimated, and so began a series of events that would see both locomotives not only preserved, but eventually repatriated to within a few miles of their original place of work.

With the new millennium came a new look for the line as significant investment was made in improving the experience for visitors. However, it also signalled the end of the line for *Woolwich* and *Carnegie* together with much of the rolling stock.

Carnegie had always been more of a locomotive than the railway really needed and its huge weight and power did little to ease running costs and track maintenance. By 2000, *Woolwich* was out of its 10-year boiler ticket and facing the prospect of major refurbishment. Together with *Budley*, the locomotives and much of the rolling stock was sold to the Royal Gunpowder Mills at Waltham Abbey in Essex, a 170-acre heritage site and visitor attraction commemorating more than 300 years of the production and development of explosives and rocket propellants before its closure in 1991.

In 2000, Alan Keef Ltd, of Ross-on-Wye, Herefordshire was commissioned to build a new engine, a 5.5-ton 0-4-0 diesel-powered replica tank engine locomotive for the line. It was named *Sir Walter Raleigh* in recognition of the area's close historical links with the Elizabethan explorer. The commission also included a set of four new 24-seater semi-enclosed passenger carriages.

In 2007, *Bicton* was sent to Alan Keef Ltd, for mechanical refurbishment and a rebuild that would complement the scale and appearance of *Sir Walter Raleigh*. Together, these locomotives share the workload providing a regular service for visitors throughout the year.

Woolwich is now being restored at the Crossness Engines Trust's works adjacent to the old Royal Ordnance factory at Woolwich, where it is planned to have it in steam once again. •

Chapter 19

REVIVING THE SOME[RSET & DORSET]

The Somerset & Dorset Railway Joint Railway is a real enigma. It was closed under Beeching on March 7, 1966 owing to comparatively poor patronage, it has since acquired legendary status: it appears that more books and DVDs have been published on it than any other British cross-country route. Much of its fame came from the 'Pines Express', which ran over it, carrying holidaymakers from Manchester Piccadilly and Liverpool lime Street to the Sunny South. Today, three sections of it are back in railway use, while restoration continues at others.

The Somerset & Dorset Railway – almost always referred to as "the S&D" – is one of the best-loved of Britain's lost lines. Its hallmarks were doubleheaded holiday trains to Bournemouth climbing over the Mendip Hills that were steam hauled to the end.

Its main line linked Bath Green Park to Bournemouth West via the Mendip Hills, with its principal branch, the company's original main line, from Evercreech Junction to Burnham-on-Sea, and a shorter branch to Bridgwater.

It was never a high-speed line: its winter business was carrying freight and local passenger traffic over the Mendips, but in the summer season it came into its own, carrying a heavy service of Saturday holiday trains from northern towns to Bournemouth.

These trains brought unusual traffic combinations to the route, and the home fleet of BR Standard 5MTs 4-6-0s and 9F 2-10-0s were augmented by strangers such as Bulleid West Country light Pacifics from the Sunny South.

As assistance over the steep gradients was usually required, the original S&D class 7F 2-8-0s – two of which survive, No. 53808 at the West Somerset Railway and No. 53809 at the Midland Railway-Butterley – were pressed into service to assist, or handle lighter trains on their own.

The S&D was often referred to as "the Slow and Dirty", or "the Slow and Doubtful", but it always commanded a considerable loyalty from railway enthusiasts, especially as it passed through photogenic hilly countryside and the spectacular sight of its doubleheaded trains. When it closed in 1966 it was widely mourned. Here, the work of legendary photographers, most notably Ivo Peters, has left an outstanding record for both those who knew the line pre-1966 and those coming to it since.

The route remained steam-worked almost entirely until closure, though some diesel multiple units ran over the line on a couple of excursions in the final years. After closure, diesels worked demolition trains, and some diesel workings ran to Blandford Forum after the line had closed.

THE 'PINES EXPRESS'

The 'Pines Express ran daily between 1910 and 1967, although it wasn't until September 26, 1927 that it carried that name for the first time. It had been named after the pine trees growing in the chines around Bournemouth.

When the service first ran, unnamed, on October 1, 1910, it was a joint effort by the Midland Railway and LNWR, introduced to compete with a LSWR/GWR service between Birkenhead and Bournemouth.

The final 'Pines Express' to run over the S&D was on September 1962, hauled by

ABOVE: At Midsomer Norton on March 12, 1955, S&D 7F 2-8-0 No. 53800 collects loaded coal wagons from the Down line. It had arrived at the Up Mome signal with the 6.05am Templecombe-Bath freight, leaving it there while shunting. LMS 'Jinty' 0-6-0T No.47557 (hidden to the left) had drawn these out from Norton Hill Colliery. It later ran back (bunker-first) to Radstock attached to the front of No. 53800. IVO PETERS, COURTESY JULIAN PETERS

ABOVE: Ivo Peters' wonderful 60-year-old photo of the northern entry to Chilcompton Tunnel cutting reveals both the current end of land being leased by the revivalist trust and also the site of its proposed run-round and platform, earmarked for the bottom of the field to the right. On May 19, 1956, BR Standard 5MT 4-6-0 No. 73047 heads an eight-coach relief 'Pines Express' – the 10.30am Liverpool Lime Street-Bournemouth West, no assisting engine needed. IVO PETERS COLLECTION; COURTESY JULIAN PETERS

106 Making Fresh Tracks to the Sunny South and West

RSET & DORSET

ABOVE: The way it was: a summer Saturdays-only Nottingham-Bournemouth train passes Midsomer Norton South on August 4, 1962, with Somerset & Dorset 7F 2-8-0 No. 53808 in charge. DAVE COBBE COLLECTION/RAILPHOTOPRINTS.CO.UK

9F No. 92220 *Evening Star*, which in 1960 was the last steam locomotive built for BR.

The train was then diverted over ex-GWR metals via Oxford, Reading, Basingstoke and Southampton. In 1964 a 'Pines Express' became the last passenger service worked over the Didcot, Newbury & Southampton Railway before that line closed to all traffic between 1965-67.

From October 4, 1965, the 'Pines Express' was extended to Poole, but the last train was run on March 4, 1967.

That would not be the end of a Sunny South legend. InterCity (British Rail) revived the name for several years as part of the CrossCountry network, but all named CrossCountry trains finally lost their names as part of Virgin CrossCountry's Operation Princess in 2002.

THE S&D MENDIP MAIN LINE PROJECT

For decades after the 1966 closure, most of the S&D route succumbed to either redevelopment for new uses or reabsorption by nature or farming. As we have seen, only at Radstock did one preservation project establish a foothold in the early 1970s, using the stub to Writhlington Colliery. With the demise of the North Somerset Coalfield in 1973, the Somerset & Dorset Railway Trust's project could not compete with redevelopment pressures, and its exodus to Washford station on the West Somerset Railway followed in 1975-76.

It then seemed like the S&D would never enjoy anything like the revivals springing up elsewhere. The 1980s and 1990s saw yet more destruction of the infrastructure, albeit with notable exceptions such as Charlton Viaduct and Bath Road Viaduct at Shepton Mallet. From the mid-1990s onwards, the off-road cycling movement laid claim to many sections of trackbed and, with Lottery and local authority support, significant lengths were at least saved for public access. This included much-needed protection for disused viaducts, tunnels and bridges.

In 2016, restoration activity of varying types by heritage groups exists at four sites on the S&D 'main line' from Bath to Bournemouth

ABOVE: The 'Pines Express' relief nearing Shoscombe & Single Hill Halt in 1959, with the 10.20am Liverpool Lime Street to Bournemouth West following 25 minutes behind the packed main train, headed by LMS Fowler 7F 2-8-0 No. 53807 piloting Bulleid West Country light Pacific No. 34040 *Crewkerne*. BEN BROOKSBANK*

ABOVE: Now on static display inside the National Railway Museum at York, *Evening Star* hauled the last 'Pines Express' over the Mendip Hills. ROBIN JONES

Making Fresh Tracks to the Sunny South and West

ABOVE: First steam at Midsomer Norton since 1966: In July 2005, visiting LMS 'Jinty' 0-6-0T No. 47493 masqueraded as 47496, a Radstock locomotive. JULIAN JEFFERSON

BELOW: Midsomer Norton looking southwards on September 11, 1961. This scene was mostly restored by 2016. JOHN EYERS; SOUTH WESTERN CIRCLE, EYERS COLLECTION

ABOVE: Representing two scrapped Somerset & Dorset Sentinels in LMS black livery, No. 7109 stands alongside Midsomer Norton South signalbox. Antiques expert Paul Atterbury officially renamed *Joyce* at Midsomer Norton on July 9. BOB EDWARDES

BELOW: On Sunday, March 6, 2016 the exact 50th anniversary of the closure of the Somerset & Dorset system, visiting LMS 3F 'Jinty' 0-6-0 No. 47406 blasts away from Midsomer Norton station with the 1pm departure, while Sentinel No. 7109 waits in the Up platform. JULIAN JEFFERSON

– Midsomer Norton, Shillingstone, Spetisbury and Midford, while private owners at Masbury station are also sympathetic to the railway's heritage.

However, the S&D Mendip Main Line Project is the most advanced. That project title implies grander ambitions than simply restoring Midsomer Norton station and a short section of running line. Here we look at the achievements over 20 years, and consider what greater aspirations are being entertained. How realistic are they, and how true they can be to the historic S&D spirit?

RESURRECTION STARTS

In the early 1990s, a new S&D group – the Somerset & Dorset Railway Trackbed Trust disaffected by the original S&D Trust's exile to the WSR, sought safeguarding of the S&D route and infrastructure for sympathetic uses, including any potential railway presence.

This strategy was largely dependent on the goodwill of landowners and local authorities. In 1996 S&DRTT seized a rare opportunity and secured a three-year lease on one of the few surviving stations, at Midsomer Norton, and staved off yet another threat of redevelopment. At that stage, there was little prospect of an operating railway, but the station became the HQ and base for the embryonic project.

In 1998, the newly emerging Bath & North East Somerset Council gained control of the station site and the prospect of longer-term security of tenure by S&DRTT seemed to evaporate amid rumours of sale and redevelopment. By getting recognition of the tourism value of the project, securing a regeneration grant from the regional development authority, and submitting a planning application, the by-then-renamed Somerset & Dorset Railway Heritage Trust overcame the council's resistance and obtained a 25-year lease in 2001 (since extended to 99 years). By that time it was already reaching out to trackbed owners further south in anticipation of extending a running line towards Chilcompton and operating public trains.

While Midsomer Norton was an iconic location, it has clear physical limitations – not least the trackbed being 'book-ended' by the missing Silver Street bridge north of the station and the landfilled Chilcompton Tunnel cutting to the south. The unrelenting 1-in-53 gradient south of the station would also present operational challenges. Yet it would have been tragic to give up on what was then the only available S&D site because of a few constraints. The lease covered only 300yds of trackbed, barely enough to contain the 'station limits', let alone give a steam train a decent outing.

The station restoration itself would occupy the trust for years to come, but sights were soon set on southward extension of the running lines – plural, because the aim was always to recreate a significant length of double track, partly to remain historically true, but also for eventual S&D-type train operations on both Down and Up lines. To date, double track only extends for about 600yds – round the corner and out of sight of the station. The priority now is to extend one (Down) running line southwards as far as the trackbed is clear.

Reassembling a railway from fragmented ownership has proved a serious challenge, with three separate parcels beyond the station for the first mile. Each lease secured has been followed by successful planning applications and brisk construction.

Negotiation of the third lease – with the Duchy of Cornwall – has been especially protracted, the breakthrough finally coming in November 2015 and a planning application for track-laying being approved in February 2016. Completion of this extension will give the project the 'magic mile' before more substantial obstructions to further expansion.

The newly leased trackbed was cleared and regraded by May 2016 and the first panel of track laid during June. It is planned to complete tracklaying by the winter of 2016-17 and open the extension to trains in time for the 2017 season.

A WORKING RAILWAY AGAIN

Running closely behind extension of the running line has come the establishment of regular train operations since 2009 – through the revived historic S&DJR Company. There have been interruptions for various reasons, including motive power (un)availability, recruiting and training sufficient staff as well as the need to meet the many ORR regulations.

Diesel haulage has been the norm, using the trust's Class 08 shunter D4095, but occasional hiring of steam locomotives from 2005 onwards has naturally proved a great attraction.

That year, history was made when visiting LMS 'Jinty' 0-6-0T No. 47493 from the Spa Valley Railway, masquerading as No. 47496, a Radstock locomotive, became the first steam locomotive to run on the S&D since 1966.

The next big step here, however, was for Midsomer Norton to have a 'S&D' locomotive of its own. Its first resident steam locomotive – former Croydon Gas Works' 28-ton Sentinel 0-4-0VB No. 7109 *Joyce* – attained its boiler ticket in February 2016, just ahead of the S&D's 50th anniversary commemoration.

Joyce may never have run on the S&D in its working life, but is representative of a distinct type that did.

No. 7109 was the first of eight locomotives of this type, built by the Sentinel Waggon Works at Shrewsbury in 1927, with a pair of transverse engines at the front and a vertical water-tubed boiler at the rear of the cab. It uses both gears and chains to transfer the drive to the axles and its central section houses a 4in-thick cast-iron water tank to provide ballast as well as hold water.

Test results gave sufficient confidence for two similar units to be purchased by the Somerset & Dorset Joint Railway Company for use at Radstock: built in 1929, the pair were built to a reduced loading gauge as they had to pass under Tyning Arch, which had only 10ft 10in clearance.

Given the S&DJR numbers 101 and 102, they replaced three older Highbridge-built saddle tanks, Nos. 24A, 25A and 45A, for shunting coal wagons on the colliery branches around Radstock.

They were taken into LMS stock in 1930 and renumbered 7190–7191 and became 47190-47191 under British Railways. Their bell-shaped front-ends made them an eye-catching locomotive in the Ian Allan locospotters books of the day.

No. 47191 was withdrawn in 1959 from Bath Green Park and No. 47190 in 1961 from Bristol (Barrow Road). Sadly, both were scrapped.

In 1968, No. 7109 *Joyce* became part of Alan Bloom's Bressingham Steam Museum collection, and later the private Shropshire Collection of industrial locomotives, later being acquired by the Somerset & Dorset Locomotive Company Limited, which moved it to Tyseley Locomotive Works to begin restoration. In December 2004, it was bought by a consortium of 18 members of the Somerset & Dorset Railway Heritage Trust, the group that has restored Midsomer Norton station, and in September 2010 was acquired by one of the members, Andy Chapman from Chippenham, and his colleague Nigel Dickinson from Bath.

On February 18, 2016, it emerged from the station shed, 56 years after it retired in 1960, and steamed in public over the weekend on February 27-28.

No. 7109 differs from the Radstock Sentinels in several respects. The SDJR pair had a lower cab roof, square cab windows, oval as opposed to round buffers, an injector as opposed to a cab-mounted boiler feed pump, a deeper step into the cab, a flat (as opposed to curved) sloping plate for the lower cab rear panel and more elaborate lamp brackets.

The chain/axle adjustment radius rods linked to the rear on the Radstock pair but to the front on No. 7109. The leading engine mount is visible at the front on No. 7109 but not on the SDJR versions.

However, these differences are comparatively minor, and No. 7109 is set to appear not only as *Joyce*, its correct identity, but as No. 47109 (a BR-style number incorporating its works number) and No. 47189 (the number before Radstock's No. 47190).

It has been fitted with vacuum brakes so it can haul coaches. Tests showed that the original pair were capable of hauling 1000 tons on the flat.

So, with hired-in Jinty 0-6-0 No. 47406 from the Great Central Railway, the Midsomer Norton project in 2016 staged two 50th anniversary-of-closure weekends with two representative steam locomotives working on the actual S&D for the first time in more than 50 years. This was indeed a remarkable threshold for the project.

One BR Mk.1 SK carriage is operational, with a second, a BSK, rapidly being restored, and the loan of a third under negotiation, to make up a typical three-coach local set in BR(MR) maroon livery. A second set in BR(SR) green is a longer-term aspiration. A collection of brake vans and assorted wagons enable works trains and demonstration freights to be assembled.

ABOVE: The interior of Midsomer Norton station's Anderson shelter. JULIAN JEFFERSON

MORE ATTRACTIONS AT MIDSOMER NORTON

Apart from the railway, locomotives and rolling stock, the Midsomer Norton set-up currently includes two static museums – an S&D-themed one in the former stables and a military-themed one in a Second World War pillbox, a shop in the station, a workshop in the goods shed, a buffet coach, the renowned greenhouse and gardens, a lineside walk, a nature reserve and wildlife habitats along the railway corridor.

Creation of a depot on the Somervale sidings site south of the station will offer visitors the chance to see restoration work on locos and rolling stock. As well as running routine train operations, the project stages regular special events, notably at Easter, midsummer, the national Heritage Open Days (early September) and Christmas. Recent themed events have included the First World War, the Home Guard and transport heritage.

DEVELOPMENT PLANS

So, what are the prospects for further development in the short-, medium- and longer-term? In 2016 both the next line extension and the Somervale depot scheme

ABOVE: The permanent-way team pauses after installing the first rail and fishplate on June 20, 2016. JOHN EYERS; SOUTH WESTERN CIRCLE, EYERS COLLECTION

RIGHT: The 2016 extension: Looking northwards from the toe of Chilcompton Tunnel cutting on May 22, 2016, after the trackbed regrading. PETER RUSSELL

ABOVE: Yugoslavian-built pirate copy Southern railway 'USA tank' at Shillingstone in early 2016. PROJECT 62
RIGHT: Shillingstone station refurbished in Southern Railway colours. GILLETT'S CROSSING*

were under implementation. A regular timetable of public trains is operating for the 2016 season, albeit only monthly until more safety critical staff to cover weekly operations are recruited and trained. A one-mile running line by the 2017 season should place the project on a par with other short heritage railways.

The next infrastructure scheme will be a run-round and platform near Chilcompton Tunnel, requiring a level site on the Down side of the 1-in-53. This facility will increase operational flexibility considerably, perhaps allowing operation of two trains simultaneously.

Although the trust's and the company's main energies have recently focused on the operational railway, they have long been exploring the potential for more substantial expansion both southward and northwards. It is common knowledge that this would require overcoming major physical obstacles and raising serious capital funding well beyond anything achieved so far.

Most initiatives are planned, some reactive. A 2013 appeal to buy Masbury station was a brave, if unsuccessful, attempt to capture another iconic S&D site when an unexpected opportunity arose. This would have secured a second base for longer-term development, admittedly stretching volunteer and financial resources, but such openings are too rare to ignore. It could also have enabled a pincer movement to link the two bases in due course.

In 2016, the trust launched two funding appeals – the first for track materials to complete the latest extension, the second to create the Somervale running and maintenance depot. This will provide vital covered accommodation for historic locomotives and stock, as well as space for engineering and other activities currently occupying the station.

To extend southwards beyond the first mile requires firstly the removal of the Chilcompton Tunnel landfill, something akin to the Bluebell Railway's monumental work on Imberhorne Cutting, albeit about one third of the size. A feasibility study is an essential prerequisite, and implementation could cost at least £1 million. Then there is the occupation of both tunnel bores by a local gun club on a lease from the former BR Property Board.

If both the cutting and one tunnel could be re-opened, the trackbed further south is

relatively unobstructed as far as the former site of Chilcompton station, apart from the recently under-filled Baker Robinson's bridge. Land ownership is again fragmented, although the curve between the tunnels and Redan Bridge is in a single holding.

There are some significant obstructions through the rest of Chilcompton but a clearer run through Moorewood to Binegar. Binegar station again presents some built obstructions, but a largely clear section ensues to Masbury and on to Shepton Mallet.

The Mendip District Local Plan has helpfully safeguarded the trackbed for 'sustainable transport' uses throughout its jurisdiction.

Northbound down to Radstock, the railway corridor is in council hands as a linear park with a cycleway, which could be realigned alongside a single-track railway.

Two major bridges (Silver Street and Welton Road) are missing. Replacing the former would require substantial alterations to the raised highway and cost upwards of £500,000.

The Welton Road case is simpler, with plenty of headroom between the remaining embankments, but probably with a similar cost to Silver Street. From Welton Road to the centre of Radstock, the trackbed is clear.

Regaining access through Radstock would be complex but could offer the tantalising prospect of a link to the extant but mothballed North Somerset Railway line to Frome and thence the national network. This would necessitate reinstating the notorious level crossing and running alongside Waterloo Road, plus a tight reverse curve through a coal waste tip and Ludlows Colliery. The trust has sought safeguarding of this narrow corridor by the authorities, as part of regeneration plans.

IDEALISM AND REALISM
The project is under no illusions about the physical and financial hurdles to major extensions in either direction.

Serious consideration would probably need at least a 30-year development plan to reconnect Radstock with Shepton, big capital to match, and the backing of appropriate authorities. The current generation of activists will mostly be long gone by then, but supporters need to hold on to the dream. Meanwhile, the trust keeps planning for a greater S&D, but for now consolidation is the key – a viable, operational, albeit short railway conveying something of the S&D spirit.

For more information about the project and how you can help visit www.sdjr.co.uk

THE S&D REVIVAL IN DORSET
The Shillingstone Railway Project is in many ways a counterpart on the southern section of the S&D to the more advanced Midsomer Norton scheme.

After the closure of Shillingstone station along with the main line in 1966, Dorset County Council purchased the trackbed for a proposed village bypass.

Afterwards, various furniture manufacturing companies were sited in the station yard over the years, occupying industrial buildings constructed in the late 1970s, some of them making partial use of the station building.

By December 2002, the bypass plan had been shelved and the station was unoccupied. Dorset County Council decided to dispose of the redundant station, and, after protracted negotiations, the North Dorset Railway Trust took over the lease in July 2005, with a view to reopening the station as a heritage railway venue.

Restoration work began in 2003 and has continued steadily ever since.

In 2009, 210ft of the Up main track through the station was laid and ballasted. When it was moved out of its shed that year, a Ruston & Hornsby diesel shunter (since sold) became the first standard gauge locomotive on the Somerset & Dorset main line south of the Mendips since the demolition train departed in July 1967, exactly 42 years previously.

Progress in 2010 included acquiring a tracked Priestman Mustang excavator, finishing construction of the Up platform wall, re-grading of the cattle dock trackbed and preparations for tracklaying, and the connection of the station to the mains drainage system.

In August 2015, low-cabbed Class 08 shunter No. 08995 was bought for future use at the station, where it is intended to add another 1200ft of running line and a loop.

The station building currently houses a waiting/refreshment room, shop and offices. The former parcel shed contains a small museum. The south end of the Up platform has been rebuilt and the picnic area above landscaped, while the bicycle shed has been rebuilt from its foundation ring.

STEAM BACK AT SHILLINGSTONE

A pair of 'USA tanks' have arrived on Somerset & Dorset metals in time for the 50th anniversary of the closure of the system.

Project 62, which owns Yugoslavian-built 'pirate' copies of USATC 0-6-0Ts Nos. 30075 and 30076, reunited them at the North Dorset Railway Trust's headquarters at Shillingstone station in January 2016.

Both of the locomotives were built to the design of the original USA tanks that were introduced during the Second World War and were used both in the UK and mainland Europe.

No. 30075 was constructed in 1960 and worked at the Store Steel works in Yugoslavia from where it was originally purchased for preservation in 1990 and transported to the UK. It was returned to working order and initially saw service on the Swanage Railway.

Not currently serviceable and requiring work on its boiler, firebox and running gear, assessments will now be undertaken to see how to progress the work in order to get it into operational condition as soon as possible.

No. 30076, which was built in 1954, was similarly in industrial use in Bosnia Herzegovina, after Project 62 members from the ArcelorMittal Zenica works acquired it in 2006. It has been estimated that it will cost at least £50,000 to return this locomotive to working order and this will be a longer-term project. Both locomotives were allocated as Class 62 locomotives in their industrial use, hence the name of the owning group.

Both locomotives carry mock BR numbers, which would have been the next in sequence of the USA class, an original example of which, as we saw earlier, can be seen running on the Kent & East Sussex Railway.

The pair were loaded and moved to their new home on January 20. No. 30075 was collected from the Great Central Railway's (Nottingham) base at Ruddington while 30076 was moved from secure storage in the West Midlands, with both locomotives coming together for the first time in several years at Rownhams Services on the M27. The last time they were together was at the Mid Hants Railway.

Shares are still available in both locomotives and details can be found on Project 62's website at www.project62.supanet.com

Details of the North Dorset Railway Trust and the Shillingstone Station Project can be found at www.shillingstone-railway-project.org.uk The station site is normally open on Saturday, Sunday and Wednesdays.

THE GARTELL LIGHT RAILWAY

Situated just south of Templecombe, where the Somerset & Dorset Joint Railway crossed the Southern Railway's main line from Waterloo to Exeter, the 2ft gauge Gartell Light Railway has been running trains over a section of the S&D trackbed for the last quarter of a century, although the origin of the line goes back further than that.

In 1984 agricultural engineer, John Gartell, and his father, Alan, acquired a job lot of 2ft gauge locomotives, wagons and track panels from agricultural firm Fisons on the Somerset Levels. Their intention had been to construct a small private railway, probably no more than 200yds in length.

Gradually track length increased beyond that originally planned. By this time John and his father had been joined by a number of local enthusiasts and the line found its way on to the nearby S&D formation, where further track was laid.

In response to public demand, the first tentative open day took place in 1990 and proved a great success. Since then the story of the Gartell Light Railway has been one of constant development and improvement.

The small industrial diesels acquired from Fisons have long since gone and the motive power register now includes two steam locomotives, an 0-4-2T and an 0-4-0T+T, both built specially to cope with the steep gradients and sharp curves that are a feature of the line. They are joined on front-line services by a Bo-Bo diesel hydraulic that bears more than a passing resemblance to a Crompton 33/2, the so-called 'Slim Jim' version of the class built specially for the Hastings line with its restricted clearances. There are also two smaller diesel locomotives, normally used only for shunting or hauling works trains.

Gone, too, are the open-sided coaches, which came to the GLR from a Butlin's holiday camp, and for several years constituted the line's passenger fleet. These have been replaced by fully enclosed coaches built in the GLR's extensive workshops and turned out in contrasting liveries to reflect the line's S&D heritage. Set 100, with wooden bodies and finished in Southern Railway malachite green, forms the 'Pines Express'.

The first rake of all-steel coaches (set 101), in Midland red, was constructed in 1998. Finally, a second batch of all-steel coaches (set 102), this time finished in S&D dark blue, entered service at the beginning of the 2002 season. Two of the three sets have a compartment specially adapted to accommodate a visitor in a wheelchair.

Goods rolling stock includes a variety of vans and open wagons, a milk tanker, a bogie permanent-way crew and tool van and two brake vans. Some of the goods stock has been sign-written with the names of local firms. Although used from time to time to make up a demonstration goods train, the various vans and wagons serve more than just a cosmetic purpose and are frequently used in works trains.

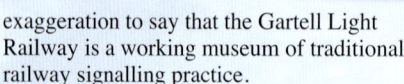

NORTH TO TEMPLECOMBE
The GLR is unusual in that the line is Y-shaped. From the main terminus at Common Lane the line climbs steeply, first at 1-in-32 and then at 1-in-50, through a series of curves to join the S&D trackbed at Pinesway Junction.

From here, depending on the timetable in use, trains can either continue south along the former S&D route to the line's southern terminus at Park Lane, or the loco can run-round and the train can head north towards Templecombe, crossing over the branch from Common Lane by means of a flyover.

The latter option, the so-called 'double cross' timetable, is the one invariably used when the railway is open to the public. This has the advantage of permitting what may well be a unique feature in the heritage sector: two trains departing simultaneously and running side by side, albeit for only a short distance. From Pinesway Junction station, one train descends at 1-in-50 on its way back to Common Lane, while the other climbs at 1-in-38 along the S&D trackbed towards Tower View, the line's northern terminus. Tower View, 37 miles south of Bath Green Park, takes its name from Alfred's Tower, a folly at Stourhead, visible on the northern horizon nine miles away. At Tower View, where there is a seven-lever ground frame, the locomotive runs round and the train proceeds non-stop to Park Lane, the site of a level crossing in S&D days, where there is a five-lever ground frame. Here the loco runs-round once more before heading north on the final stage of its journey back to Common Lane. At Pinesway Junction station it halts briefly and then departs at the same time as the following service from Common Lane, the two trains running side by side before crossing one over the other at Pinesway Flyover.

SIGNALLING EXCELLENCE
First-time visitors to the GLR are invariably astonished by the number and variety of working signals. Of Southern and Great Western provenance, they are operated from two full-size, fully operational signalboxes at Common Lane and Pinesway Junction respectively. Apart from the run-round at Tower View and Park Lane, every train movement is governed by the signalmen on duty in the two 'boxes. It is therefore no exaggeration to say that the Gartell Light Railway is a working museum of traditional railway signalling practice.

Of the two signal boxes the one at Pinesway Junction is the more interesting. Built in 1892 by the LSWR as a Type 5 with a ground-level frame, it controlled the farm crossing at Wyke between Sherborne and Yeovil Junction on the Waterloo-Exeter main line. After becoming redundant in 1964, it served as a farm building before being rescued by GLR volunteers in 1993. Extended by six feet and equipped with a 30-lever McKenzie & Holland frame that was once used on the Becton Gasworks railway in East London, it replaced the original seven-lever box at Pinesway, as the station was then called, in 1995.

All 30 levers at Pinesway Junction are in use and during the course of a normal open day the signalman there is required to make some 900 lever movements, arguably making the 'box the busiest in the entire UK heritage sector.

Due recognition was received in 2014 when Pinesway Junction signalbox and the impressive five-arm gantry it controls were awarded a Highly Commended certificate as part of the National Heritage Awards scheme. Just opposite the 'box, on the other side of the line, the restored Whitaker tablet-exchanging apparatus from Stalbridge has been erected, providing another reminder of the GLR's S&D heritage.

Built by GLR volunteers in traditional style, the signal box at Common Lane is equipped with an 18-lever frame made for the LSWR by Stevens & Son in 1896 and became operational in 1991. Offering a splendid overview of the terminus, it is only marginally less busy than its counterpart at Pinesway Junction, since it controls all arrivals and departures, as well as empty stock and light engine movements as trains are shunted from Platform 1, the arrival platform, to Platform 2 ready for departure.

On public open days, the railway is open at 10am, and an intensive three-train service is operated with the first train of the day departing at 10.30am. Thereafter trains depart every 20 minutes throughout the day, with the last service leaving at 4.30pm. The programme of public open days follows a regular pattern. The first of the season is on Easter Monday, followed by the two May bank holiday Mondays. The line is then open on the last Sunday in June and July, August bank holiday Monday and the last Sundays in September and October. An hourly service is also run on two days in February when the GLR hosts a model railway exhibition.

On open days the line is signposted from the A357 at Templecombe and the A30 at Henstridge.

MIDFORD AND SPETISBURY
TWO smaller restoration projects are based at Midford station on the northern section of the S&D, and Spetisbury station on the southern.

Midford station is now owned by the New Somerset and Dorset Railway, which was formed in 2009 with the very ambitious aim of restoring the complete S&D from Bath to Bournemouth.

It has plans to rebuild the station building and re-lay the track, when the Two Tunnels Greenway cycleway, which passes through the site, will be diverted or accommodated. The site has been cleared to uncover the remains of the old station.

At Spetisbury in May 2012 volunteers started to clear the overgrown and derelict station site, working under licence from landowners Dorset County Council.

The long-term ambition is to restore the platforms and reconstruct the buildings as close to the originals as possible, to form a railway heritage centre based around this rare surviving Dorset Central Railway station, subject to agreement with local residents and authorities as well as the usual planning permission. The Spetisbury Station Project has no intention to lay any track and supports the Dorset County Council Trailway, which uses the trackbed between the platforms at Spetisbury.

A shot-term goal is to erect a small timber building on the Down platform, which will act as a cafe and information point for the station and Trailway, in keeping with the site's railway heritage. ●

RIGHT: Spetisbury station today. The station was opened on September 1, 1860 and was closed in 1956 as part of an economy campaign. SPETISBURY STATION PROJECT

Chapter 20

LEFT: Former Groudle Glen Railway Bagnall 2-4-0T *Polar Bear* in action at Amberley on July 13, 2014. CLIFF THOMAS

CHALK, STEAM AND A POLAR BEAR!

Amberley Museum and Heritage Centre, which was set up in a chalk quarry in Amberley, West Sussex, in 1979, boasts one of the most important collections of industrial railway equipment in the UK.

The Amberley Musuem railway boasts an extensive and varied collection of locomotives and rolling stock ranging from 18in gauge to 5ft 3in gauge, and runs passenger trains using a mixture of steam, internal combustion and battery-electric traction.

Its site was originally a chalk quarry operated by Pepper & Sons, with its own internal standard gauge line linked to the LBSCR at Amberley station. The track was lifted when the site was abandoned in the late 1960s.

A registered charity, the museum was founded in 1979 by the Southern Industrial History Centre Trust and has previously been known as the Amberley Working Museum, Amberley Chalk Pits Museum or plain Amberley Museum.

At first, a small industrial railway was envisaged, operating typical narrow gauge industrial trains. The first locomotive to arrive on site was the Motor Rail Hibberd 1980/1936, donated to the museum by Southern Water and previously used at the city of Chichester's sewage works at Apuldram.

The first locomotive to run under its own power at Amberley was Peter Smith's Ruston & Hornsby four-wheeled diesel mechanical shunter No. 187081 of 1937.

In 1982, the local Thakeham Tiles Co replaced its short narrow gauge railway in favour of a conveyor-belt system. The company donated the entire railway, track, wagons and locomotives to the museum. Some of the track, one of the locomotives and the wagons are still in use at Amberley today.

In 1982, the collection of industrial and narrow gauge items formerly kept at Brockham Museum's site near Dorking came to Amberley. Brockham Museum's collection dated back to 1960, when the Dorking Greystone Lime Co of Betchworth, Surrey, disposed of its railway stock and the company's general manager, Major Taylerson, was keen to see the locomotives preserved.

The London Area Group of the Narrow Gauge Railway Society purchased one of the pair of 3ft 2¼in gauge Fletcher Jennings tank locomotive, *Townsend Hook*. Initially this was placed on display at Sheffield Park station on the embryonic Bluebell Railway, while efforts were made to find an alternative home.

A site was found at a disused chalk pit in Brockham, only a stone's throw from *Townsend Hook's* old stomping ground at Betchworth, and the locomotive moved there in 1962, when two Orenstein & Koppel diesels were acquired, No. 6 *Monty* and No. 7, later named *The Major* in honour of Major Taylerson.

In 1967 the now-flagship of the museum fleet was acquired, 1905-built Bagnall 2-4-0T No. 1781 of 1905 *Polar Bear* from the then-closed but since revived 2ft gauge Groudle Glen Railway, a seaside line on the east coast of the Isle of Man.

By the early 1980s the limited access to the site forced a transfer away from Brockham, and Amberley was deemed the best location.

A 2ft gauge running line was built at Amberley from 1982-84 running along one side of the pit between Amberley and Brockham stations. The inaugural train was hauled by *Polar Bear*, which had been returned to steam.

In the mid-1980s Decauville 0-4-0WT *Barbouilleur* entered service, and following *Polar Bear's* boiler being condemned around 1987, was the sole steam locomotive available until 1993. *Polar Bear* re-entered traffic in its original yellow livery with a new boiler in 1993, and was joined that same year by Bagnall 0-4-0ST No. 2067 of 1918 *Peter*. The latter was a 3ft gauge machine for the Canadian Forestry Commission but was returned to Bagnall after the First World War and was then rebuilt to 2ft gauge and purchased by the Cliffe Hill Granite Co in Leicestershire, where it worked until 1949 when it was stored out of service. It was then acquired by the Narrow Gauge Railway Society and first went to Brockham.

The main line runs from Amberley station near the museum entrance along the side of the pit past the De Witt lime kilns to Brockham station. From Brockham the line curves round the top of the pit and passes the running shed and ends up at Cragside station, across the pit from Brockham.

The running line was extended with the extension round the top of the pit to the new Cragside station opening in mid-2007.

The industrial non-passenger lines connect to the main line at Brockham station, which has a small siding on Platform 2, as well as the LBSCR ticket office from Hove station. In addition there is the Betchworth Hall shed, used for the restoration of *Townsend Hook*; it will eventually will be used as a museum to display the Dorking Greystone Lime Co exhibits.

The railway holds its annual gala weekend on the second weekend of July each year, in addition to two industrial trains days in April and October.

The railway made an appearance in the 1985 James Bond film, A View To A Kill, with the tunnel appearing as the entrance to Mainstrike Mine. Two engines went to Pinewood Studios along with several wagons to film scenes 'inside the mine'.

In 2010, four of the museum's Hudson flat wagons were sent to the same studios for use in the film Captain America: The First Avenger.

■ More details of the museum and its railway can be found at www.amberleynarrowgauge.co.uk ●

ABOVE: The Hampshire Narrow Gauge Railway Trust's Hunslet 0-4-0ST *Cloister* and Bagnall 0-4-0ST *Wendy*, both former residents of Amberley, revisited the line for the July 12-13, 2014 gala weekend. *Wendy* is seen pulling away from Brockham station with the freight set. CLIFF THOMAS

Making Fresh Tracks to the Sunny South and West 113

Chapter 21

IT'S A SMALL WORLD!

Peco is famous for its model railway products. However, the company also runs its own passenger-carrying steam railway at its headquarters at Beer in East Devon.

ABOVE: Single Fairlie 2-4-4T *Claudine* built at Beer Works in 2005 heads past a display of the Beer Heights fleet. BHLR
RIGHT: No. 3 *Dickie*, an 0-4-2 built in 1976 by David Curwen in Wiltshire, steams past the trees. BHLR
BELOW: Beer Heights locomotives *Mr P* and *Caroline* passing Station Gallery. BHLR

The very attractive Sunny South village of Beer in East Devon never had a station of its own, at least in the steam era, so if you wanted to travel there by train for your summer holiday, the Seaton branch was the only way.

However, Beer is renowned throughout the world for railways.

For it is also the headquarters of the Pritchard Patent Product Company – familiar to model railway enthusiasts worldwide as PECO, one of the foremost manufacturers of railway modelling track and now in its 70th year of trading.

After years of keeping scale modellers everywhere supplied with its acclaimed flexible track and kits, it seemed a logical steam for PECO to build a railway on its own doorstep.

The Beer Heights Light Railway was first conceived in 1974 by PECO founder, Sydney Pritchard, who first established a factory and then the adjacent PECO Modelrama exhibition on the hillside above this historic fishing village with its shingle beach. It was decided that a 7¼in gauge miniature railway would further add to visitors' experience.

On July 14, 1975, Rev Wilbert Awdry of Thomas the Tank Engine fame officially opened the short length of track from Much Natter station with the first steam locomotive being christened *Thomas Jnr* to suit.

The following decades saw the little railway blossom into a tourist attraction in its own right, with thousands upon thousands of visitors every year. In that time the line was extended out toward Devil's Gorge, under the attraction's car park through a long, dark tunnel and out to Wildway, an area of woodland around the pond, Lake Charlotte.

The result is a railway a mile in length, with the number of resident locomotives serving the line also increasing over the years.

At present, rolling stock consists of 11 resident locomotives including eight steam, one electric tram *Alfred*, one diesel, *Jimmy*, and a new liquid propane gas locomotive, *Ben*, named for the 40th anniversary of the line in 2015 by BBC news correspondent Ben Ando.

The locomotives are a third the size of British narrow gauge rolling stock, with *Linda*, built in 1983, being a scale model of the Penrhyn Quarry Hunslet of the same name, which runs on the Ffestiniog Railway in Wales.

The railway operates to a high standard of railway practice incorporating both semaphore and electric signalling systems and radio contact between all railway staff.

At the helm since 1991 is Chief Mechanical Engineer, John Macdougall, responsible for the construction of both *Mr P* and *Claudine* named in honour of the late Sydney Pritchard and his wife, as well as the day-to-day running of all railway operations.

Throughout each year a series of special events takes place with PECO Loco Week and the August bank holiday railway gala being highlights.

During these events, guest locomotives are invited from far and wide to run doubleheaded passenger services as well as special goods trains.

Pecorama, within which the Beer Heights Light Railway is situated, has also expanded in size and nature considerably over the years.

The Millennium Celebration Garden opened in 2000 and offers a wonderful display of flora throughout the season through the distinct celestial themes of the Sun, Moon and Rainbow Garden Rooms.

Orion, a Pullman carriage built in 1951 for use on the 'Golden Arrow' service to London Victoria, serves morning coffee and afternoon tea at Beer Victoria station, a full-scale platform built opposite the site's main office building using remnants of former local stations. These facilities, as well as the 10-hole crazy golf course, Garden Room Restaurant and Pecorama Play Station indoor soft play area, have established Pecorama as a great day out for all the family.

The site is open daily from 10am- 5pm throughout the season, in 2016 until October 29. Information on upcoming special events can be found at www.pecorama.co.uk where tickets can also be purchased at a discount. ●

■ An in-depth summary of the history of the line can be found in, A Pecorama Guide to the First 40 Years of the Beer Heights Light Railway, available at www.pecopublications.co.uk

LEFT: *Thomas* Jnr was launched into traffic in 1975 by Thomas the Tank Engine creator Rev Wilbert Awdry. BHLR

ABOVE: The Beer Heights Light Railway under construction. BHLR

Chapter 22

TOP OF THE SOUTHERN!

The highest point on the Southern Railway network was Woody Bay station on the legendary Lynton & Barnstaple Railway, which has been reborn as a heritage line and has all the makings of a major contributor to Exmoor's tourist economy.

The Lynton & Barnstaple Railway – always known to its many admirers simply as the L&B – is often described as the premier narrow-gauge railway in England.

Opened in 1898 and closed in 1935, decades before Dr Beeching wielded his axe in the 1960s, it died young and its legend has glowed brightly ever since.

More books have been written about the line and more photographs – and even cine films – were taken of it than of any comparable railway, and it has also inspired modellers all round the world.

Part of the railway's appeal, of course, lay – and still lies – in its glorious Exmoor setting: every summer its solidly built carriages filled with happy holidaymakers who had travelled from all over the country to revel in the delightful Devon scenery.

Even the third-class carriages included open-sided compartments to enable the passengers to savour the countryside, and it is said that children liked to pick flowers from the hedgerows as the carriages trundled past.

Constructed to the gauge of only 1ft 11½in to save money and to allow for tighter curves

ABOVE: *Lew* it isn't – but it's as near as we will probably ever get to the long-lost original Lynton & Barnstaple Railway Manning Wardle 2-6-2T, which may still exist somewhere in the Brazilian jungle. Ffestiniog Railway near-replica *Lyd* brought a very familiar and much-loved outline back to the Exmoor hills after a gap of 75 years when it steamed at Woody Bay station in September 2010. ROBIN JONES

ABOVE: Manning Wardle 2-6-2T No. 761 *Taw* passing one of the L&B's impressive first-class observation saloons at the end of a Lynton-bound train headed by sister *Yeo* at Blackmoor on August 5, 1935, only a few weeks before the railway closed. GN SOUTHERDEN

LEFT: Privately owned Bagnall 0-4-2T No. 3023 of 1953 *Isaac* climbs the gradient towards Woody Bay on September 6, 2015. Isaac was one of four Bagnall locos built for the South African Rustenburg platinum mine. When the 2ft-gauge track at Rustenburg was altered to 3ft 6in, the four, all now preserved, became redundant. One of a pair taken to the Welsh Highland Heritage Railway, in April 1982, was the mine's No. 3, which was sold to a private purchaser and moved to Wakefield for further restoration work. The restoration was completed by the Ffestiniog Railway's Boston Lodge Works in 2012, and it was renamed *Isaac*. It arrived at Woody Bay on November 29, 2013. TONY NICHOLSON/L&B

ABOVE: Southern Railway No. 188 *Lew*, then just a year old, and sister Manning Wardle 2-6-2T *Taw* doublehead a service from Barnstaple in 1926. L&B ARCHIVES

RIGHT: The stuff that dreams are made of: *Lew* climbing towards Chelfham, as depicted by artist Eric Leslie, whose beautiful watercolours adorn many L&B publications, from books to Christmas cards and the revivalists' quarterly magazine. L&B

ABOVE: *Lyn* taking water at Blackmoor station shortly before the railway closed in 1935. L&B archives

LEFT: Manning Wardle 2-6-2T *Lyn* at Barnstaple Town station in 1935. L&B

as it climbed on to the shoulder of Exmoor, the L&B was a main line in miniature with numerous cuttings through solid rock and 80 bridges, including two viaducts. Indeed, it was the only narrow gauge railway in Britain which, under the terms of its enabling Act, had signalling to main line standards.

Following the opening of the Devon and Somerset Railway to Barnstaple, there were calls for an extension to serve the twin villages of Lynton and Lynmouth, which were popular with wealthy Victorian holidaymakers.

Through the middle of the 19th century, several schemes were proposed, from established railway companies and independent developers. The successful scheme was supported by Sir George Newnes, publisher of Titbits and The Strand Magazine who became chairman of the railway company, and became MP for Newmarket in Cambridgeshire.

The Lynton & Barnstaple Railway Bill was passed on June 27, 1895, and the line opened on May 11, 1898 with public service commencing five days later connecting with trains from Waterloo via the Ilfracombe branch at Barnstaple Town. At a time when the great age of railway building was long over, the Sunny South was still very much extending its empire.

The magnificent eight-arched Chelfham Viaduct curves 70ft above the valley floor and has now been fully restored to enable it to carry trains once more, but the less substantial viaduct at Lancey Brook was blown up during the Second World War by Royal Engineers practising for D-Day.

The other source of the L&B's perennial attraction was its handsome little Manning Wardle locomotives, which were unique to the line. Three 2-6-2Ts were ordered from the Leeds manufacturer of that name for the opening of the railway and named after local rivers – Yeo, Exe and Taw – but when the Lynton and Barnstaple Railway Company

RIGHT: A pair of Manning Wardle 2-6-2Ts haul the last train on the Lynton & Barnstaple on September 29, 1935, crossing the embankment near Rowley Cross in Parracombe. The A39 Parracombe bypass can be seen on the left. RL KNIGHT

ABOVE: The first steam locomotive to run on the revived Lynton & Barnstaple railway was Jim Haylock's freelance 0-4-0T *Emmet*, pictured at Woody Bay in May 2004. ROBIN JONES
RIGHT: *Lyn* at Woody Bay c1925. L&B ARCHIVES

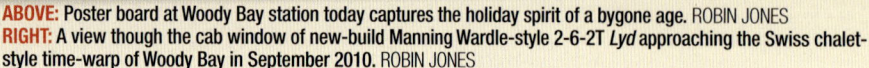

ABOVE: Poster board at Woody Bay station today captures the holiday spirit of a bygone age. ROBIN JONES
RIGHT: A view though the cab window of new-build Manning Wardle-style 2-6-2T *Lyd* approaching the Swiss chalet-style time-warp of Woody Bay in September 2010. ROBIN JONES

decided it needed a fourth locomotive, the firm had been on strike and a 2-4-2T was purchased from Baldwin of Philadelphia instead. Officially named *Lyn*, it was always known by the staff as the Yankee. A fourth Manning Wardle, christened *Lew*, was acquired in 1925.

RESURRECTION OF A LEGEND
The day after the railway closed, a wreath of bronze chrysanthemums was placed at the end of the line at Barnstaple Town station. Sent by Cpt Thomas Woolf of Woody Bay, who described himself as "a constant user and admirer", it bore the inspiring message: "Perchance it is not dead, but sleepeth". Those memorable words have sustained lovers of this little railway for 80 years.

In 1979 a small group of enthusiasts formed the Lynton & Barnstaple Railway Association, dedicated to rebuilding as much of the legendary line as possible.

Remarkably little development has taken place on the route of the railway since it closed and in 1995 the association was able to purchase the picturesque Woody Bay station, which had survived virtually unaltered since 1898.

The association then became a charitable trust and made Woody Bay its headquarters for the project to rebuild the L&B, evocatively recaptured by the superb paintings and drawings of the railway's resident artist Eric Leslie.

Woody Bay station was officially reopened on May 11, 2003, the 105th anniversary of the opening of the line. The first passenger-carrying trains since 1935 came into service on July 17, 2004, hauled by a Hunslet diesel locomotive.

During the following autumn, Edmund Nuttall Ltd, the civil engineering company, which had constructed most of the original railway in 1896-98, very generously rebuilt the next bridge on the line towards Barnstaple, No. 67, at its own expense.

Since 2009 the Lynton & Barnstaple Railway Trust has operated its own steam engine *Axe*, which had been built by Kerr Stuart in 1915 for service in the First World War. Two members also keep their own locomotives at Woody Bay, *Isaac* and *Charles Wytock*, and you may well see one of those in action.

The Lynton & Barnstaple Railway Trust is a registered charity belonging to its members. Membership currently numbers more than 2500 and is steadily growing.

The railway is operated by a not-for-profit Community Interest Company (CIC), which is controlled by the trust and owns the delightful Chelfham station next to the famous viaduct.

Chelfham station is open to the public every Sunday (sat nav EX31 4RP). You can also buy shares in the CIC to help the railway grow.

In 2014 the trust received the Heritage Railway Association Award for Small Groups for "an outstanding achievement in railway preservation".

WOODY BAY STATION
Idyllic Woody Bay station (called Wooda Bay until 1902) has the sort of sylvan setting that film location agents dream about.

Situated on the open moor by the side of the A39 but shaded by mature trees planted by the company to hide the scars of construction, it appears to be stranded in the middle of nowhere. On a sunny day, visitors can enjoy sweeping views down the valley to the sea five miles away. Barnstaple is 16 miles distant (marked by a plate on the platform side of the stable) but feels like another world.

The attractive station building, constructed of local stone under a tiled roof, is a very substantial structure for such a remote spot.

At 964ft above sea level, it was also the highest station on the Southern Railway. It has now been lovingly restored to all its Southern Railway charm.

Like Lynton and Blackmoor (but unlike the other stations on the line) it was built in the so-called Swiss chalet style at a time when the Victorian promoters of Lynton were marketing the area as "the English Switzerland".

Its isolated location meant that the station also served as a house for the stationmaster, who was supplied with a kitchen, parlour and scullery downstairs and two cosy bedrooms upstairs. The Barnstaple end of the building incorporated a booking hall (still fulfilling that purpose), office and ladies' waiting room. Gentlemen, however, were exiled to an open-roofed lavatory outside. The Station Hotel – now called Moorlands – was built shortly after the station.

Woody Bay was intended to be a junction station for a short branch line to Woody Bay itself, described by its optimistic promoter Col Benjamin Greene Lake of Martinhoe Manor as a "rising seaside watering place".

A cliff lift from the branch line to the sea was planned like the cliff railway between Lynton and Lynmouth, and a pier was built in 1896 to encourage passing steamers to call. But it was badly damaged by gales in 1899 and was eventually demolished in 1902.

Meanwhile Col Lake, a wealthy London solicitor, had been declared bankrupt in 1900 and imprisoned a year later for spending his clients' money on the development of Woody Bay. He died a broken man and Woody Bay remains delightfully undeveloped.

However, at the insistence of the colonel when he gave the railway the land on which to build the station, a clause had been inserted into the Act of Parliament authorising the construction of the Lynton & Barnstaple Railway stating that: "The company shall construct and for ever efficiently maintain near Martinhoe Cross... a station available for passenger and goods traffic to be called Woody Bay station..."

Historians have speculated since that the Southern Railway closed the L&B illegally in 1935. It is certainly true that the Southern lifted the track from a point just west of Woody Bay Station through to Lynton – but not the other way – only a few weeks later.

ABOVE: Carrying Southern Railway Maunsell green livery as No. 190, and making its third visit to the Lynton & Barnstaple Railway, Manning Wardle replica 2-6-2T *Lyd* climbs the 1-in-50 approach to Woody Bay on October 4 during the line's 2014 autumn gala, with the award-winning rake of original coaches. A fourth rebuilt coach was delivered in April 2015. TONY NICHOLSON

STEAMING TO A BRIGHT FUTURE

Today's revived railway runs nearly a mile from Woody Bay westwards to Killington Lane, a temporary terminus short of the village of Parracombe.

In 2015, this comparatively short heritage line carried 48,000 passengers: if you compare that mile for mile with Britain's top steam railways, the L&B might well come out several points ahead at the top of the table.

However, the revivalists' long-term goal is to do what the railway says on the tin – reconnect both towns in its name.

At the time of writing in summer 2016, they had obtained planning permission to relay the original line from Blackmoor Gate to Wistlandpound Reservoir, a local tourist attraction; this would give the revived line a meaningful, albeit temporary destination, before the next push west to Barnstaple.

Furthermore, the revived railway company hopes to buy the former Blackmoor station, which was converted into the Old Station House Inn, and is now a successful pub and restaurant complex. The revivalists aim to purchase the establishment through a share offer and continue to run it in its present format, while building a new platform alongside.

The Exmoor National Park Authority was to decide on the railway's application for planning permission to rebuild the line from Killington Lane to Blackmoor in the autumn of 2016.

One of the stated aims of the revivalists was to restore the 19¾-mile railway as far

ABOVE: A railway heritage milestone: new-build Manning Wardle-style *Lyd* heading a train of two coaches borrowed from the Ffestiniog Railway carries a commemorative wreath as it climbs the 1-in-50 to Woody Bay, the highest point on the Southern Railway, the sea clearly visible on the horizon on September 25, 2010. ROBIN JONES

ABOVE: Perchance it is not dead but merely sleepeth? Seventy-five years after the legendary wreath and card were placed on the smokebox door of the last original L&B train, new-build L&B Manning Wardle-style 2-6-2T *Lyd* debuting at Woody Bay in September 2010 carries a similar floral tribute. ROBIN JONES

ABOVE LEFT: A rake of modern Lynton & Barnstaple Railway freight wagons. ROBIN JONES
ABOVE RIGHT: A 7¼in-gauge scale replica of Manning Wardle 2-6-2T *Yeo* on the 140yd miniature railway at Woody Bay station. ROBIN JONES
LEFT: Then Old Station House Inn was once Blackmoor station, and could so easily be so again. ROBIN JONES
BELOW: The superb rake of rebuilt original Lynton & Barnstaple Railway carriages in the platform at Woody Bay station in May 2015. ROBIN JONES

as possible in its original form, rather than simply build just another narrow gauge heritage line on the track.

Buying the old trackbed piece by piece over several decades is just one hurdle. Another facing the revivalists is that none of the original locomotives survived.

All but one were sold for scrap within weeks of the line closing. One of them, however, Manning Wardle 2-6-2T *Lew*, which was supplied to the Southern Railway in 1925, was sold for export to Brazil.

At Swansea Docks in 1936, *Lew* was loaded aboard the *SS Sabor* destined for the port of Recife in Brazil. However, once it left Britain, it became lost in the mists of history and like so much of the L&B, became the stuff of legend.

It has not been possible to find any record of *Lew* being unloaded, and as most of the relevant shipping records were destroyed during the Second World War, there is no means of discovering its eventual destination.

Did it reach Brazil, or was it dumped overboard to lighten the ship's load in a storm? Did it steam in South America? Was it scrapped, or just laid up and left to rot in a rainforest somewhere?

Nobody can answer these questions, and despite enthusiasts making numerous enquiries and trips to Brazil in search of the engine, its fate remains a mystery. It is difficult to believe that in these days of mass global communications someone would not have taken a picture of it and shared it.

Even if a miracle happened and *Lew* was found, it is likely that it would be fit only for static display.

A project to build a new L&B Manning Wardle was launched in 1996 by the Ffestiniog Railway at Boston Lodge Works, which has, in the heritage era, built new or replica locomotives for its own line. It was to be closely based on *Lew*.

The £300,000 locomotive, named *Lyd* after the L&B tradition of choosing names of Devon rivers with three letters, first moved under its own steam at Boston Lodge on August 5, 2010 as the culmination of a project, which was worked on as money and resources became available.

Its first scheduled appearance came at sister line the Welsh Highland Railway's Superpower event on September 11-12 that year. After that, it appeared at the Launceston Steam Railway, whose owner Nigel Bowman had supported the project throughout.

However, the climax to its debut month was undoubtedly its visit to the autumn gala at Woody Bay on September 25-26, when for the first time in the 75 years since the line closed, a L&B Manning Wardle locomotive was heard climbing the 1-in-50 gradient to Woody Bay!

Thousands packed the little line's autumn gala to see the 'new *Lew*' haul former L&B coach No. 15 and Ffestiniog Railway observation car No. 102, which had been based on an L&B design. Ffestiniog general manager, Paul Lewin, loaned the pair to run behind *Lyd* for the big occasion.

Although clearly externally similar to *Lew*, *Lyd* has several modern design and construction techniques to improve overall efficiency.

In August 2011, it was taken into the paint shop at Boston Lodge to be turned out in the livery everyone wanted to see – Southern Railway lined Maunsell green, as carried by *Lew* on the L&B, and numbered 190.

Lyd returned to Woody Bay for the May 2013 especially to haul No.7 and No.17 – the first two original L&B carriages to be restored by volunteers, using vehicles that had survived as garden outbuildings. No.11 and No.16 have since joined the pair: it is as if a complete authentic L&B rake has appeared out of nowhere! That fact was not lost on the Heritage Railway Association, which in 2013 named the L&B as the winner of its Annual Award (Small Groups).

Lyd was booked for the L&B's autumn gala on September 24-25, 2016, and is likely to make regular repeat visits from North Wales.

However, the modern-day L&B has long yearned for a replica original locomotive of its own.

There is a long-running project to build a new version of 2-6-2T *Yeo*. However, 2017 is set to see the launch of a replica of the original Baldwin *Lyn*, on May 13 at the spring gala.

The original *Lyn* was built in Philadelphia in 1898, the year the railway opened. Between July 1897 and January 1898, workers at several British engineering companies were on strike in support of demands for an eight-hour working day, leaving UK locomotive builders with large backlogs of unfulfilled orders.

Needing an extra locomotive quickly, the L&B looked to the far side of the Atlantic.

Baldwin 'flatpacked' *Lyn*, which was shipped as a kit of parts, and assembled it at the L&B's Pilton works near Barnstaple. Its distinctive American shape meant that *Lyn* was referred to by staff as 'The Yankee'.

The 762 Club, the registered charity behind the seven-year project to build the new locomotive, raised funds by selling shares at £762 a time.

The new *Lyn* is being re-created as closely as possible to the original 1898 locomotive.

However, the new *Lyn* is, unlike the original, all British. The all-welded boiler was made by Bennett Boilers of Highbridge in Somerset, while the wheels were cast at the Trefoil Steel Company plant in Tinsley, Sheffield.

It will also differ in that it will incorporate many 21st-century features to increase the power, reliability and economy in order to haul 50% more carriages than the original.

The new locomotive will appear in the condition that the original returned from a rebuild at Eastleigh Works in 1929, further enhancing the Sunny South credentials!

The revived Lynton & Barnstaple Railway could easily do for North Devon what the narrow gauge Ffestiniog and Welsh Highland Railways have done for the tourist economy of Snowdonia. The revivalists also hope that a park-and-ride service can be provided to Lynton.

In terms of major tourist attractions, the new L&B is the West Country's sleeping giant. If as the critics claim, Brexit will cause more Brits to take holidays at home because of poor European exchange rates, the L&B is exactly what its locality needs.

NEWNES' SECOND LYNTON RAILWAY

Sir George Newnes, who owned a large house at nearby Hollerday Hill, did so much to make the L&B happen. He was also largely responsible for financing the water-powered Lynton & Lynmouth Cliff Railway, designed by George Croydon Marks, later Baron Marks of Woolwich, which opened on Easter Monday 1890, and is still with us today.

The high cliffs separating the two towns proved a major obstacle to economic development in Victorian times. The remoteness of the area, and rugged geography, meant that villagers relied on sea transport for most deliveries of coal, lime, foodstuffs and other essentials, which had then to be carried by packhorses and carts up the steep hill to Lynton.

Holidaymakers began to arrive at Lynmouth on paddle steamers from Bristol, Swansea and other Bristol Channel ports, from about 1820. Ponies, donkeys and carriages were available for hire, but the steep gradients meant that the animals had only short working lives.

Building of the 3ft 9in gauge parallel-tracked cliff railway began in 1887 and took three years. An Act of Parliament formed the Lynmouth & Lynton Lift Company in 1888, and a further Act gave the company perpetual rights to water from the West Lyn River, obtained through mile-long pipes.

The railway is now classified as a listed monument. It not only still serves an invaluable purpose, but is a fascinating working example of Victorian transport technology.

Newnes later produced plans for Bristol's Clifton Rocks Railway, an inclined lift from Hotwells Road to the garden of No. 14 Princes Buildings, which now includes the modern-day Avon Gorge Hotel, in a bid to resurrect Clifton as a spa resort. This funicular opened on March 11, 1893 but was never a great success and closed on October 1, 1934.

The tunnels have survived and a charitable trust aims to preserve and restore the railway. ●

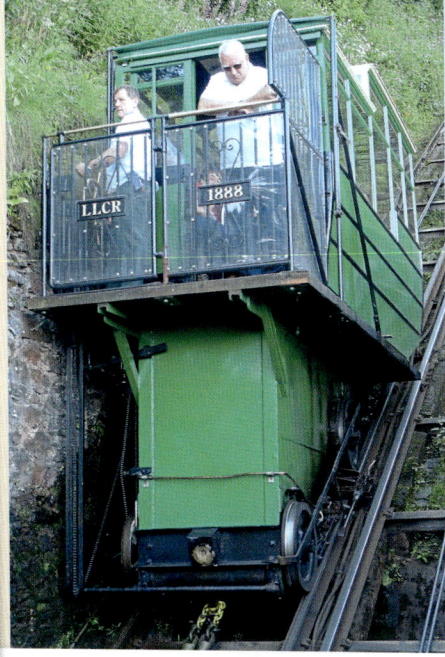

RIGHT: One of the funicular railway cars approaching the Lynmouth base station. ROBIN JONES
BOTTOM: The Lynton & Lynmouth Cliff Railway: Victorian technology still very much providing an invaluable service today. ROBIN JONES

Chapter 23

STEAMING BACK TO

Exmouth was another classic Sunny South destination, and from the ea­
holidaymakers. However, an enforced move saw the owners move wes­

When East Devon District Council drew up plans for an £18-million redevelopment of Exmouth seafront, there was no longer space for longstanding traditional attractions such as a seaside fun park, crazy golf course and the Railway Carriage Café and model railway, which had been there since the 1970s.

Sadly, model railway owners Keith and Sara Southwell could do nothing to halt the tidal wave that was the Exmouth Splash scheme, which involved a multi-screen cinema, an outdoor water splash zone and a seafront restaurant. When their lease ran out at the end of 2014, their time was up.

British Railways chairman, Dr Richard Beeching, did not axe the Exmouth Junction to Exeter branch, but the council had called time on the model trains. The council wanted to demolish the building housing the model railway, which was used by the Home Guard during the Second World War.

Keith, who first became interested in the Exmouth model railway while working there as an 11-year-old doing a Saturday job, had leased it for 25 years, but the council decided that it did not fit into the scheme of new things.

Undeterred, the Southwells looked for pastures new – and bought the 15in gauge Lappa Valley Steam Railway at St Newlyn East in Cornwall.

The 1½ mile-long railway, which attracts around 50,000 visitors a year, runs from Benny Halt to East Wheal Rose, along part of the trackbed of the GWR branch from Newquay to Perranporth and Chacewater, which closed under Beeching on February 4, 1963.

It was founded by Eric Booth in 1974. He ordered a new steam locomotive, 0-6-4PT *Zebedee*, to be built by Severn Lamb. Four carriages were built locally and the first passenger services ran on June 16, 1974.

Three more locomotives including Curwen/Berwyn Engineering 0-6-0 *Muffin* arrived from the Longleat Railway in 1976, when more carriages were built.

Ownership of the park passed to his four children in 1992 and they had run the park ever since, with the help of general manager, David Milne, but they decided to sell so they could retire.

The venue is a sizeable entertainment complex which also includes two miniature railways, one 7¼in gauge and the other 10¼in, as well as a Grade II listed Cornish mine engine house, Wheal Rose, with a visitor viewing platform, boating lake, crazy golf course, cafe, an adventure playground, wildlife lake, pedal and electric car tracks, a brick path maze depicting Richard Trevithick's first railway locomotive and several woodland walks.

LEFT: Lappa Valley Railway locomotives *Zebedee* and *Muffin*. LVR

ABOVE: The Carriage Café in its previous location on Exmouth seafront. ROBIN JONES
LEFT: Triple header: *Ruby*, the latest addition to the Lappa Valley Railway fleet, leads *Zebedee* and *Muffin* on a special train to mark the line's 40th anniversary. EMILY WHITFIELD-WICKS/LVR
RIGHT: A head of steam at the Lappa Valley Railway. LVR

EAST WHEAL ROSE

0s, a popular model railway on the seafront entertained
ds – to buy the Lappa Valley Railway at St Newlyn East near Newquay.

Keith said: "It is a great shame that the council couldn't see its way to incorporate this unusual attraction into its new plans, but Devon's loss is Cornwall's gain."

The 1956-built restored BR Mk.1 coach, which housed the Carriage Café on Exmouth seafront, was moved to the Lappa Valley by the couple as they embarked on a five-year programme of significant enhancements for the leisure park.

In July 2015, another steam locomotive was added to the fleet, in the form of *Ruby*, an 0-4-2T built by Exmoor Steam.

East Wheal Rose is the largest remaining Cornish engine house and its 120ft chimney stack, is a landmark that can be seen for miles. It was also the site of the largest mining disaster in Cornwall's history, when in 1846 a flash flood claimed the lives of 39 local men resulting in the closure of the mine.

The origin of the trackbed dates back to 1849, when local minerals magnate, Joseph Treffry, developed a transport network to export ore. He built the harbour at Par, and later a series of tramways, including one from Newquay to East Wheal Rose mine.

The network was eventually taken over by the Cornwall Minerals Railway, which in 1896 became part of the GWR, and pounced on an opportunity to boost its passenger trade in Cornwall, in competition with the London & South Western Railway, by linking the increasingly popular holiday resorts of Newquay, Perranporth and St Agnes.

The East Wheal Rose branch was upgraded to carry passenger trains and became part of a new route beginning at Chacewater on the main line from Penzance to London. The completed passenger line was opened to the public in 1905 and greatly improved the mobility of local people who could now travel to the market town of Truro.

From the 1930s until the late 1950s, the branch to the coastal resorts was very busy, particularly with holidaymakers. However, by the early 1960s road transport was becoming increasingly competitive and after Beeching was appointed to stem the soaring losses of British Railways, it became one of many country routes earmarked for closure.

The rails were lifted, and nature took its course, reclaiming much of the formation, before Eric Booth moved in a decade later.

The railway has won the Family Attraction and Overall Winner awards in recent Primary Times reader Star Awards.

Visit www.lappavalley.co.uk for full details of events and opening times. ●

ABOVE: The Lappa Valley Railway is the centrepiece of a sizeable family entertainment complex. ROBIN JONES
RIGHT: The bulk of East Wheal Rose engine house towers over the 15in gauge railway below. LVR

Making Fresh Tracks to the Sunny South and West

Chapter *Helston*

THE MOST SOUTHERLY STEAM OF ALL!

It may be still be early days, but Cornwall's Helston Railway, which is restoring part of the GWR branch into the town, has already returned steam to the line and carried off a major national award against stiff competition. After winning a major planning battle, it is on the move again.

The 8½-mile line from Gwinear Road on the GWR Paddington to Penzance main line to the town of Helston, world famous for its Flora Day celebrations in May, was the southernmost branch line in the UK.

It was built to open up the agricultural district of south-west Cornwall and opened on May 9, 1887, but also carried a sizeable number of holidaymakers in the summer.

In 1903, Helston station found itself at the heart of a transport revolution, when, rather than spend £85,000 on building a light railway from there to Lizard Town, it tested the market with bus services on the route. They were the first successful bus services operated by a British railway company, and within a year, the GWR was running 46 motor buses. Here, buses eliminated the need to build a railway: by the 1950s and '60s, they were helping to phase out rural railways.

The branch was sharply curved and steeply graded, with ruling gradients of 1-in-60 and 1-in-54. In 1922 it had eight trains in each direction; by 1939 this had grown to 10 on weekdays and 11 on Saturdays. Helston had a small engine shed there.

Freight traffic, most of which was agricultural, accounted for about two-thirds of the branch's revenue. During the Second World War, especially during the D-Day preparations in 1944, Nancegollan station, the railhead for the fishing port of Porthleven, experienced extensive military traffic.

The branch's postwar demise mirrored that of so many other rural routes: passenger services ended on November 3, 1962 and goods traffic on October 4, 1964. The track was lifted by the middle of the following year.

Against the odds of the Beeching era, several of Cornwall's GWR branches survived: those to St Ives, Falmouth, Newquay, Looe and Gunnislake (the truncated Callington branch), are very much still with us. In 1994, a group of British Rail officials surveyed the remains of the Helston branch with a view to a feasibility study, but decided the figures would not stack up.

Eight years later, a dozen people founded the Helston Railway Preservation Society, and on April 28, 2005, work began on clearing the overgrown trackbed. The society has the ultimate goal of restoring four miles of the branch as a tourist attraction.

The Victorian tourist attraction of Trevarno Gardens, which a stretch of the trackbed passed, became the society's base, and a half-mile section of track was laid by 2010. Trevarno was the home of William Bickford Smith – the first chairman of the original Helston Railway.

On July 25-26 that year, the fledgling heritage line welcomed steam for the first time, in the form of cut-down Port of Par Bagnall 0-6-0ST No. 2572 of 1934 *Judy* from the Bodmin & Wenford Railway, during the celebration of the completion of the latest station platform on the line, at Trevarno, and the newest since Truthall Platform in 1905.

Although *Judy* was in steam and operating on the railway, the line was unable to carry passengers, as the new Helston Railway Company was not authorised to operate passenger trains at the time.

At the National Railway Heritage Awards ceremony in the Merchant Taylors' Hall in London on December 1, 2010, the railway was announced as the surprise winner of the Ian Allan Publishing Heritage Railway of the Year Award.

The award was presented by pop mogul Pete Waterman to Helston Railway director, Stuart Walker; general manager Alan Burton, and society vice-president Chris Heaps OBE.

Passenger services started in December 2011, at the Trevarno Gardens Winter Wonderland event.

The final lengths of track on the railway's Truthall extension were declared fit for use on July 19, 2012 and the first public train ran the same day to give an overall length of around a mile.

Around 2000 customers were carried throughout 2012, the train comprising a Rushton Hornsby diesel shunter and a BR brake van.

However, the revivalists received a major setback that summer of when they were told to move out the station and cafe in Trevarno Gardens pending a sale of the property, which attracted around 800,000 visitors a year.

The railway was told that potential buyers did not want public access through the estate.

The railway was given eight weeks to relocate its main operating base to Trevarno Farm, where a new car park was planned along with a temporary platform at Prospidnick.

The next battle began in the spring of 2014, when nearly 50 local residents objected to the railway's plan to extend its running line by around 400yds and add sidings at Trevarno Farm.

Together with organic skincare company Organic Trevarno, the railway submitted an application for planning permission, but residents said it was wrong to turn a peaceful rural hamlet into an industrial site.

Cornwall Council refused permission, the railway appealed, but following a local enquiry, a planning inspector upheld that decision. However, the railway welcomed comments made in the inspector's decision notice, saying that the refusal was "a very finely balanced decision".

That spurred on the railway to submit a fresh application to Cornwall Council the following spring, for an extension to the track beyond the Prospidnick road bridge, a new platform behind Trevarno Farm and to retain a 60-space car park... only for it to be refused again.

It was third time lucky when the railway appealed. In the summer of 2016, Government planning inspector, Neil Pope, granted permission.

He said: "Most developments result in some adverse impact and where these impacts are significant it may be necessary to withhold permission. In this instance, there would be no serious loss of privacy or significant noise disturbance."

In giving his decision, he acknowledged the benefits that heritage railways bring to local economies.

"I find that the benefits outweigh the limited adverse impacts upon the living conditions of some neighbouring residents," he said. "While some interested parties have queried the extent of the economic benefits that would arise from the scheme, the proposal would benefit tourism interests in this part of Cornwall and assist in strengthening the local economy.

"Social benefits would also ensue with rail enthusiasts taking part in the reinstatement of a further section of rail track and in assisting visitors.

"The proposal would also offer educational benefits. In this regard, I note the letter of support from the College of Humanities at the University of Exeter, as well as the engagement with local schools. These benefits carry considerable weight."

Heritage Railway Association chairman, Brian Simpson, said: "The planning decision is good news for the Helston Railway, and it's great news for all UK heritage railway operators.

"All the data says that heritage railways bring truly valuable benefits to their communities, with little, if any disadvantages. The trickle-down benefits of heritage railway operation can be widespread and lasting."

The railway's mile of track is open to the public on Thursdays, Sundays and bank holiday Mondays from Easter to October each year, currently with diesel-hauled brake van rides, a buffet and well-stocked gift shop. Entry to the railway is free, as are train rides for the under-fives.

Future projects include the re-opening of what will be the most southerly station in Britain at Truthall Halt, with a re-creation of the traditional GWR pagoda station building that once stood there.

It is also intended to build a new station complex at Trevarno Farm together with a new access road.

Looking further ahead, it is hoped that the line will eventually be relaid over the four-arch Cober Viaduct to Water-Ma-Trout on the outskirts of Helston where a new station would be needed, as the site of the original is not available.

Didn't the Swanage Railway start its public services over just a few hundred yards of track?
■ More information about the Helston Railway is available www.helstonrailway.co.uk ●

TOP: Steam returned to the Helston branch for the first time in 48 years on July 25-26, 2010, in the form of diminutive Bagnall 0-4-0ST *Judy* from the Bodmin & Wenford Railway, Cornwall's only other standard gauge heritage line. HRPS
ABOVE LEFT: Thanks to the decision of a planning inspector who highlighted the benefits that heritage lines can bring to localities, the Helston Railway is able to continue its push towards the outskirts of the town. HRPS
ABOVE RIGHT: Current regular Helston Railway service trains comprise one of two Ruston Hornsby 165DS shunters and a BR brake van.
BELOW LEFT: The Helston Railway aims to restore Trusthall Halt to its original GWR condition. HRPS
BELOW RIGHT: VA Park Royal Class 103 DMU, which ran services on the West Somerset Railway in its early years, is now over by the Helston Railway and is a long-term restoration project. HRPS

Chapter 25

RETRACING THE 'ACE'

The route of the 'Atlantic Coast Express' over the LSWR 'Withered Arm' west of Exeter, and an associated branch, now boasts three excellent heritage railways, each offering a very different package.

On September 4-6, 2011, Steam Dreams ran an 'Atlantic Coast Express' to Padstow – despite the fact that the tracks to the North Cornwall port, world famous for its May 1 Padstow Obby Oss festivities, were lifted shortly after its station closed on January 30, 1967.

However, the Guildford-based operator did not let a minor hindrance like that get in the way of a luxury dining train.

The 12-coach train carrying 360 passengers – with all dining classes sold out – ran from Waterloo to the Atlantic coast, but reaching it via the GWR branch of Newquay, 12 miles down the coast road from Padstow. From there, passengers could be taken by coach to Padstow station, where the surviving platform edge fronts on to a bus and coach park.

Alternatively, passengers could choose to alight at Bodmin Parkway, once the junction for GWR services to Padstow. From there, they were taken on an evening trip behind 1899-built 'ACE' veteran LSWR T9 4-4-0 'Greyhound', a class of locomotive, which once made the Waterloo to Padstow route its own, to Boscarne the westernmost point of the surviving line and the nearest modern-day railhead to Padstow, before returning to Bodmin General for onward transfer by coach to Padstow and their accommodation.

THE LONG ROAD TO PADSTOW

In 1834, the Bodmin & Wadebridge Railway became the first standard gauge railway to open in the West Country, the first in the region to carry passengers and possibly the first in Britain to offer cheap excursion tickets.

When the Cornwall Railway, which was in the GWR camp, obtained powers in 1846 to build a line from Plymouth to Falmouth, the LSWR reacted by buying the Bodmin & Wadebridge – even though it was several counties away from its nearest line at that time. The line ran from Wadebridge to a station in Bodmin, later Bodmin North, with a mineral branch from Boscarne to Wenfordbridge on the western side of Bodmin Moor.

In 1882, the North Cornwall Railway received an Act of Parliament allowing construction of the line from Halwill to Padstow's South Quay, which would be worked by the LSWR. However, the first train did not run into Padstow until March 23, 1899.

Not only did Padstow handle through LSWR/SR trains to Okehampton, Exeter or Waterloo and local trains to Wadebridge and Bodmin North, but also GWR/WR local trains to Bodmin Road (now Parkway).

When the Cornwall railway was built, for engineering reasons it missed out Bodmin, which subsequently lost its county town status to Truro. On May 27, 1887, the GWR made some amends late in the day by opening a branch from Bodmin Road to Bodmin General. The following year, a new line was built by the GWR around the edge of the town to link to the Bodmin & Wadebridge line at Boscarne Junction, with Bodmin General station becoming a Y-shaped junction.

This point became an interactive meeting point between two great rival railway cultures, those of the GWR and LSWR.

THE BODMIN & WENFORD RAILWAY

Beeching's report proposed the closure of the lines serving Padstow. Freight ended in 1964, followed by most of the through passenger trains to Waterloo, including the 'Atlantic Coast Express'. All through services ceased in September 1966 followed a month later by the closure of the North Cornwall line, and the line from Padstow to Wadebridge was closed on January 30, 1967.

Freight trains continued to run between Bodmin Road and Wadebridge

126   Making Fresh Tracks to the Sunny South and West

ABOVE: Padstow 'Atlantic Coast Express' veteran LSWR T9 'Greyhound' No. 30120 back on Southern territory at Boscarne on Sepember 3, 2010, when it was officially relaunched into traffic following its overhaul by the Flour Mill workshop at Bream. ROBIN JONES

TOP RIGHT: Bodmin & Wenford or the Bluebell Railway? Beattie well tank No. 30587 as scrapped sister No. 30586 passes Westheath Road on April 17. BEN OLIVER RAIL PHOTOGRAPHY/BWR

LEFT: Bulleid West Country light Pacific No. 34007 *Wadebridge*, banked by LSWR T9 No. 3010, heads past Westheath Road towards Bodmin General on May 4, 2014. BARRY BATEMAN/BWR

RIGHT: Bodmin's LSWR pair: Beattie well tank No. 30587 and T9 No. 30120 side by side at Bodmin General. ROBIN JONES

BELOW: GWR 57XX pannier tank No. 4612 heads past Westheath Road with a service train on March 25, 2014. BARRY BATEMAN/BWR

until September 1978, and the line to Wenfordbridge remained open for china clay traffic until October 3, 1983, when complete closure of the route took place.

Efforts to preserve the branch line, with a view to re-opening it as a heritage railway, began shortly after closure, with the formation of the Bodmin Railway Preservation Society in July 1984. To raise the £139,600 needed to purchase the line from Bodmin Parkway to Boscarne Junction, the Bodmin & Wenford Railway plc was formed by the society. The company successfully purchased the track, and North Cornwall District Council secured the land, from British Rail.

The revivalists held their first open day on Sunday June 1, 1986, former Devonport Dockyard Bagnall 0-4-0ST No. 19 gave shunting demonstrations at Bodmin General Station, which were the first authorised train movements in the preservation era.

The necessary Light Railway Order was obtained on August 31, 1989, and regular services between Bodmin Parkway and Bodmin General were restored on June 17, 1990. A new intermediate station known as Colesloggett Halt was brought into use.

The line from Bodmin General to Boscarne Junction was re-opened on August 15, 1996, with a new station built at the latter – the only point where the heritage line runs over former Southern Railway metals.

The Bodmin & Wenford has not only emerged as a major attraction in the heart of Cornwall, easy to reach from most resorts in the Duchy, but has built up an impressive fleet of steam and diesel locomotives. Many of them ran in Cornwall or represent locomotive types that did – a Cornish railway museum by the back door!

Examples include *Alfred* and *Judy*, the two diminutive cut-down Bagnalls that ran at Par docks, GWR prairie No. 5552, a type that ran on most GWR Cornish branch lines; GWR panniers Nos. 4612 and No. 6435; GWR heavy freight 2-8-0T No. 4247, which once hauled china clay trains from St Blazey to Fowey Docks, and former West of England Main Line veteran Class 50 No. 50042 *Triumph*.

However, the two LSWR stars are the abovementioned T9, and LSWR 0298 class 2-4-0 Beattie well tank one of three ancient locomotives that were used for many years on the mineral branch from Boscarne Junction to Wenfordbridge until the early 1960s, their longevity down to their short wheelbase, which enabled them to work the notoriously tight curves on the mineral line. Back in the1950s, enthusiasts would travel from all over England to see them at Wadebridge shed.

The LSWR pair are part of the National Collection and were, like others in the Bodmin

ABOVE: BR Pacific No. 70000 pulls into Okehampton with Steam Dreams' 'ACE' on the afternoon of September 6, 2011. It was almost certainly the first time that a 'Brit' would have visited Okehampton as the Southern-based examples would have been replaced at Exeter Central if they had ever ventured that far west. It was also the first main line steam tour over the Dartmoor Railway for seven years. DAVID HUNT

LEFT: Class 08 shunter D4167 *Bluebell Mel*, at Darlington in 1962, is staple motive power on Dartmoor railway heritage services. DR

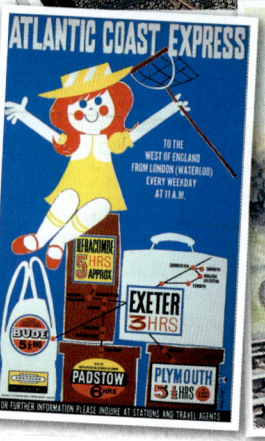

locomotive fleet, overhauled to running order by Bill Parker's Flour Mill workshops.

However, the revivalists never did reach the Wenford in their title. They had hoped to run real china clay trains on the Wenfordbridge line, as well as heritage brake van rides, but were thwarted when neighbours mounted a successful legal challenge to overturn the Light Railway Order for the branch in 1998.

On its return to London, the Steam Dreams' 'ACE' took a brief diversion to take in another part of the lost route to Padstow, the Exeter-Okehampton line.

THE DARTMOOR RAILWAY

Okehampton was one of the great unlikely survivors of the Beeching report, which called for the eradication of inter-city routes that 'doubled up', hence the 1968 closure of the Southern main line from Exeter to Plymouth in favour of the GWR alternative via Dawlish and Newton Abbot.

However, the section from Exeter to Okehampton escaped the axe. Despite, in Beeching's day, having a falling population of less than 4000, and only about 50 regular users per day, Okehampton's passenger services to Exeter survived until June 5, 1972.

The line from Coleford Junction survived, however, for freight, because of the British Rail granite ballast quarry at Meldon, three miles west of Okehampton, which had an output of 300,000 tons per year.

The privatisation of British Rail in the early 1990s saw the quarry operation sold to Leicestershire-based Aggregate Industries UK Ltd, along with the 18-mile line.

The company, together with Devon County Council, Dartmoor National Park and RMS Locotec, formulated the concept of the Dartmoor Railway. Their aim was to create a community railway that would enable visitors to access and enjoy the National Park without the use of a car. The county council has sponsored the Sunday Rover trains between Exeter and Okehampton, which were introduced in 1997.

Heritage trains, mainly diesel hauled, were introduced on the line as an additional revenue stream, initially between Okehampton and Meldon Quarry and later extended to Sampford Courtenay on Saturdays.

In 2008 the Dartmoor Railway was leased by US-based Iowa Pacific Holdings, and placed along with the Weardale Railway in County Durham under the control of its subsidiary, British American Rail Services.

The freehold of the Dartmoor Railway is still owned by Aggregate Industries. For the past two years it has been trying to sell both the railway and Meldon's dolerite quarry, which closed in 2011 owing to the global recession.

It was decided to axe the regular heritage services in favour of themed special event trains, such as diesel-hauled dining trains and Wild West re-creations, which had proved commercially more lucrative. At Christmas 2012 the railway, along with its Weardale counterpart, ran the 'Polar Express' based on the book by Chris Van Allsburg and the Warner Brothers' film of the same name. On both railways, it was a huge success. Further 'Polar Express' events were staged in November and December 2013, 2014 and 2015.

However, the line's supporting volunteer body, the Dartmoor Railway Supporters Association, which refused to provide free labour to run commercial services, in early 2014 reached agreement to run its own heritage services at weekends and bank holidays under the banner of Granite Line Ltd.

The heritage services use a variety of rolling stock, including a Southern Region Class 205 'Thumper' unit restored to its original livery and number. Services are also operated using restored diesel locomotives in push-pull and top-and-tail mode with a variety of coaching and ex-EMU stock. Steam-hauled services have also operated occasionally.

At Meldon, passengers can walk across the stunning Meldon Viaduct and a buffet carriage is open on a seasonal basis selling light refreshments.

There is also a Devon County Council-funded service operated by Great Western Railway between Exeter and Okehampton on summer Sundays.

The popular Old Station Tea Rooms at the beautifully restored Okehampton station, refurbished in the 1990s by a consortium of councils and the Dartmoor National Park, is open seven days a week serving a full breakfast and lunch menu as well as afternoon and Devon cream teas.

The station, which also has a museum and a shop, is a great base for a number of walks and access to Dartmoor. It is also located at the start of the Granite Way footpath/cycleway that runs alongside the railway to Meldon and then a further 11 miles on the old trackbed to Lydford.

Main line trains could one day return to the line. Following the collapse of the Dawlish sea wall in the storms of February 2014, leaving Plymouth and Cornwall cut off from the national network until emergency repairs were completed, there were many calls for the reinstatement of the Southern line from Exeter to Plymouth. Although this is considered a shortlisted option by both the government and Network Rail, at the time of writing, no decision had been made.

NORTH WALES COMES TO MID-CORNWALL

Launceston (otherwise Dunheved), the ancient capital of and acknowledged gateway to Cornwall, sits astride the A30 one mile from the border with Devon. Dating back to Celtic times, the whole of Launceston is steeped in history, and is dominated by its castle built by Robert de Mortain, half-brother of William I, in the 11th century.

Launceston was once served by two railways. The GWR built a broad gauge branch from Plymouth via Tavistock in 1865, (converted to standard gauge in 1892 and closed in 1962) alongside which the later North Cornwall Railway built its station, reaching Launceston in 1886.

In 1965, trainee teacher Nigel Bowman rescued Hunslet 0-4-0ST No. 317 *Lilian* from the Penrhyn slate quarry in North Wales, and restored it to working order at his home in Surrey. He then set about looking for a site to build a 2ft gauge for *Lilian* to run on, and settled on Launceston in 1971, after considering stretches of trackbed from Guildford to Horsham and part of what had been the Lynton & Barnstaple Railway.

The purchase of the Launceston trackbed and legal complications took 12 years to resolve, but Nigel received full backing from the local council which, quite rightly, saw the railway as an excellent attraction congruous with the history of the town, and the first half-mile mile of the Launceston Steam Railway opened on Boxing Day 1983. The railway was extended progressively, the latest opening to Newmills in 1995 bringing the line to its current 2½-mile length.

The railway's Launceston station is located among buildings in which gas was once made, and are now workshops and an engineering museum. However, part of the GWR station site was saved and is now the car park for the line.

The railway is now home to four Quarry Hunslet locomotives, all more than 100 years old, which are maintained on site. They have made this little length of the 'ACE' route a little piece of Snowdonia in exile.

Visitors are often surprised to learn that the railway is self-sufficient and that all engineering is carried out on site. Boilers are made and repaired and new parts are produced, often using machinery that is as old as the locomotives themselves. Parts of the workshops are open for viewing.

The journey starts from the station built by the railway on the former trackbed, where the fine canopy rescued from Tavistock North station can be seen, as well as an original Launceston station sign.

Shortly after leaving the station, the line passes first under a road bridge and then under the old Priory Leat, which crosses on a cast-iron aqueduct. At one time the leat was owned by Sir Francis Drake, latterly it provided power to the town mills, and although the mill is now incorporated into housing, it still remains, now owned by the Launceston Steam Railway.

The leat is the one small feature of Launceston Priory, which has remained in use over the centuries. Lying below and to the north of the town are the ruins of the priory, founded in 1126 by the then Bishop of Exeter alongside the River Kensey: pedestrians can still cross the river by means of the ancient clapper bridge.

Once the wealthiest and most important priory in Cornwall, but following Henry VIII's dissolution of the monasteries, it was razed and never rebuilt.

It was only when the North Cornwall Railway was being constructed that it was rediscovered, and sufficient of the foundations were revealed to enable the size and layout of the buildings to be established. The Launceston Steam Railway occupies part of the priory site with a viewing area and interesting display.

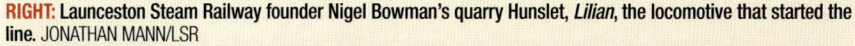

RIGHT: Launceston Steam Railway founder Nigel Bowman's quarry Hunslet, *Lilian*, the locomotive that started the line. JONATHAN MANN/LSR
BELOW: Quarry Hunslet 0-4-0ST *Dorothea* at the modern-day Launceston station, the third in the town's history. JONATHAN MANN/LSR
BOTTOM LEFT: Launceston Steam Railway founder Nigel Bowman's wife Kay rebuilt Quarry Hunslet 0-4-0ST No. 763 of 1901 *Dorothea* from scratch. In 2000, *Dorothea* ran along the line, but with a borrowed boiler. Her achievement earned her the Heritage Railway Association's John Coiley Award for Locomotive Restoration the following year. Since then, as time permits, Kay has restored the boiler. On Sunday, November 13, 2011, Kay drove *Dorothea* the length of the line without incident, celebrating the locomotive's 110th birthday. *Dorothea* entered service in October the following year. In October 2013, Kay received one of *Dorothea's* original long-lost works plates after it was rediscovered in a box of scrap metal in South Wales. LSR

Making Fresh Tracks to the Sunny South and West

Once the River Kensey is crossed, the railway follows it through unspoilt countryside to the hamlet of Newmills, the present terminus, and is very convenient for another attraction, Newmills Farm Park.

ALL CHANGE FOR WADEBRIDGE!

The Bodmin & Wenford Railway has long hoped to extend back to Wadebridge, and to have a new terminus on the route of the 'ACE'.

The formation of a new unitary authority for Cornwall has raised high hopes of a fresh start for an extension over the modest 4¼ miles of the old trackbed to the town, now occupied by the popular Camel Trail cyclepath and footpath.

Padstow and Wadebridge saw their last passenger trains depart on January 31, 1967, the North Cornwall line from Halwill Junction and Launceston having closed on October 1 the previous year. At Wadebridge the line to Padstow remained for a quarter of a mile beyond the level crossing to allow access to the lines serving the quays on the river. The quay lines were lifted in April 1973, but Wadebridge station continued in use for freight until 1978. The last locomotive-hauled passenger train, a 12-coach special from the Midlands hauled by Class 25 No. 25080, ran on September 30, 1978, while a charity DMU shuttle from Bodmin, was the last passenger train of all, on December 17 that year.

Working with Cornwall Council, the heritage line is looking at the potential, which could be unlocked by reaching Wadebridge. As well as heritage services, talks have also looked at running community trains, possibly DMUs, to Bodmin Parkway.

The cost of relaying from Boscarne to Wadebridge was estimated in 2016 at £9.1 million. A new basic terminus would be built in a traditional style south of the suburb of Guineaport.

ABOVE: The famous iron bridge on the curve over the River Camel where trains passed for the last mile into Padstow. It now carries the Camel Trail cyclepath. ROBIN JONES COLLECTION

The railway could input £6 million a year input into the Wadebridge economy. So, Wareham in 2017 – Wadebridge the sooner the better!

When that happens, it is likely that the Bodmin & Wenford Railway will change its name back to that of the original company on the route; the Bodmin & Wadebridge.

There is no chance that the railway would ever be allowed to run to the old Wadebridge station – now converted into the Sir John Betjeman Centre and a youth club – tram-like through the town's streets to pick up the formation on the other side. Several years ago, another option was considered, taking the railway along the riverbank to the western end of the great stone bridge, which gave the town its name. However, since then, blocks of luxury flats have been built on the waterfront, blocking the way.

Sadly, while extending the railway back to Padstow would bring huge benefits to that town too, if only in terms of alleviating summer traffic congestion, it is now a non-starter. Padstow's station building is today home to the town council, with the former yard now a public car park.

Back in the 1980s engineer, Brian Taylor, drew up plans to lay a 15in gauge railway between Padstow and Wadebridge, but was refused planning permission.

Instead, he and his wife Doreen founded the 3½-mile Kirklees Light Railway on the trackbed of the Lancashire & Yorkshire Railway's branch from Clayton West to Shelley Woodhouse. Brian designed a locomotive for that line, which opened in 1991, Cornwall's gain being Yorkshire's loss. Had Brian's Padstow scheme succeeded, it would have been one of the most beautiful steam lines in the UK, rivalling the Dartmouth Steam Railway, but the formation is now the busiest part of the Camel Trail, and by virtue of its stunning estuarine scenery, deservedly so. •

ABOVE: The classic North Cornwall railway station at Padstow, which opened on March 27, 1899, survives as the town council offices. ROBIN JONES

RIGHT: End of the line: outside the Shipwrights Arms on Padstow's North Quay stands this 259-mile railway milepost representing the distance from the port to Waterloo, and therefore the westernmost point of the Southern Railway. ROBIN JONES